Making Health Services More Accessible in Developing Countries

Other titles from IDE-JETRO:

Hiroshi Sato and Mayumi Murayama *(editors)*
GLOBALISATION, EMPLOYMENT AND MOBILITY
The South Asian Experience

Takashi Shiraishi, Tatsufumi Yamagata and Shahid Yusuf *(editors)*
POVERTY, REDUCTION AND BEYOND
Development Strategies for Low-income Countries

Mariko Watanabe *(editor)*
RECOVERING FINANCIAL SYSTEMS
China and Asian Transition Economies

Daisuke Hiratsuka *(editor)*
EAST ASIA'S DE FACTO ECONOMIC INTEGRATION

Hisayuki Mitsuo *(editor)*
NEW DEVELOPMENTS OF THE EXCHANGE RATE REGIMES IN DEVELOPING
COUNTRIES

Tadayoshi Terao and Kenji Otsuka *(editors)*
DEVELOPMENT OF ENVIRONMENTAL POLICY IN JAPAN AND ASIAN
COUNTRIES

Masahisa Fujita *(editor)*
ECONOMIC INTEGRATION IN ASIA AND INDIA

Masahisa Fujita *(editor)*
REGIONAL INTEGRATION IN EAST ASIA
From the Viewpoint of Spatial Economics

Akifumi Kuchiki and Masatsugu Tsuji *(editors)*
INDUSTRIAL CLUSTERS IN ASIA
Analyses of Their Competition and Cooperation

Mayumi Murayama *(editor)*
GENDER AND DEVELOPMENT
The Japanese Experience in Comparative Perspective

Nobuhiro Okamoto and Takeo Ihara *(editors)*
SPATIAL STRUCTURE AND REGIONAL DEVELOPMENT IN CHINA
An Interregional Input-Output Approach

Akifumi Kuchiki and Masatsugu Tsuji *(editors)*
THE FLOWCHART APPROACH TO INDUSTRIAL CLUSTER POLICY

ntents

v

les and Figures

Figures

Chapter 4

Chapter 6

Chapter 7

Chapter 8

Contributors

Anugrah Abraham
Development consultant, India

Cheryl D'Souza
Development consultant, India

Masako Ii
Professor, School of International and Public Policy, Hitotsubashi University, Japan

Banri Ito
Lecturer, School of Economics, Senshu University, Japan

Seiro Ito
Associate Senior Research Fellow, Development Studies Centre, Institute of Developing Economies, IDE-JETRO, Japan

Hisaki Kono
Research Fellow, Area Studies Centre, Institute of Developing Economies, IDE-JETRO, Japan

Kensuke Kubo
Associate Senior Research Fellow, Development Studies Centre, Institute of Developing Economies, IDE-JETRO, Japan

Hiroko Uchimura
Associate Senior Research Fellow, Inter-disciplinary Studies Centre, Institute of Developing Economies, IDE-JETRO, Japan

Tatsufumi Yamagata
Senior Research Fellow, Inter-disciplinary Studies Centre, Institute of Developing Economies, IDE-JETRO, Japan

Hiroko Yamane
Professor, National Graduate Institute for Policy Studies, Japan

Preface

Health is increasingly a critical concern in the context of poverty reduction. Poor people suffer most from ill-health and disease; by the same token, people are more likely to fall into poverty because of ill-health. Health is a fundamental human right and the attainment of better health is an essential worldwide social goal. In addition, reflecting the vicious cycle of poverty and ill-health, health is a focal issue in development. In fact, three of the eight Millennium Development Goals (MDGs) require substantial improvements in the health sector by 2015, namely, reduction of child mortality, improvement of maternal health, and combating of HIV/AIDS, malaria and other diseases.

Although international concern about health is increasing, health outcomes do not appear to be improving at a steady rate. A fundamental problem is that necessary and affordable services do not reach those in need. The most vulnerable are the least protected. What factors hinder the poor from accessing the healthcare services they need? This is our fundamental concern.

Family characteristics, such as economic or education level, affect the behaviour of family members when they seek healthcare services. Other issues, such as health service provision, will affect the availability or affordability of healthcare services. The limited capacity for provision of healthcare services in developing countries is a critical concern in the health sector, and a major bottleneck for improving the access of people to needed healthcare services. The bottleneck is our underlying focus in this research project. To examine the bottleneck, we highlight the function of health systems, in particular the key elements of health systems, that is, finance and resources. Each chapter focuses on an element that is essential for a workable health system. We attempt to clarify what is happening in health systems and why it is happening. Our attempts provide solid analyses; however, by the same token, they tend to limit the analyses to specific cases. Given these merits and limitations, we throw light on the principal issues broadly shared among the developing countries which aim to strengthen their health systems.

This book is based on the final product of a two-year research project (FY2006-FY2007) conducted by the Institute of Developing Economies, IDE-JETRO. The research project team was composed of in-house and external experts. At the frequent meetings of the project members over the two-year period, the members discussed the fundamental concern of this project, and they shared their focal issues, which are expressed in each chapter, with the entire membership of the group.

In the process of implementing the research project, we were indebted to people in various fields for their cooperation and valuable comments. We would like to express our thanks to Rouselle F. Lavado, Ichiro Otani, Margit Molnar, Yunguo Liu, Shuo Zhang, Xiaoling Wang, Liejun Wang, Maria Antonio, Maria Ofelia Alcantara, Yurika Suzuki, Masaakira James Kondo, and Johannes Jütting. With regard to conducting the research in rural Andhra Pradesh, we would like to thank C. Mohanudu, M. Sunanda, Hanumappa Sudarshan, Prashanth, Cheryl D'Souza, Anugrah Abrahams for discussions, and staff at the M. Venkatarangaiya Foundation for their cooperation, especially, Shantha Sinha, Venkat Reddy, J. Bhaskar and his team, and Srinivas. Fusao Yoshimi of IDE provided execellent work in contractual and budget management. We also would like to express our gratitude to the developers of TeX and its associated programmes, the core team of R and its package lattice developer, Deepayan Sarkar. We would like to thank, last but not least, the anonymous reviewers for their valuable comments. All errors and opinions remain solely the responsibility of the authors.

Hiroko Uchimura

Introduction: Key Factors for Functioning Health Systems

Hiroko Uchimura

Health in development

Health status significantly differs between developed and developing countries. The gradient is found in the relationship between income level and health status (Preston 1975; Backlund et al. 1999). The upward trend linking per capita income and life expectancy is known as the Preston curve. Preston (1975) pointed out that an increase in per capita income relates to an improvement in health (that is, an increase in life expectancy) more strongly in low-income countries than in high-income countries.

In addition to the determinants of health status at the national level, the determinants of health disparities among people within a country have drawn attention (Flegg 1982; Bidani and Ravallion 1997; Deaton 2002; Deaton and Lubotsky 2003). Socioeconomic status, such as occupational status or education level, closely relates to the health disparity among people in a country (Grossman 1972; Feinstein 1993; Schultz 1993; Elo and Preston 1996; Fuchs 2004). Education has an impact on health even when the income effect is controlled (Elo and Preston 1996). Since education affects people's healthcare-seeking behavior, it has been pointed out that education of the mother has a significant impact on child health (The Cebu Study Team 1991; World Health Organization (WHO) 2005).

The geographical situation, that is, the distance to health institutions where people can obtain needed healthcare services, has also been pointed to as an important factor affecting the utilization of health services (Thomas et al. 1996; Palmer 2008). Long-distance travel to health institutions is an indirect cost for obtaining health services. The supply-side factors, such as the scale and allocation of health resources, affect the availability and affordability of healthcare services. In particular, public

1

health institutions which provide free or low-price services play an essential role in providing healthcare services for the poorer of the poor (Russel 2008; Ranson et al. 2008). The deployment of public health institutions is critical to improving accessibility of healthcare services, especially in poor regions.

Meanwhile, there exist several routes through which ill-health impoverishes people. A direct impact arises from the expense of medical treatment (Sala-i-Martín 2005). Another arises from the reduction in family income when work is discontinued due to illness (McIntyre and Thiede 2008). In some cases, a family might be able to manage the health expenses; however, in cases of heavy expenses (such as hospitalization) or perpetual expenses, health expenses will cause serious economic damage. A family may be forced to sell scarce assets or even livestock which is essential for the family's livelihood. This type of selling of family capital may not only impoverish the family but may also increase their difficulty in extricating themselves from poverty.

If the leading income earner of the household falls seriously ill or dies of disease, the negative impact may extend beyond the current generation. Such a family may not be able to invest in its children, and the children may forfeit an opportunity to free themselves from poverty (Hulme 2003). In addition, episodes of disease in childhood may reduce adult earning power due to reduction in productivity caused by weakened physical strength or lost educational opportunities. Such direct and indirect costs of illness can be reduced by establishing effective risk-pooling systems (World Bank 2006). The systems to control financial risks associated with uncertain illness will provide the poor with financial protection and contribute to breaking the vicious circle between ill-health and poverty.

The focus of this study

As we discussed, various factors interact, and these factors ultimately improve or worsen people's health status. Among those factors, our underlying focus in this study is on the bottlenecks that obstruct provision of physically and financially accessible healthcare services. To examine the bottlenecks, it is important to highlight the interrelated structure and functional relationships of the factors, that is, health systems (Roemer 1993a, 1993b). It is stressed that a workable health system is required so that the healthcare services needed are accessible to those in need in developing countries (World Health Organization 2000; Blas and Hearst 2002; Hanson et al. 2003; UN Millennium Project 2005).

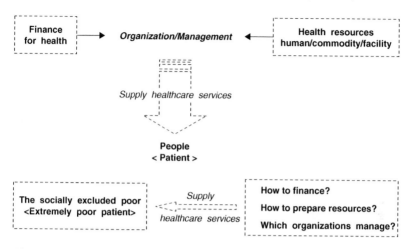

Figure 1: Principal components and our focal issues in health systems
Note: Author's compilation.

The scope of health systems is enormously broad, encompassing almost all the aspects of social and human relations that influence health. We need to focus our study on the key elements in the health systems that affect the availability and affordability of healthcare services. To examine health systems, Roemer (1993a, 1993b) presented five principal components of health systems – finance, resources, organization, management and service delivery. These components can be identified in any health system (Roemer 1993a). Based on this concept, a health system is defined as the combination of finance, resources, organization and management that leads to the delivery of health services (Roemer 1993a, 1993b). This can be the basis of the broad definition of health systems presented by the World Health Organization (2000) which highlights the importance of health system performance to attain better health.[1]

Figure 1 summarizes the structure of our study based on the above concept. To examine the factors that affect the availability and affordability of healthcare services, we focus on two of the principal components in health systems, finance and resources. We also are concerned with which organizations manage the two components and how they manage them. Through our analyses, we attempt to clarify what is happening in the health system and why it is happening. We then consider the obstacles and key factors pertaining to each component for making health systems function.

Each component is clarified as follows (Roemer 1993a, 1993b). Finance is generally based on public finance (tax revenue), social insurance, voluntary insurance, charity and personal spending. Their relative proportions and combination form health financing systems, which influence various aspects of health systems. In addition, external funds (foreign aid) are also important in developing countries. The resources consist of human resources, health facilities, commodities (drugs, equipment, and so on), and knowledge. The major organizations that form and implement health programmes or policies are governments at several levels, other governmental agencies, voluntary health agencies, enterprises, or a private healthcare market. These organizations manage the activities in the health system. An organization or a combination of organizations plan and administer health projects, or establish health-related regulations and legislation. The combination of these components will lead to the delivery of healthcare services.

Our study is composed of eight chapters, of which Chapters 1 to 7 focus on elements of the focal principal components in health systems, respectively. Chapters 1 to 4 examine the elements of finance in turn – public finance (Chapter 1), health financing systems (Chapter 2), social insurance (Chapter 3), and external funds (Chapter 4). Chapter 5 focuses on the elements of resources – drugs and knowledge. Chapter 6 examines another element of resources, human resources, and Chapter 7 also examines elements of resources, health facilities as well as human resources. Chapter 8 considers all components of the health system in the provision of healthcare services to the socially excluded poor (the extreme poor) in developing countries.

The recent state of key elements in health systems and an overview of the study

Finance

One of the most serious barriers preventing the poor from accessing healthcare services is the heavy burden of out-of-pocket payments (OOP). In addition, the high OOP is a major factor in the vicious circle of ill health and poverty in developing countries. Table 1 presents OOP as a percentage of total health expenditure in developing countries. It shows that the OOP level differs between developing regions. The OOP level is particularly high in South Asia, and relatively high in Southeast Asia and East Asia. In addition, OOP did not decrease substantially in those regions between 2000 and 2004.

Table 1: OOP as percentage of total health expenditure

	2000	2001	2002	2003	2004
Northern Africa	47.7	46.0	46.9	46.3	47.2
Sub-Saharan Africa	50.3	49.4	48.5	46.9	46.2
Latin America	38.2	38.5	36.9	36.3	35.1
The Caribbean	33.5	33.5	31.7	33.0	32.3
Eastern Asia	57.5	58.4	56.4	54.6	52.4
Southern Asia	71.8	73.2	73.9	74.7	74.5
South-Eastern Asia	53.2	52.3	51.7	52.2	51.6
Western Asia	37.1	35.6	36.9	31.2	26.9
Oceania	12.5	11.4	11.3	11.0	10.7
CIS Europe	40.9	42.0	40.9	40.7	40.9
CIS Asia	56.6	55.2	56.4	54.9	53.8

Note: Author's calculation based on data from WHOSIS (WHO Statistical Information System). The regional groupings adopted here are those defined by 'Millennium Development Indicators: World and regional groupings'. The number of countries included in each region depends on the grouping definition and the data availability. The calculated figures are population-weighted averages for each region. The population used to calculate population-weighted average is the data from 2005.

Why is OOP persistently high in those regions? A distinguishing feature in those regions is the low contribution of general government expenditure on health (Table 2). The general government expenditure accounts for less than 40 per cent of total health expenditure in those regions, which is significantly lower than other regions. In addition, among those regions, the percent contribution of social security expenditure to general government expenditure is low in South Asia and Southeast Asia (Table 2).

Chapter 1 examines the role of public finance (government expenditures) in the health sector. Public finance is supposed to play a significant role in the health sectors of developing countries, since the individual's financial capacity is scarcely sufficient to access needed healthcare services. In addition, public finance can promote equity in health by providing health services on the basis of health needs (Roemer 1993a). However, as we observed, public finance does not necessarily meet expectations, and the individual consequently bears much of the financial burden of accessing healthcare services in developing countries.

The scale of fiscal outlay for the health sector and the patterns of government expenditures in the health sector critically affect the outcomes. Central as well as local governments are key organizations in this context. In particular, local government, which is in direct contact with local

Table 2:   General government expenditure and social security expenditure on health

	General government expenditure on health as % of total expenditure on health					Social security expenditure on health as % of general government expenditure on health				
	2000	2001	2002	2003	2004	2000	2001	2002	2003	2004
Northern Africa	46.5	48.4	47.5	47.9	47.0	21.5	21.0	21.8	21.9	22.0
Sub-Saharan Africa	38.7	39.5	39.2	40.7	41.5	2.2	2.8	2.7	2.6	2.2
Latin America	49.2	48.7	50.8	51.5	52.7	34.4	35.0	34.4	34.6	34.2
The Caribbean	54.3	54.0	55.4	54.0	55.2	5.9	5.4	5.3	4.6	4.3
Eastern Asia	39.5	37.1	37.2	37.6	39.3	56.9	55.0	54.7	53.4	55.1
Southern Asia	22.4	21.2	20.7	20.0	20.5	6.2	6.1	6.4	6.1	5.7
South-Eastern Asia	33.3	35.9	36.4	35.8	36.4	8.4	10.2	11.5	12.1	12.3
Western Asia	55.8	57.9	56.4	61.9	66.1	38.5	35.5	36.8	38.0	38.1
Oceania	81.1	81.7	82.3	82.6	82.4	0.4	0.4	0.4	0.2	0.2
CIS Europe	59.8	58.6	60.2	60.6	60.8	26.3	27.0	26.3	26.4	27.0
CIS Asia	41.0	41.7	40.7	42.4	43.6	5.8	5.5	5.6	7.8	7.8

Note: General government expenditure on health comprises the outlays on health by all tiers of government, social security agencies, and direct expenditure by parastatals and public firms. Other notes are same as Table 1.

people, is positioned as a vital actor in the improvement of local health. The intergovernmental alignment of fiscal responsibility and authority will hence have a critical impact on health outcomes.

Chapter 1 focuses on the influence of public finance, particularly the local fiscal capacity, on health services by taking China as a case study. Although local governments play a significant role in the health sector in China, there are large gaps among local fiscal capacities. This chapter examines the impact of local fiscal capacity on local health resources and the overall design and funding schemes of new medical insurance programmes in China.

The author finds that local own fiscal revenue has a significant effect on the level of health resources at each locality. In addition, she indicates that although the fiscal transfer from central to local governments has contributed to reduction of the disparity in local fiscal capacities recently, it does not necessarily lead to reduction of the disparity in local health expenditures. In China, a large part of the fiscal transfer from central to local governments is earmarked transfer that does not include much transfer for health purposes. In addition, the Chinese government frequently provides earmarked transfers on a matching-fund basis that requires co-financing by local governments. Therefore, this design of fiscal transfers tends to change the allocation of local governments' budgets. The empirical analysis shows that the changes in the allocation of the local budget have a larger impact on the local health resources than does the transfer allocated for health purposes. The health conditions in poor regions would be improved more effectively by providing local governments with transfers on a full-cover basis.

The author also raises critical issues regarding the medical insurance programmes, that is, the unity of the insurance programmes and the portability of the insurance. At present, each locality modifies the grand design of the insurance programmes; in addition, the insurance programmes are segmented based on urban and rural registration in China. This design of the insurance system fixes the health disparity between urban and rural areas or across regions. The author suggests that a concrete measure for improving the unity and portability of insurance would be to raise the pooling level of the insurance funds from the city/county level to the provincial level. It would also be possible to apply a cross-subsidy scheme to the insurance funds between city/county levels. This issue is critical for the reduction of the health disparity across regions and areas in China.

Developing countries generally combine several funding schemes to finance health systems, and so their financing systems are frequently fragmented (World Bank 2006). Government funds public health institutions to provide free or low-cost health services for poor people. At the same time, a social health insurance system is established to mobilize resources and pool the risks. Government frequently subsidizes a part of the social insurance funds, particularly when a country aims to include the poor in social health insurance. In such mixed systems, the method of managing the financial resources significantly affects the scale and allocation of the resources in the health sector and the effectiveness of the resource utilization.

Chapter 2 features a study of a health financing system by drawing on the experiences of the Philippines. A health financing system is a mechanism to mobilize resources, pool resources and purchase health services. The design of health financing systems will hence critically influence the scale and allocation of resources as well as the effectiveness of resource utilization. As was seen in Table 1, a large part of total health expenditure is covered by out-of-pocket payments in developing countries. In addition to weak public health finance, malfunction of health financing systems is another major factor that causes high OOP. This chapter clarifies the health financing mechanism of the Philippines and considers the key factors in reducing the financial burdens on the individual for obtaining health services.

The Philippines has been reforming its health sector since the late 1990s. A focus of the reforms is the health financing system, which aims to improve Filipinos' financial access to health care services by mobilizing resources and reducing OOP. Nonetheless, the share of OOP in total health expenditure has not been reduced much since the middle of the 1990s. The author finds that the health service price level is substantially inflated, and the inflated costs are mostly borne by individuals' payments, that is, OOP.

The author suggests that three major factors cause the malfunction of the health financing system in the Philippines. The first and the most serious problem is the lack of a fee schedule for health services (user fees). Health service price (user fee) is not on schedule in the Philippines, which means that providers can basically charge the patients what they want. This allows providers to capture the health insurance benefits as *rent* by charging different service fees to the insured and the uninsured. In addition, the social health insurance scheme facilitates capturing. The present scheme is a 'first peso coverage up to a cap' scheme. Social health insurance covers a part of health service costs up to a certain cap, but the remaining costs need to be covered by the patients. The costs incurred by the patients are neither on schedule nor capped. Another factor is the method of remuneration for providers. As in other countries, it is better to regulate the health service prices (user fees). However, as this might not be a realistic option for the Philippines at least from a short-term perspective, the author considers the effectiveness of an indirect mechanism to control the health service price inflation, but indicates her doubts concerning its effectiveness. She suggests that the social health insurance scheme will require modification so as not to facilitate the capturing of insurance benefits by providers.

Social health insurance systems mobilize resources, and control the insurance members' financial risks associated with uncertain illness. It is a challenge for developing countries to include people in the agricultural sector or informal sector in social health insurance systems.[2]

Chapter 3 retraces the experiences of Japan, which had a pro forma universal insurance system at the end of 1930s and attained formal universal coverage of social health insurance in 1961. This chapter investigates how Japan established its social health insurance system.

A representative country whose health systems are based on social insurance is Germany (Roemer 1991, 1993b; Hiroi 1999). In Germany, voluntary health insurance was initially organized for low-income workers; afterwards, mandatory legislation was formed for the insurance in 1883 (Roemer 1991, 1993b). In contrast to current developing countries, it is pointed out that the percentage of the population in the informal sector, especially in the agricultural sector, was already low in Germany at that time (Hiroi 1999). A distinctive feature of Japan's experience is that mandated social health insurance was attained at a time when people not employed in the formal sector comprised a large proportion of the total population (Hiroi 1999; Hiroi and Komamura 2003; JICA 2004).

The origin of the health insurance system in Japan dates back to the early 20th century. The Factory Law, which aimed to protect factory workers, was introduced together with the rise of modern industry in Japan. About 30 years later, the National Health Insurance Law was enacted, the purpose of which was to insure the general population in rural areas, mainly farmers. To implement this insurance system, each municipality formed a National Health Insurance Association and became an insurer. The author points out an interesting feature of the municipality insurer. The general population in rural Japan had a sense of solidarity that had been developed through irrigation and rice-farming activities in each village, which created a sense of local community and mutual assistance. The author suggests that such a sense of local community suited the scheme in which the municipality was the insurer, and that contributed to the implementation of the social health insurance system targeting farmers. After the Second World War, the social health insurance system was restructured and attained formal universal coverage. The social insurance system ensures equitable access to healthcare services for the whole population in Japan.

The present social health insurance system, however, needs to be reformed to respond to emerging issues. In addition to the insurance premium, general tax revenues also fund the insurance fund in Japan, as mentioned above, which is a common feature in developing countries. This mixed system has caused problems in the role of insurers. The author suggests that the role of insurer should be clearly and appropriately designed, and who has the responsibility for the balance of the insurance fund also should be clarified. In addition, Japan's experience in struggling to respond to the aging population will also provide suggestions to some developing countries that are predicted to face aging problems in the mid-term perspective.

The public finance and social health insurance systems contribute to mobilizing domestic financial resources for health. However, the domestic financial resources are so limited in developing countries that external funds are expected to play an important role in health development. Chapter 4 focuses on the external funds for health. Table 3 shows that the contribution of the external fund is exceptionally high in sub-Saharan Africa and Oceania. Moreover, the external fund contribution appears to polarize toward those two regions. Sub-Saharan Africa suffers from a heavy burden of serious diseases, such as HIV/AIDS, which might be a reason for the concentration of external funds in that region.

Official Development Assistance (ODA) has been a major source of the external funds for health. However, the share of funds for health in ODA was only around 10 per cent in the late 1990s (OECD-WHO 2003). Meanwhile, GHPs (Global Health Partnerships) have been increasing their presence as emerging external funds for health in recent decades. For instance, the Global Alliance for Vaccine and Immunization (GAVI) or the Global Fund to Fight AIDS, Tuberculosis, and Malaria (the Global Fund/GFATM) raises substantial amounts of finance and plays significant roles in improving health in developing countries. Since its inception in 2002, the Global Fund had committed US$9.9 billion as of the end of 2007.

Chapter 4 examines the fundamental situation of GHPs and, furthermore, conducts in-depth empirical analysis of the Global Fund. The chapter finds that GHPs tend to be implemented in countries that suffer from a heavy burden of diseases but whose capacity for governance is weak. In contrast, through econometric analysis of the Global Fund grant programmes, the author finds that the performance of grant programmes depends on the governance, in particular the effectiveness of government, the rule of law and control of corruption, of the recipient countries. This implies that just funding for the health sector is not sufficient to attain the desired results. The international aid community, aiming at better health in developing countries, will also need to support developing countries to build their governance capacity. Despite the increasing presence of GHPs, little study has been conducted to examine GHPs' actual deployment or the grand performance mechanism. To fill this gap, this chapter presents a comprehensive analysis of GHPs and a detailed empirical analysis of the Global Fund, which provides new findings.

Health resources

Chapters 5 to 7 focus on the elements of the resources in health systems: pharmaceuticals, knowledge, human resources and health facilities. All these resources are indispensable for making needed healthcare services accessible to those in need. First, Chapter 5 focuses on the issue of availability of pharmaceuticals. The issue of human resources is examined

Table 3: External resources for health

	External resources for health as % of total health expenditure					Per capita external resouces (US$)				
	2000	2001	2002	2003	2004	2000	2001	2002	2003	2004
Northern Africa	0.6	0.6	0.5	0.6	0.6	0.5	0.5	0.4	0.4	0.5
Sub-Saharan Africa	14.7	13.7	12.5	15.9	19.0	4.3	3.9	3.7	5.7	8.4
Latin America	1.1	1.1	1.0	1.0	0.7	3.0	3.0	2.3	2.3	2.0
The Caribbean	8.2	7.1	5.6	4.2	4.2	12.3	11.2	9.3	6.7	7.3
Eastern Asia	0.1	0.0	0.3	0.8	1.0	0.1	0.0	0.2	0.6	0.9
Southern Asia	2.7	3.6	2.1	2.5	2.5	0.5	0.8	0.5	0.7	0.8
South-Eastern Asia	4.9	3.1	3.2	2.8	3.5	1.8	1.2	1.3	1.3	1.8
Western Asia	5.9	5.2	3.3	3.7	2.4	13.8	11.8	7.7	9.6	7.1
Oceania	21.6	23.2	32.5	25.0	26.9	9.2	9.7	13.7	11.7	14.7
CIS Europe	0.4	0.4	0.4	0.3	0.3	0.4	0.5	0.5	0.4	0.7
CIS Asia	2.8	4.4	5.7	4.6	4.6	0.9	1.4	2.0	1.8	2.4

Note: The unit of per capita external resources is US$ at annual average exchange rate. Other notes are the same as for Table 1.

in Chapter 6, and Chapter 7 discusses the issues of human resources and health facilities.

Pharmaceuticals

The per capita spending on pharmaceuticals of low-income countries is far lower than that of high-income countries (WHO 2004).[3] However, the principal source of pharmaceutical expenditure is private spending, both in high-income and low-income countries (WHO 2004: 45–6). In several developing regions, more than 30 per cent of total health expenditure is spent on pharmaceuticals (Table 4). As observed above, private health expenditure is mostly borne by OOP in developing countries. This suggests that pharmaceutical pricing critically impacts the accessibility of appropriate pharmaceuticals in developing countries.

The international concern about the prevalence of HIV/AIDS calls for increased access to antiretrovirals (ARVs), the most effective treatment of HIV/AIDS, in developing countries. To respond to this concern, some GHPs concentrate their projects on HIV/AIDS. Those GHPs aim to improve the availability of necessary medicines and treatment for these

Table 4: Pharmaceutical expenditure and ARV therapy coverage

	Total expenditure on pharmaceuticals as % of total health expenditure		Estimated antiretroviral therapy coverage (%)
	1995	2000	December 2006
Northern Africa	36.6	33.8	27.0
Sub-Saharan Africa	26.4	24.0	21.4
Latin America	20.3	23.6	71.6
The Caribbean	22.3	20.1	59.6
Eastern Asia	50.6	44.0	27.0
Southern Asia	19.2	18.3	2.9
South-Eastern Asia	27.0	30.2	25.0
Western Asia	23.2	24.3	–
Oceania	26.8	29.4	8.0
CIS Europe	13.5	17.4	11.6
CIS Asia	17.9	15.6	9.7

Note: Author's calculation based on the following data: total expenditure on pharmaceuticals as % of total health expenditure from *The World Medicines Situation* (WHO 2004), estimated antiretroviral therapy coverage from *Towards Universal Access* (WHO, UNAIDS and UNICEF 2007), and each country's population from WHOSIS (WHO Statistical Information System). Other notes are the same as for Table 1.

diseases. The necessary treatment, however, does not yet adequately reach those in need in developing countries. The estimated antiretroviral therapy coverage is still very low in most of the developing regions (Table 4).

Chapter 5 examines the pricing mechanism of HIV/AIDS drugs, specifically antiretrovirals (ARVs). The availability and affordability of a drug in developing countries is closely related to 'spread of technology (knowledge)' (Roemer and Roemer 1990), so this chapter focuses on how the spread of technology is associated with the availability/affordability of a drug; that is, the pricing mechanism of pharmaceuticals. The pricing of pharmaceuticals affects the types, quantity and quality of pharmaceuticals that people can obtain. Various factors interact in the pharmaceutical market: pharmaceutical firms, price regulation and patents, for example. This complicated interaction fuels debates on the issue of pricing.

There is some concern that market domination by originator pharmaceutical firms will keep prices high because the level of competition is low in the market: patents may exclude generic firms from the market, which will hinder the poor from accessing low-price pharmaceuticals in developing countries. Others suggest that originator pharmaceutical firms can price the pharmaceuticals differently in high-income countries and low-income countries if certain conditions are met. All these matters are still being debated, and solid evidence has been limited. The sparse data availability constrains more solid, empirical analysis of this issue. Chapter 5 attempts to fill this gap by using data from the price-reporting mechanism of the Global Fund.

The authors find that originator pharmaceutical firms price ARVs differently in high-income countries and low-income countries. They indicate a clear tendency for originator firms to offer lower prices in low-income countries. They also estimate the process by which the identity of the winning bidder is determined in procurement tenders. The results suggest that originator firms are likely to bid lower prices than generic firms in low-income countries, whereas generic firms tend to bid lower prices than originator firms in middle-income countries. Regarding the controversial issue of patents, the analysis in this chapter does not find a clear impact from patents on the pricing of ARVs. The results do not broadly respond to questions on the issue of general pharmaceutical pricing because the authors use specific data on a particular treatment for their analysis. Nonetheless, their analysis provides an evidence for debate, in the form of a solid picture of the complicated pricing mechanism.

Table 5:   Density of physicians (1997–2004)

	Number of physicians per 1000 population
Northern Africa	0.74
Sub-Saharan Africa	0.17
Latin America	1.52
The Caribbean	2.68
Eastern Asia	1.12
Southern Asia	0.57
South-Eastern Asia	0.35
Western Asia	1.31
Oceania	0.12
CIS Europe	3.93
CIS Asia	3.12
Developed countries	2.82

Note: The year of the data is any year from 1997 to 2004, depending on the availability of the data in each country. Other notes are the same as for Table 1.

Human resources and health facilities

The insufficiency of health workers is also a serious bottleneck to providing appropriate healthcare services in developing countries. The low density of physicians in Oceania, sub-Saharan Africa and Southeast Asia is distinct from other regions (Table 5). The number of physicians is absolutely insufficient in some countries (WHO 2006). For instance, the number of physicians per 1000 population was 0.05 in 2000 in Papua New Guinea, which is included in the Oceania region, and 0.13 in 2003 in Indonesia, which is included in the Southeast Asian region.[4] Meanwhile, the largest need for health workers exists in sub-Saharan Africa, where many countries suffer from HIV/AIDS (WHO 2006). In addition to the problem of absolute shortage, the distribution problem also draws attention. Health workers are unevenly distributed not only among countries but also within countries.

In recent times, migration of health workers from developing countries to developed countries has increasingly become an international concern because such migration has the potential to aggravate the uneven global distribution of health workers and lead to a serious shortage of health workers in developing countries.

Chapter 6 focuses on the issue of health workers, particularly the migration of health workers. Both demand-side and supply-side factors are at the root of the migration. Demand for health workers is growing in developed countries where the population is rapidly aging, while health workers from developing countries are moving to developed countries to seek better opportunities.

Vis-à-vis these increasing concerns, international attempts have been initiated to provide solid evidence on the global flow of health workers (WHO 2006; OECD 2007). These studies indicate that the outflow of health workers is increasing recently from smaller African countries, in addition to outflows from the traditional major source countries such as the Philippines and India. Destinations are also diversified. Health workers migrate not only to the major developed countries but also to the Middle East; moreover, they have even become mobile among the developing countries in recent years. To further develop this recent attempt, Chapter 6 examines case studies both of sending and receiving countries: the Philippines and South Africa as sending countries, and Saudi Arabia, the United Kingdom and the United States as receiving countries.

The author finds that the volume and destination of migrant health workers significantly change over time, and the changes depend not on the sending countries' situations but on the receiving countries' domestic conditions and policy changes. The author suggests that the supply of health workers from lower-income countries is positioned as an *adjustment valve* to fill the gap between supply and demand of domestic health workers in richer countries. This finding provides a new perspective on this issue for the current international debate which has been mostly concerned with the volume of migrants from developing countries. This function as an adjustment valve causes uncertainty for the sending countries because the sending countries cannot predict the volume of health workers who will leave their health sectors. Health workers or students who seek better opportunities in richer countries will also face uncertainty concerning the demand in those countries.

Although a conclusive answer to this issue cannot be provided, the author suggests two possible policy responses. The first is to establish formal bilateral agreements on migration of health workers between sending and receiving countries. The other suggestion is to enhance medical tourism, but this suggestion will be controversial. The author emphasizes the positive spillover effect from medical tourism for host countries (developing countries). Healthcare services provided by hospitals with advanced skills and technology organized for medical tourism to treat foreign patients would possibly spill over into host countries. Such a spillover effect would contribute to improving the quality of care in developing countries (host countries), and medical tourism would also enhance retention of health workers in developing countries (host countries) by increasing their wages.

However, we should note that it is the rural areas that suffer severely due to a lack of health workers in developing countries. Medical tourism could aggravate the maldistribution of health workers within a developing country. Health workers who are seeking better opportunities would perhaps increasingly attempt to seek workplaces in urban areas where the working conditions and remuneration would be superior through enhanced medical tourism, and this would not necessarily ameliorate the lack of health workers or improve the quality of care in rural areas. The effect of medical tourism on host countries (developing countries) is still controversial; nevertheless, the author's suggestion is worth consideration as a policy option for this emerging issue.

Provision of healthcare services in rural areas is a serious challenge for developing countries. In many developing countries, public health institutions are placed in rural areas to provide primary health services free of charge or with low user fees. However, such public health institutions frequently do not function as intended. Chapter 7 provides a case study of the function of a primary health centre (PHC) in rural Andhra Pradesh, India. Various constraints exist. Their deployment is not sufficient or appropriate, such that rural population cannot physically access the public health institutions. Other problems include the lack of availability of pharmaceuticals and medical equipment and the absenteeism of physicians or vacant positions in public health institutions. Chapter 7 examines PHC deployment and factors causing the malfunction of PHCs.

The authors find that although the number of PHCs has increased in rural Andhra Pradesh, the distribution is still biased. There are significantly fewer primary health centres in areas inhabited by scheduled tribes. They also find that a lack of necessary medical goods and physicians hinders the poor from obtaining healthcare services at PHCs. They suggest that the critical factor that causes physician absenteeism is the large difference in the remuneration between PHCs and private health institutions. The authors indicate that the large differences in remuneration create an incentive that substantially influences the absence of PHC physicians as well as the quality of their care.

The first response should be to raise the remuneration of PHC physicians. It is, unfortunately, not a realistic option for the government of a developing country, in particular a local government, to provide remuneration for physicians of PHCs that is comparable to that of private institutions. To improve physician attendance at PHCs, the authors suggest that the remuneration should be linked to the performance of a physician; the remuneration of PHC physician is generally based on seniority at present. The most important but difficult challenge is measuring performance. The authors argue that performance evaluation could be composed of personal evaluation and medical evaluation. The medical evaluation assesses whether the treatment provided is medically appropriate. The personal evaluation could be performed by the patients treated or by the community in which the PHC is located. In line with improvement in data availability, further elaborate work will be required to examine the effectiveness of the performance evaluation schemes.

Healthcare services for the extreme poor

Chapter 8 reviews the experiences of the NGO Asha Kiran Society that provides healthcare services to the socially excluded poor in Orissa, India. Public health services frequently do not reach the socially excluded poor who inhabit remote areas. In response to the questions of 'Who will be able to provide health services for those poor people?' and 'How is it possible to provide health services for those socially excluded poor', the Asha Kiran Society started its activities to provide healthcare services for the largely tribal groups of Southern Orissa in 1991.

Based on their experiences, the authors cite four major barriers to improvement of access for the excluded poor to basic healthcare services. The first is a sort of a cultural barrier. The socially excluded tribes generally do not have knowledge about modern healthcare services, and this forms a psychological barrier that prevents them from accessing healthcare services. This type of demand-side barrier sometimes exists, and its removal is critical to reaching the socially excluded poor. Geographical barriers are also critical because the targeted poor inhabit remote areas. It is not physically easy, and sometimes not even possible, for them to access public health institutions. This geographical problem leads to another barrier, that is, the economic barrier. Public transportation is generally not available in such remote areas. If the extreme poor in these areas therefore need to use private transportation, the fare costs impose a heavy financial burden. In addition, as discussed in Chapter 7, PHCs are unlikely to function as intended. The authors cite this malfunction of PHCs as an organizational barrier. In that case, patients need to pay user fees to obtain healthcare services, which further impoverish the poor.

How did the Asha Kiran Society approach the poor people and overcome the barriers? Village-level health visits and community health workers' activities contributed to bridging the geographical barrier. In addition, Asha Kiran took an effective approach by training semi-literate village women as health assistants. This approach was effective not only in overcoming the geographical barrier but also in bridging the cultural barrier. Involving the community in the activities also contributed to the sustainability of the health service provision.

To provide the poor with financial protection, particularly against in-patient financial burdens, the Asha Kiran Society established a community health insurance scheme. The authors indicate that a distinguishing feature of this insurance is the building of the insurance scheme on the existing system of solidarity within local communities. This appears to share features with the experience of Japan's insurance system in the pre-war period, as discussed in Chapter 3. This experience provides a lesson for establishing a sort of health insurance system in societies where a formal economy is not well organized.

One of the most significant outputs of the Asha Kiran Society's activities was to generate awareness of healthcare services among the socially excluded poor, who had hardly received the services before. As a result, their health-seeking behaviour changed; this led to better health service utilization and an improvement in their health knowledge, nutrition and maternal health.

Providing healthcare services for the excluded poor is an important challenge in the context of health and poverty. However, the extreme poor are socially excluded, so that the general health sector reforms usually do not respond to this issue. The experiences reviewed in this chapter provide lessons for this delicate and often neglected issue.

This introductory chapter has summarized the issue of health in development as well as the focus of our study, namely the key elements of health systems. We observed the recent state of the key elements in developing regions in the overview of this study. The following chapters provide in-depth analyses of each element.

Notes

1. WHO (2000) defined a health system as one including 'all the activities whose primary purpose is to promote, restore, or maintain health', and stated 'all health systems carry out the functions of providing or delivering personal and non-personal health services; generating the necessary human and physical resources to make that possible; raising and pooling the revenues used to purchase services; and acting as the overall stewards of the resources, powers, and expectations entrusted them'.
2. Korea and Taiwan achieved universal coverage through mandated social health insurance between the late 1980s and the early 1990s when they

became middle-income countries (Hiroi and Komamura 2003). More recently, Thailand achieved universal coverage by introducing what is known as the '30 baht insurance scheme', although the scheme still has problems related to of financial sustainability and harmonization between insurance programmes (Pannarunothai 2008).
3. WHO (2004) indicates that, in 2000, average annual per capita spending on medicine was US$4.40 in low-income countries and US$396 in high-income countries. Considering the substantial differences in total health expenditure per capita between developing countries and developed countries, that is a serious financial burden for obtaining medicine in low-income countries.
4. The data is from WHOSIS (WHO Statistical Information System): www.who. int/whosis/en/index.html.

References

Backlund, Eric, Paul D. Sporlie and Norman J. Johnson (1999) 'A Comparison and the Relationships of Education and Income with Mortality: the National Longitudinal Mortality Study', *Social Science and Medicine*, Vol. 49: 1373–84.

Bidani, Benu and Martin Ravallion (1997) 'Decomposing Social Indicators Using Distributional Data', *Journal of Econometrics*, Vol. 77: 125–39.

Blas, E. and N. Hearst (2002) 'Health Sector Reform and Equity-Learning From Evidence?' *Health Policy and Planning*, Vol. 17 (Suppl 1): 1–4.

Cebu Study Team (1991) 'Underlying and Proximate Determinants of Child Health', *American Journal of Epidemiology*, Vol. 133, No. 2: 185–201.

Deaton, Angus (2002) 'Policy Implications of the Gradient of Health and Wealth', *Health Affairs*, Vol. 21, No. 2: 12–30.

Deaton, Angus and Darren Lubotsky (2003) 'Mortality, Inequality and Race in American Cities and States', *Social Science and Medicine*, Vol. 56: 1139–53.

Elo, Irama T. and Samuel H. Preston (1996) 'Education Differentials in Mortality: United States, 1979–85', *Social Science and Medicine*, Vol. 42. No. 1: 47–57.

Feinstein, Jonathan S. (1993) 'The Relationship Between Socioeconomic Status and Health: A Review of the Literature,' *The Milbank Quarterly*, Vol. 72: No. 2: 279–322.

Flegg, A. T. (1982) 'Inequality of Income, Illiteracy and Medical Care as Determinants of Infant Mortality in Underdeveloped Countries,' *Population Studies*, Vol. 36, No. 3: 441–58.

Fuchs, Victor R. (2004) 'Reflection the Socio-Economic Correlates of Health', *Journal of Health Economics*, Vol. 23: 653–61.

Grossman, Michael (1972) 'On the Concept of Health Capital and Demand for Health', *The Journal of Political Economy*, Vol. 80, No. 2: 223–55.

Hanson, Kara, M. Kent Ranson, Valeria Oliveira-Cruz and Anne Milles (2003) 'Expanding Access to Priority Health Interventions: A Framework for Understanding the Constraints to Scaling-up', *Journal of International Development*, Vol. 15: 1–14.

Hiroi, Yoshinori (1999) *Nihon no Shakai Hosho* (in Japanese) (Social Security Systems in Japan), Tokyo: Iwanami Shoten.

Hiroi, Yoshinori and Kouhei Komamura (eds) (2003) *Asia no Shakai Hosyo* (in Japanese) (Social Security Systems in Asia), Tokyo Daigaku Syuppankai.

Hulme, David 2003. 'Conceptualizing Chronic Poverty', *World Development*, Vol. 31, No. 3: 403–23.

Japan International Cooperation Agency (JICA) Institute for International Cooperation (2004) *Nihon no Hoken Iryo no Keiken* (in Japanese) (Development of Japan's Health Systems), Tokyo: JICA.

McIntyre, Di and Michael Thiede (2008) 'Illness, Health Service Costs and Their Consequences for Households', in Sara Bennett, Lucy Gilson and Anne Milles (eds) *Health, Economic Development and Household Poverty*, 75–89, London and New York: Routledge.

OECD (2007) *International Migration Outlook 2007*, Paris: OECD.

OECD-WHO (2003) *Poverty and Health*, Paris: OECD.

Palmer, Natasha (2008) 'Access and Equity: Evidence on the Extent to Which Health Studies Address the Needs of the Poor', in Sara Bennett, Lucy Gilson and Anne Milles (eds) *Health, Economic Development and Household Poverty*, 61–74, London and New York: Routledge.

Pannarunothai, Supasit 2008. 'Improving Equity in Health Through Health Financing Reform: A Case Study of the Introduction of Universal Coverage in Thailand', in Sara Bennett, Lucy Gilson, and Anne Milles (eds) *Health, Economic Development and Household Poverty*, 189–202. London and New York: Routledge.

Preston, Samuel H. (1975) 'Changing Relation Between Mortality and Level of Economic Development,' *Population Studies*, Vol. 29, No. 2: 231–48.

Ranson, M. Kent, Tara Sinha and Mirai Chatterjee (2008) 'Promoting Access, Financial Protection and Empowerment for the Poor: Vimo SEWA in India', in Sara Bennett, Lucy Gilson and Anne Mills (eds) *Health, Economic Development and Household Poverty*, 203–24, London and New York: Routledge.

Roemer, Milton I. (1991) *National Health Systems of The World, Volume One: The Countries*, New York: Oxford University Press.

Roemer, Milton I. (1993a) *National Health Systems of The World, Volume II: The Issues*, New York: Oxford University Press.

Roemer, Milton I. (1993b) 'National Health Systems Thought the World', *Annual Review of Public Health*, Vol. 14: 335–53.

Roemer, Milton I. and Ruth Roemer (1990) 'Global Health, National Development, and the Role of Government,' *American Journal of Public Health*, Vol. 80, No. 10: 1188–92.

Russel, Steven (2008) 'Coping with the Costs of Illness: Vulnerability and Resilience Among Poor Households in Urban Sri Lanka', in Sara Bennett, Lucy Gilson and Anne Milles (eds) *Health, Economic Development and Household Poverty*, 90-114, London and New York: Routledge.

Sala-i-Martín, David. (2005) 'On the Health-Poverty Trap', in Guillem López-Casasnovas, Berta Rivera and Luis Currais (eds) *Health and Economic Growth*, 95-114, Cambridge MA and London: MIT Press.

Schultz, T. Paul (1993) 'Mortality Decline in the Low-Income World: Causes and Consequences,' *The American Economic Review*, Vol. 83, No. 2: 337–42.

Thomas, Duncan, Victor Lavy, and John Strauss (1996) 'Public Policy and Anthoropometric Outcomes in the Côte d'Ivoire', *Journal of Public Economics*, Vol. 61: 155–92.

UN Millennium Project 2005. *Who's Got the Power? Transforming Health Systems for Women and Children*, Task Force on Child Health and Maternal Health, World Bank.

WHO (World Health Organization) (2000) *The World Heath Report 2000: Health Systems; Improving Performance*, Geneva: World Health Organization.

WHO (2004) *The World Medicine Situation*, Geneva: World Health Organization.

WHO (2005) *The World Health Report 2005: Make Every Mother and Child Count*, Geneva: World Health Organization.

WHO (2006) *The World Health Report 2006: Working Together for Health*, Geneva: World Health Organization.

World Bank (2006) *Health Financing Revisited*, Washington: World Bank.

WHO, UNAIDS, UNICEF (2007) *Towards Universal Access: Scaling Up Priority HIV/AIDS Interventions in the Health Sector*, Geneva: World Health Organization.

1
What is the Role of Public Finance in Health and How Should It Be Fulfilled?: A Study of China

Hiroko Uchimura

Introduction

Health is a critical concern in developing countries. Improving health at the national level as well as reducing health disparity within a country is an important challenge for developing countries (WHO 2004a, 2005a). Various factors influence health disparity in a country. Income levels of households can affect affordable health services. Education levels would influence people's healthcare-seeking behavior. Such differences in demand-side factors lead to disparity in health among people. The scale and allocation of health resources affect availability and accessibility of healthcare services in every region. Such differences in supply-side factors also lead to disparity in health between regions. This chapter focuses on supply-side factors by examining the case of China, a country that faces serious disparity in health across regions and areas.

Before the economic reforms, provision of health services was basically financed through state-owned enterprises (SOEs) in urban areas and people's communes in rural areas. After the economic reforms began in the late 1970s, the economy rapidly developed, and socioeconomic conditions significantly changed in China. The changes, however, brought about decay in the conventional health system based on SOEs or people's communes. Instead, central and local governments required direct financing for the health system, and individuals also became to bear financial burdens of obtaining healthcare services (Li 2004; Wong et al. 2006).

Since priority was given to economic development, reforming the health system was not undertaken promptly in China. As a result, out-of-pocket payments (OOP) for health services soared, and health improvement stagnated through the 1980s and the 1990s. Although the financial role of government became increasingly important in reforming the health system, the central government transferred most responsibilities to local governments (Blumenthal and Hsiao 2005). The fiscal capacity of local governments came to have a substantial impact on provision of health services at their localities. In this context, this chapter highlights the influence of government financing on the availability and accessibility of healthcare services in China. In particular, it examines the impact of local fiscal capacity on the strength of local health resources, and overall design and funding schemes of the new medical insurance programmes.

There are several financial sources for health, such as general tax revenues, social insurance or direct personal payments. Among these sources, general tax revenues have the merit of supporting equity in health by providing health services on the basis of health needs (Roemer 1993). Public finance is hence expected to contribute to reducing health disparity in a country (World Bank 2006). In this sense, in addition to providing public goods or correcting insurance market failures, subsidizing the poor to obtain needed health services also justifies the intervention of government in financing health systems (Musgrove 1996; Gertler 1998; World Bank 2006).

Considering such characteristics of public finance for health, our underlying concern in this chapter is how government financing influences health disparities between regions or areas in China. By examing the impact of local fiscal capacity on health resources or medical insurance function, we consider how public finance can improve the health service provision in poor localities and reduce health disparities in China as a whole. The next section observes the health status as well as the scale and allocation of health resources in China. Section 2 summarizes patterns of Chinese government financing for health systems. Section 3 clarifies the intergovernmental fiscal relationship between central and local governments. In order to examine the relationship between local fiscal capacity and local health resources, this section provides basic information on public finance in China. Section 4 includes econometric analysis of government financing and local health resources. It also examines functions of the new medical insurance programmes. The last section presents conclusions.

1.1 Health status transition in China

1.1.1 Mortality levels

Figure 1.1 presents changes in the under-five-years old mortality rate (U5MR) and economic growth (per capita GDP) in China and developing

(1) Changes between 2000 and 1990

Growth ratio of per capita GDP of 2000 to that of 1990:
per capita GDP (2000)/per capita GDP (1990)

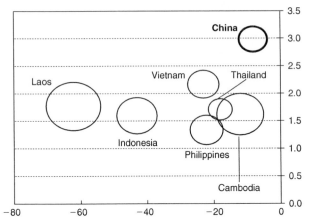

Reduction in U5MR between 2000 and 1990:
U5MR of 2000 − U5MR of 1990

(2) Changes between 2005 and 2000

Growth ratio of per capita GDP of 2005 to that of 2000:
per capita GDP (2005)/per capita GDP (2000)

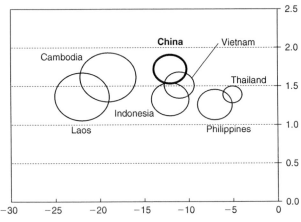

Reduction in U5MR between 2005 and 2000:
U5MR of 2005 − U5MR of 2000

Figure 1.1: Changes in mortality levels and economic growth in China and developing Asian countries: U5MR and per capita GDP

Notes: Author's compilation based on data from *The United Nations Site for the MDG Indicators*, United Nations, and *World Economic Outlook*, IMF.
Size of the circle in (1) indicates the level of U5MR for each country in 1990.
Size of the circle in (2) indicates the level of U5MR for each country in 2000.
In both cases, lager circles indicate higher mortality levels.
Per capita GDP is on a purchasing-power-parity basis.

Per 1000 live births

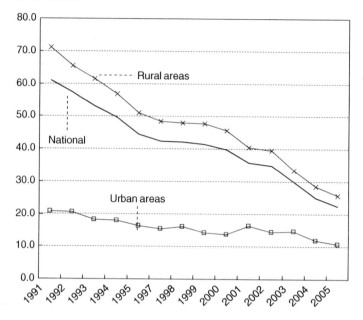

Figure 1.2:   Changes in U5MR in China
Note: Author's compilation based on data from *Health Statistical Yearbook of China* (Ministry of Health, China).

Asian countries. Compared with the latter, China's economic growth was impressive between 1990 and 2000. In fact, the Chinese economy has achieved over 9 per cent growth per year since the 1990s. However, improvement in its health status was the most sluggish in the Asian countries (Figure 1.1). After 2000, the pace of China's improvement in the health status caught up with that of other Asian countries.

Looking at the health indicators within a country, the trend and level of indicators differ between urban and rural areas in China (Figure 1.2). The U5MR were more than three times higher in rural areas than in urban areas in the 1990s. The disparity gradually began to decrease after 2000. The mortality level of the whole of China is strongly affected by that of rural China, which reflects the heavy weight of the rural population as a proportion of the national population. This suggests that, in order to improve health status in China, rural health status must be improved. Health status also varies across regions. The maternal mortality rate (MMR) significantly differs between provinces (Figure 1.3).

Per capita GDP
by province (1000 RMB)

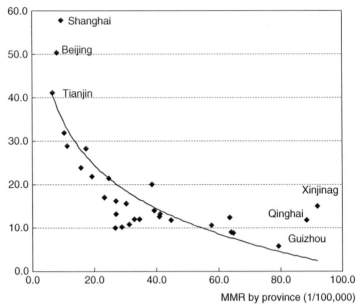

Figure 1.3: Maternal mortality rate and per capita GDP by province (2006)

Notes: Author's compilation based on data from *Health Statistical Yearbook of China* and *Statistical Yearbook of China*.
Data include 30 provinces. Tibet is excluded because its MMR is exceptionally high (244.1, 2006).

The MMR of Tianjin (6.6) or Beijing (7.9) is almost the same level as that of Japan (6.0, 2005).[1] This is less than one-tenth of the MMR of provinces that have progressed less, such as Guizhou (79.3), Qinghai (88.5) or Xinjiang (92.1). The health disparity between regions is also critical in China.

1.1.2 Health resources

In the following, we overview physical or human resources, such as the number of hospital beds or doctors per 1000 population in China (Figure 1.4). Referring to other Asian countries, for instance, the number of doctors per 1000 population is 1.57 (2003) in Korea, 0.7 (2000) in Malaysia, and 0.58 (2000) in the Philippines. As presented in Figure 1.4, compared with those Asian countries, the number of doctors per 1000 population in China is not relatively low. The number of hospital beds

Per 1000 population

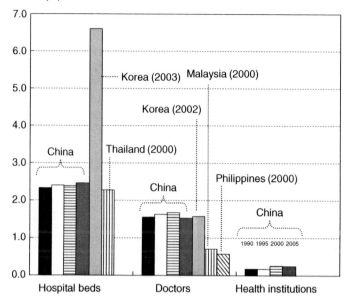

Figure 1.4: Number of health resources per 1000 population in China and other Asian countries

Notes: The number of hospital beds and doctors is from *China Statistical Yearbook* (National Bureau of Statistics, China). Calculations on the number of health institutions are based on data from *China Statistical Yearbook* (National Bureau of Statistics, China). Data for other Asian countries are from WHOSIS (WHO Statistical Information System): www.who.int/whosis/en/index.html.

per 1000 population in China is lower than that of Korea (6.6, 2002), but it is almost the same as Thailand (2.2, 2000). These figures indicate that health output level in China is not low compared with other Asian countries.

The number of doctors or hospital beds per 1000 population varies among provinces and differs between urban and rural areas in China (Table 1.1). The number of hospital beds per 1000 population is 6.79 in Beijing and 6.81 in Shanghai, which is the same level as in Korea (6.6, 2002), while it is much lower in other provinces, such as 1.69 in Guizhou or 1.98 in Jiangxi.

We further investigate the differences in the number of health institutions per 10,000 population below the province level. Figure 1.5 presents the highest and the lowest number of health institutions per 10,000 population in prefectures in a province. The Theil index captures the

Table 1.1:   Health resources by province

	Doctors	Hospital beds	Beds in township and village health centres
	(per 1000 population)		(per 1000 rural population)
National	1.52	2.70	0.80
Highest three	4.28 (Beijing)	6.81 (Shanghai)	2.38 (Shanghai)
	3.23 (Shanghai)	6.79 (Beijing)	1.29 (Beijing)
	2.65 (Tianjin)	4.58 (Tianjin)	1.29 (Jiangsu)
Lowest three	1.11 (Guanxi)	1.98 (Jiangxi)	0.55 (Guanxi)
	1.06 (Guizhou)	1.95 (Guanxi)	0.47 (Guizhou)
	1.01 (Anhui)	1.69 (Guizhou)	0.46 (Ningxia)
Standard deviation	0.68	1.21	0.36
Median	1.53	2.78	0.78
Sample	31	31	31

Notes: Author's compilation based on the following data:
The number of hospital beds per 1000 population and beds in township and village health centers per 1000 rural population are 2006 data from *Health Statistical Yearbook of China* (Ministry of Health, China). The number of doctors is based on data of 2005 from *China Statistical Yearbook for Regional Economy* (Department of Comprehensive Statistics, National Bureau of Statistics, China).

disparity in the density of health institutions among prefectures in a province. The higher the Theil index, the larger the disparity. The Theil index indicating the gap between provinces (0.05) is lower than that between prefectures in most of the provinces. It means that the disparity between prefectures in most of the provinces is larger than the disparity between provinces. In addition, the disparity level between prefectures varies among provinces. Health institutions are relatively equally distributed among prefectures in some provinces, whereas they are more unevenly distributed in others.

Those figures indicate that the health resources are not distributed well between and within provinces. The density of health resources also significantly varies between urban areas and rural areas. Improvement in the health status for China was sluggish in the 1990s when compared with its impressive economic growth. In addition, the serious problem in China is the health disparities between regions or urban and rural areas.

Before the economic reforms, health service provision was basically financed through state-owned enterprises (SOEs) in urban areas[2] and through the cooperative medical scheme (CMS) based on people's communes in rural areas (World Bank 1997; Li 2004; Wong et al. 2006). Along

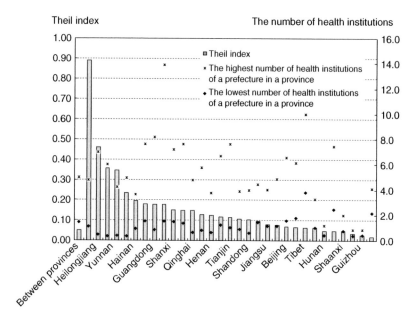

Figure 1.5: Number of health institutions (per 10,000 population): disparity among prefectures in provinces, 2005

Notes: Author's calculation based on data from *China Statistical Yearbook for Regional Economy* (Department of Comprehensive Statistics, National Bureau of Statistics, China).

with the penetration of the market economy, SOEs began to suffer from deficits. A main reason for the deficit was the heavy financial responsibility of SOEs to provide their employees and retirees with healthcare services (Nakagane 1999; Zhu 2004; Li 2004). SOEs, suffering severely from the deficit, came to be unable to finance health service provision (Liu 2002; Wong et al. 2006). Another result of introducing the market system was an increase in non-SOE type of enterprise, such as private and foreign-affiliated companies. The conventional health system did not cover employees of those non-SOEs.

Along with the economic reforms in rural areas, the rural health system, i.e., the cooperative medical scheme (CMS), began to malfunction. Agricultural production, administration or social services were based on people's communes in rural areas. Economic reforms, however, moved the production base from collectives to the household by initiating household production responsibility system. This brought about the disbandment of the people's commune that was the organizational and financial basis of the CMS, which ultimately weakened the function of the CMS (World Bank 1997, Li 2004, Zhu 2004).[3] The conventional health system needed to be reformed. The health system, however, was not restructured with changes in socioeconomic conditions. Particularly, health system reform in rural areas was almost ignored. Such a failure was a critical factor in the health problems of China in the 1980s and the 1990s (Blumenthal and Hsiao 2005).

Instead of SOEs or people's communes, governments were required to take substantial responsibility for financing health service provisions. However, the central government tightened its fiscal investment in the health sector over the 1990s, and left most responsibilities for health service provision to local governments (Blumenthal and Hsiao 2005). It was pointed out that local governments in poor regions, suffering from a lack of fiscal resources, did not take sufficient responsibility (World Bank 1997, 2005). The fiscal capacity of local governments in China began to have a critical effect on health service provision at their localities.

1.2   Patterns of public finance for health

In general, there are mainly two methods that government finances a health system: financing publicly provided health services or financing the payments for obtaining health services (Musgrove 1996). In other words, public finance improves the access of people to healthcare services by either making the services or supporting their purchasing (Chalkley and Malcomson 2000). Developing countries usually mix these methods in order to finance their health systems (World Bank 2006). China also applies both methods to its health system.

1.2.1   Health expenditure level

Before examining each of the methods in China, this sub-section reviews the trend of total expenditure on health after the 1990s. Total expenditure on health (THE) as percentage of GDP has gradually increased since the mid-1990s (Figure 1.6). In contrast, government expenditure on health as percentage of THE continuously decreased over the 1990s, reaching about 15 per cent in 2000, which is almost 10 per cent lower than the level in 1990. This trend corresponds with that the government tightened its investment in the health sector over the 1990s. Since 2003, however, government contribution to total health expenditure has gradually expanded. Although recent increases are still modest, the government's recent attempt at health sector reform appears to be reflected in the change in fiscal expenditures for health.

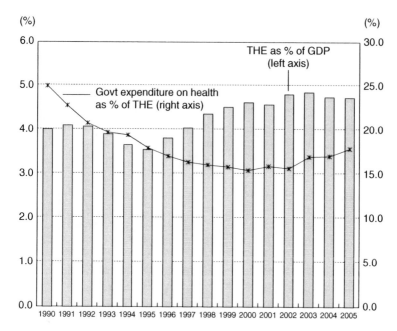

Figure 1.6: Total expenditure and government expenditure on health
Note: Author's compilation based on data from *China National Health Accounts* (China National Health Economic Institute, 2006).

1.2.2 Supporting health service provision

The government subsidizes publicly owned health institutions in China. However, it does not fully fund publicly owned health institutions but rather subsidizes a part of the budget of health institutions (World Bank 1997, 2002; Blumenthal and Hsiao 2005). Alternatively, the government allowed publicly owned health institutions to charge user fees for healthcare services provided in order to keep their financial balance (Liu 2004; WHO 2005b).[4] In this sense, the government does not quite make healthcare services but rather *supports* making healthcare services in China.

The subsidy covers a part of the running costs of health institutions. Budgeting depends on the number of personnel or beds in health institutions, but there is no unified scheme set by the central government. In practice, budgeting is mostly passive depending on prior levels; moreover, it critically depends on the fiscal capacity of local levels (World Bank 2002). Capital investment is theoretically managed through the five-year plans. Hence, budgeting is supposed to be appropriated for capital investment based on the plans. However, in actual practice, it mostly depends on the fiscal resource availability (World Bank 2002).

1.2.3   Financing medical insurance

Another instrument of government to finance health systems in China is subsidizing medical insurance programmes in urban and rural areas. In other words, the government financially supports people to obtain (buy) healthcare services. As mentioned above, user fees are charged for services, even those provided by publicly owned health services. Therefore, except for some specified services, such as state regulated immunization, patients need to pay for the healthcare services they obtain.[5]

In order to reduce individual financial burdens on accessing healthcare services as well as to lessen financial risks associated with uncertain illness, a medical insurance programme was established for urban employees in 1998 (*the urban employee basic medical insurance programme*) which is funded by premiums contributed both by employees and employers (Ministry of Labour and Social Security 1998; Li 2004; Wong et al. 2006). However, this insurance programme targets only formal employees in urban areas who have an urban registration.[6] The dependent family members of urban employees are not eligible to enrol in this insurance programme because the enrolment unit of the programme is the individual employee (Ministry of Labour and Social Security 1998).[7] In addition, rural migrants who emigrate from rural areas to urban areas and inhabit urban areas are also ineligible to enrol in the insurance programme. Therefore, a substantial portion of the urban population was uninsured.

Taking the situation seriously, in 2007 the government initiated pilot programmes of a new urban medical insurance programme (*the urban resident basic medical insurance programme*) (Ministry of Labour and Social Security 2007). Dependent family members and informal workers and the like who are urban residents are eligible to enrol in this insurance programme. Rural migrants are generally not eligible to enrol in this urban insurance programme because they are not part of the urban registered population. The government's target is coverage of 90 per cent of the urban population in 2009 and universal coverage in 2010 (Ministry of Labour and Social Security 2007). To support this insurance programme and attain the universal coverage, both central and local governments subsidize the insurance fund.[8]

Following the decay of the former cooperative medical scheme (CMS), the rural health system was not reformed until recent years. The government eventually initiated action to restructure the rural health system and established the new cooperative medical scheme (the new CMS) in 2003 (Ministry of Health 2003; WHO 2004b). The enrolment unit of the new CMS is the family (household). The premium is, however, charged on a per capita basis, and thus each household premium is the sum of all family members' premiums. All family members are required to enrol in the new CMS en masse. In order to support this scheme and restore the rural health system, central and local governments subsidize the rural insurance fund (Ministry of Health 2003).[9] The central government subsidizes insurance funds of the new CMS mainly in central-western regions where economic levels are relatively low. In recent times, the government has made efforts to increase the coverage of medical insurance. By the end of 2007, coverage of the new CMS has already reached 86.2 per cent (Ministry of Health 2008). The government aims to attain universal coverage by 2010. In China, the government supports people's purchase of health services by establishing and subsidizing the medical insurance programmes.

1.3 Intergovernmental fiscal relationships

In this section, we focus on the intergovernmental fiscal relationships between central and local governments, and provide the background for the analysis of government financing and local health resources. The intergovernmental fiscal relationship between central and provincial governments is highly decentralized in China, and this is an important factor in health disparities between regions (Mei and Wang 2006). The intergovernmental fiscal relationship below the provincial level, such as that between a province and county governments, varies across provinces. Fiscal responsibility is fairly centralized at the provincial level in some provinces, whereas it is mostly decentralized to the county level in other provinces (Uchimura and Jütting 2007).

Table 1.2 shows that local governments have substantial responsibility over fiscal expenditure. The large share of local government expenditure out of total fiscal expenditure is high even when compared to other countries around the world (OECD 2006). The expenditure responsibility of local governments is particularly high in the health sector.[10] Local governments finance more than 97 per cent of total fiscal health expenditures. Conversely, the central government shares significantly a small part of total government health expenditures. It limits the potential of central government to equalize the capacity of health service provision between localities (World Bank 2005). On the revenue side, the central government restored its authority after the tax-sharing system was

Table 1.2:   Percentage of central and local government shares in fiscal revenue and expenditure

	Fiscal revenue		Fiscal expenditure		Operating expenses for health	
	Central Govt	Local Govt	Central Govt	Local Govt	Central Govt	Local Govt
1992	27.8	72.2	28.8	71.2	2.4	97.6
1993	21.6	78.4	27.5	72.5	2.2	97.8
1994	57.7	42.3	28.9	71.1	2.2	97.8
1995	54.5	45.5	28.5	71.5	2.0	98.0
1996	51.8	48.2	27.2	72.8	2.0	98.0
1997	49.3	50.7	22.5	77.5	2.0	98.0
1998	49.5	50.5	28.9	71.1	2.1	97.9
1999	51.1	48.9	31.5	68.5	1.6	98.4
2000	52.2	47.8	34.7	65.3	1.5	98.5
2001	52.4	47.6	30.5	69.5	2.1	97.9
2002	55.0	45.0	30.7	69.3	2.7	97.3
2003	54.6	45.4	30.1	69.9	2.8	97.2
2004	54.9	45.1	27.7	72.3	2.6	97.4

Note: Author's calculation based on data from *Finance Yearbook of China* (Ministry of Finance, China).

introduced in 1994. With the increased revenue, the central government expanded its fiscal transfer to local governments.

Figure 1.7 presents the Gini coefficient, which captures the inequality level of the fiscal revenues among local governments (provinces). We find interesting differences in the trend of the Gini coefficient between local own revenue and local total revenue. The local own revenue is the province's own revenue, whereas the local total revenue includes the province's own revenue and the fiscal transfer from central government.[11] The level of the Gini coefficient is higher in local (province) own revenue than in local total revenue over the period, which means the disparity in the local own revenue among provinces is larger than the disparity in local total revenue. In addition, while the disparity in the province own revenue has further expanded since 2000, the disparity in the local total revenue has decreased slightly since the late 1990s. The fiscal transfer from central to local governments has come to be distributed in order to reduce the disparity in provincial fiscal capacities. The level of the inequality in fiscal health expenditure is lower than that in the local own revenue. However, changes in inequality in fiscal health expenditure do not exactly follow changes in inequality in local

Gini coefficient

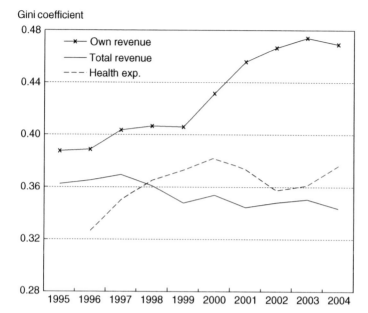

Figure 1.7: Disparities among provinces: own revenue, total revenue, fiscal health expenditure

Note: Author's calculation based on data from *Finance Yearbook of China* (Ministry of Finance, China).

total revenue. Rather, the inequality level of fiscal health expenditure fluctuated over the period.

In introducing the tax-sharing system in 1994, the central government also introduced the tax-refund system. Based on local own revenue in 1993, the amount of local fiscal revenue fell in 1994 and afterwards, due to the introduction of the tax-sharing system, has been refunded by the central government (Naito 2004; Dabla-Norris 2005; OECD 2006).[12] Obviously, this system reduced the redistributive effect of the fiscal transfer from central to local governments on local fiscal capacities (Dabla-Norris 2005; OECD 2006). Though the fiscal revenue of the central government increased after the tax-sharing system was introduced, the central government could not initially use the increased revenue effectively to equalize fiscal capacities between local governments. However, as we observed above, disparities in local fiscal capacity have been reduced since the late 1990s. Because of the increase in total tax generation, the central government increasingly has additional revenues to equalize the fiscal capacities between local governments.

The amount of fiscal transfer from central to local governments affects local fiscal resources. In addition, the design of the fiscal transfer influences the allocation of local government budgets. In China, nearly half of the fiscal transfers from central to local governments are special purpose (earmarked) transfers (Dabla-Norris 2005; OECD 2006). The earmarked transfers do not include many health-purpose subsidies, but mainly include subsidies for rural tax reforms, primary and middle-school teacher salaries, or civil servants' salary increases (OECD 2006; Mei and Wang 2006; Naito 2006). In addition, the Chinese government frequently provides earmarked subsidies on a matching-fund basis that requires co-financing by local governments (World Bank 2002; OECD 2006). Such types of subsidy force local governments to allocate their own revenue for co-financing (OECD 2006). Earmarked subsidies on a matching-fund basis change the allocation of local government budgets (Jinno 2007). Moreover, if local governments cannot afford their share of the cost (co-financing), they cannot take up the funds (earmarked transfers) (World Bank 2002; Jinno 2007). These features of fiscal transfer from central to local governments reduce redistributive effects on local financing for health in China.

1.4   Influence of public finance on health

1.4.1   Impact of local fiscal capacity on health resources

Table 1.3 summarizes the relationship between the density of health resources and local revenues. Both per capita local own revenue and per capita local total revenue correlate most highly with the number of hospital beds per 10,000 population. The number of doctors per 10,000 population also correlates highly with the local revenues. However, neither local own revenue nor local total revenue particularly correlates with the number of health institutions per 10,000 population. The number of hospital beds or doctors per 10,000 population correlates more with the local own revenue than with the local total revenue. These figures indicate that fiscal transfer, included in local total revenue, does not exert much influence on the number of per capita hospital beds or doctors at each locality.

We further investigate the relationship between the density of health resources and local own revenue or local total expenditure at the prefectural level.[13] Hospital beds per 10,000 population correlate more highly with local own revenue than with local total expenditure (Table 1.4), although the correlation level does not differ greatly. Health institutions per 10,000 population correlate more with local total expenditure than

Table 1.3: Relationships between local government revenues and health resources at provincial level (2000–2004)

	Correlation coefficient		Standard deviation	Max	Min	Median	Mean
	Per capita own revenue (RMB)	Per capita total revenue (RMB)					
Hospital beds	0.77	0.57	12.05	66.80	2.34	24.20	27.40
Doctors	0.71	0.54	7.87	47.90	2.97	14.80	16.88
Health institutions	0.14	0.30	1.10	7.05	0.53	2.75	2.74
Per capita own revenue (RMB)	–	–	1152.1	8179.5	214.3	489.6	874.2
Per capita total revenue (RMB)	–	–	1586.7	11087.4	477.1	1220.4	1750.8

Notes: Author's calculation based on data from *Health Statistical Yearbook of China* (Ministry of Health, China) and *Finance Yearbook of China* (Ministry of Finance, China). Pool data covers the period from 2000 to 2004. The revenue of local government is the aggregate revenue of all tiers of government below the provincial level. The number of hospital beds, doctors and health institutions is based on a per 10,000 population basis.

Table 1.4: Relationships between own revenue or total expenditure and health outputs at prefectural level

	Correlation coefficient		Standard deviation	Max	Min	Median	Mean
	Per capita own revenue (RMB)	Per capita total expenditure (RMB)					
Hospital beds	0.67	0.63	19.80	160.98	7.78	27.12	31.99
Health institutions	0.16	0.21					
Per capita own revenue (RMB)	–	–	1571.5	11400.0	70.3	515.0	1090.0
Per capita total expenditure (RMB)	–	–	1910.4	14013.2	140.7	1233.6	1883.3

Notes: Author's calculation based on data from *China Statistical Yearbook for Regional Economy* (Department of Comprehensive Statistics, National Bureau of Statistics, China). Pooled data covers the period of 2004 and 2005 and covers the prefectures of all provinces except Shenzhen and prefectures which do not possess any of the following four types of data: fiscal own revenue, fiscal total expenditure, number of hospital beds or number of health institutions. The number of hospital beds or health institutions is on a per 10,000 population basis.

with local own revenue; however, the correlation level is low. It suggests that fiscal transfer from the upper tiers of government does not have substantial impacts on the level of the health resources at prefectural level either.

Empirical analysis

Focusing on per capita hospital beds and per capita doctors which highly correlate with local fiscal capacity, we econometrically examine the impacts of the local fiscal capacity on health resources by using provincial panel data. Panel data covers 30 provinces over a ten-year period (1995–2004).[14] We use per capita local own revenue and per capita fiscal transfer from central to local governments as fiscal data, and the number of hospital beds per 10,000 population and the number of doctors per 10,000 population as health resource data.[15]

Analytical framework

We examine the impact of local own revenue and the fiscal transfer from central to local governments on health resources. Therefore, the dependent variable is the number of hospital beds or doctors per 10,000 population at provincial level, and the independent variables are local own revenue and the fiscal transfer from central to local governments on a per capita basis. The influence of the design of fiscal transfer on local budget allocation must be considered when the impact of fiscal transfers on health resources is analyzed. As discussed in section 1.3, earmarked subsidies on a matching-fund basis affect the allocation of local government budget because they require co-financing by local governments. Taking such an effect into consideration, the local own revenue allocated for health purposes is defined as follows:

$$OR_{hp} = OR - \delta T - OR_{nh} \qquad (1)$$

where OR denotes the overall local (provincial) own revenue, whereas OR_{hp} denotes the local own revenue allocated for health purposes. T is the fiscal transfer from central to local (provincial) governments. δ is the proportion of provincial government co-financing fund to matching funds (the matching transfer) that are allocated for non-health purposes. OR_{nh} is local (provincial) own revenue allocated for non-health purposes.

Thus, the estimation model is:

$$HR = \alpha + \beta_1(OR - \delta T - OR_{nh}) + \beta_2 \gamma T \qquad (2)$$

where *HR* denotes health resources in a province, and γ is the proportion of the transfer allocated for health purposes. Then, γT is the amount of the fiscal transfer that is allocated for health purposes at each locality. Equation (2) is transformed as follows:

$$HR = \alpha + \beta_1 OR + (\gamma\beta_2 - \delta\beta_1)T - \beta_1 OR_{nh} \qquad (3)$$

The scale of local own revenue may have a positive impact on the level of health resources in each locality. Then, the coefficient of local own revenue (β_1), which captures the effect of local own revenue on health resources controlling the influence of the transfer, is expected to be positive. The first term of the coefficient of the transfer ($\gamma\beta_2$) captures the impact of the transfer allocated for health purposes on health resources, whereas the second term ($\delta\beta_1$) captures the effect of changes in local government budget allocation due to their financing obligation for matching funds. Although the local own revenue allocated for non-health purposes (OR_{nh}) is not observed, it is considered to be specified at each province and to vary over the period. Thus, we apply a fixed-effect model with time-dummy which controls the unit (provincial)-specific characteristics and the time trend.[16] This model hence controls OR_{nh} and other provincial specific characteristics, such as provincial geographical characteristics or the ratio of rural people to urban people in a province, that are expected to affect health resources.

Results of the estimation

Table 1.5 summarizes the main results. Looking at the effects of local fiscal capacity on per capita hospital beds, the coefficient of local own revenue is positive and statistically significant. As expected, higher local own revenue is related to higher per capita hospital beds, when the influence of the fiscal transfer is controlled.[17] With regard to the effect of fiscal transfers, the interpretation is less straightforward. As we discussed above, the coefficient of transfer captures the effect of transfer itself as well as the effect of changes in local budget allocation. Hence, the coefficient of transfer (($\gamma\beta_2 - \delta\beta_1$) in equation (3)), which is negative and statistically significant, captures the overall effect of the transfer that includes both effects of transfer allocated for health purposes and changes in local budget allocation on per capita hospital beds, when the influence of local own revenue on per capita hospital beds is controlled. The negative coefficient means that the impact of changes in local budget allocation on per capita hospital beds is larger than that of the transfer allocated for health purposes.[18] Regarding impacts on the number of per capita doctors, the coefficient of local own revenue is also positive and

Table 1.5:   Estimation results

Dependent variable	The number of hospital beds per 10,000 population (ln)		The number of doctors per 10,000 population (ln)	
Independent variables				
Per capita local own revenue (ln)	0.231	(7.28)***	0.159	(4.78)***
Per capita fiscal transfer to local (ln)	−0.067	(2.88)***	0.010	(0.40)
Number of observations	300		290	
Number of groups	30		29	
R^2 (overall)	0.466		0.462	

Note: The Hubei province is not included in the data set used for analysis of the number of doctors because the data is not available for Hubei.
Numbers in parentheses are t-statistics, corrected for panel heteroskedasticity. The symbol *** indicates significance at the 1 per cent level.

statistically significant. When the influence of the local own revenue on the number of per capita doctors is controlled, the coefficient of transfer, which captures both effects of transfer allocated for health purposes and changes in local budget allocation, is positive but not statistically significant.

Discussion

The analysis indicates that the scale of local own revenue has a significant impact on the level of health resources at each locality (province). It is pointed out that after the economic reforms, the fiscal capacity of local governments has had a critical influence on health resources at each locality in China (Wang 2006a; World Bank 1997, 2002). Our empirical result supports such a situation.

A problem is that local governments in poor regions are not able to take responsibility for health service provision sufficiently. This issue is often discussed in relation to the function of fiscal transfer from the central government, and it is indicated that fiscal transfer does not effectively contribute to improving health in poor regions or reducing health disparities across regions (Zhu 2004; Mei and Wang 2006). Our empirical analysis showed that the effect of changes in local budget allocation due to local financial obligations for matching-fund on health resources (per capita hospital beds) is larger than that of fiscal transfer allocated for health purposes. As mentioned above, earmarked transfers on a matching-fund basis decrease local government own revenues which can be allocated for their own purposes because local governments must allocate their own revenues for co-financing. Such a change in the allocation of local government budgets reduces the overall effect of health-purposed transfers from central to local governments on health resources. If the central government aims at improving health resources in poor localities, it would be more effective to provide the local governments with full subsidies than to provide them with matching-fund transfers.

Another option is to increase health-purposed earmarked transfers (on a full-fund basis) or increase unconditional transfers for poor localities. Conditional transfers (earmarked transfers) will reduce the expenditure-management (decision-making) autonomy of local governments, which would weaken the responsiveness of the public services it provides. In contrast, unconditional transfers would reduce the incentives for local government to manage funds efficiently (de Mello 2000).[19] It is pointed out that local governments are more suited to provide public services in their localities than is the central government because they are well aware of their local situations (Oates 1972). In particular, providing public services such as health services, which directly link local people, requires much information on local conditions, and actual provision is primarily conducted by local governments (Jinno 2007). In this sense, an increase in unconditional transfer expands the fiscal capacity of local governments and will not reduce the autonomy of local management in providing public services for their localities. Meanwhile, the increase in conditional transfers for health purposes directly expands the fiscal resources for the local health sector. In this case, the important point is whether or not the central government can respond to the needs of localities. In addition, the actual conductor for providing services is most likely the local government, even when the transfer is conditional. Therefore, it is important to monitor the effectiveness of conditional transfers.

It is essential in any case to establish a mechanism that monitors and evaluates the outputs of local government activities in order to motivate them to provide the expected services. Improving accountability of local governments is highly important for avoiding local corruption and for achieving better health. The importance of governance at the local level, that is in terms of accountability and enforcement capacity, is stressed in the decentralization context (Lundberg and Wang 2006).[20]

1.4.2 *Funding and system design of medical insurance*

The subsidy for the medical insurance programmes (the *urban resident basic medical insurance programme* and the *new cooperative medical scheme*) from central government to localities is on a matching-fund basis. The central government subsidizes insurance funds on the condition that local governments subsidize these funds in their localities (Ministry of Health 2003). Under this funding scheme, if local governments cannot afford the co-financing fund for insurance programmes, they cannot take up the subsidy. Regarding this concern, Wang (2006b) refers to cases from pilot programmes of the new CMS. In the cases, localities that have better fiscal capacity have been assigned as pilot sites because assigned localities must meet their obligations to co-finance the new CMS. The experiences of other pilot projects of the new CMS in poor provinces, such as Qinghai, Shanxi or Gansu, indicated that a serious challenge for poor localities, in particular for the lower tier of government (mostly county level), was to raise their own funds for sustaining the new CMS (Ministry of Health, Foreign Loan Office 2002). To make the insurance programmes function in very poor localities, it would be an effective option to have the central government fully subsidize the new CMS.

Another concern is the disunity of insurance design between localities. Each insurance programme is generally managed at city level in urban areas and at county level in rural areas. The central government presents the grand design of insurance programmes, and local governments modify the grand design in actual implementation of the insurance programmes. One result of this style of management is that every locality has its own insurance design. Insurance benefits and effectiveness differ among localities, and this reflects the financial capacity of the localities. Zhu (2004) also points out that such a style of management does not reduce the health disparity across regions.

Furthermore, the critical concern is that the basic insurance scheme is segmented based on urban and rural registration (the *hukou* system), and the registration does not change even with population mobility. The insurance design and benefits differ among the insurance programmes (Table 1.A1). This peculiarity leads to a fixed disparity in the health conditions of urban and rural residents. It has been pointed out that the segmentation of the insurance programmes based on registration is one of the critical factors leading to health disparity between urban and rural areas in China (WHO 2004b). In addition, this Chinese system is not responsive to the actual social situation. At present, an increasing number of people are becoming mobile across regions or areas in China. In contrast, the medical insurance programmes recognize only the original area of the mobile population based on the *hukou* system. Based on this system, rural migrants are registered as rural population even if they live in urban areas, so that they are essentially ineligible to enrol in the urban programmes.[21] Such a mismatch between the programme design and the actual situation will lead to malfunction of the insurance programmes.

Medical insurance in China is planned so that insured people basically utilize the local health institutions in which their insurance programmes are organized. In the grand design of the insurance programmes provided by the central government, there is no particular reference to portability of insurance across regions (Ministry of Health 2003). The portability depends on each local programme. In general, if rural migrants utilize health institutions in other localities, their insurance benefits will be reduced. Insurance portability will become an increasingly critical issue in China, as the population becomes more mobile across regions. In this context, the important next step is to harmonize insurance programmes across localities and between urban and rural residents, or possibly to set up a mechanism to make insurance portable even though each locality has a different insurance design. Enrolment in medical insurance programmes should not be based on the *hukou* system but rather on the actual place where the insured person lives. A concrete measure would raise the pooling level of insurance funds from the city/county level to the provincial level or apply a cross-subsidy scheme for insurance funds between city/county levels. Hence, insurance programmes could at least be harmonized smoothly at the provincial level.

1.5   Conclusion

Since economic reforms began in the late 1970s, the Chinese economy has developed remarkably. Along with the economic development, socioeconomic conditions, which are the basis of the health system, have changed significantly. Changes in socioeconomic conditions led to malfunctions of the conventional health system in China. The health system must be restructured in order to adapt to these new socioeconomic conditions. However, health sector reforms did not take place, and the resulting situation caused the stagnation of health improvement through the 1980s and the 1990s. A further central issue is that although both central and local governments have been required to directly finance the health provision, the central government reduced its investment in the health sector over the 1990s, and transferred most responsibilities for finance to local governments.

This study has focused on the influence of government financing on health services. It examined the impact of local fiscal capacity on local health resources and the overall design and funding schemes of new medical insurance programmes in China, and considered how public finance can contribute to improving health conditions in poor regions and reduce the health disparity between regions.

Our analysis showed that the scale of local own revenue has a significant impact on the level of health resources in each locality. The fiscal transfer from central to local governments strengthens local fiscal capacity, whereas the design of the fiscal transfer influences the allocation of local budgets. Earmarked subsidies on a matching-fund basis change the allocation of local government budgets because the local government has to meet its obligation to co-finance the matching-fund projects. Our analysis indicated that the (negative) impact of changes in the allocation of local budget on health resources is larger than the impact of transfers allocated for health purposes. To improve health conditions in poor regions, it would be more effective to provide local governments in poor regions with subsidies on a full-cover basis rather than with subsidies on a matching-fund basis.

Another concern is that local governments cannot take up the (earmarked) transfer if they cannot meet their obligation for co-financing. Subsidy for the new CMS is on a matching-fund basis. It poses a serious challenge for local governments in very poor regions, particularly for the lower tier of government, for raising their own funds in order to co-finance the new CMS. To improve rural health in poor regions, it is better to provide the local governments with full subsidies for the new CMS. Particularly, it is important to lessen the financial obligation of the lower tier of government in poor localities. The use of tax revenues for health purposes needs to compete with demand from other sectors (Roemer 1993). Fortunately, tax generation has expanded more rapidly than macroeconomic growth in China since the late 1990s; therefore, the central government has the capacity to invest additional funds in health without reducing its investment in other sectors.

In addition, the critical issues affecting the effectiveness of medical insurance programmes are the unity of insurance programmes and the portability of insurance. At present, each locality modifies the grand design of the insurance programmes. Further, the insurance programme is segmented based on urban and rural registration. Such design of insurance fixes the health disparity between urban and rural areas or across regions. The portability of insurance across regions is now limited. It leads to malfunctions in insurance programmes because an increasing number of people are becoming mobile across regions and areas of China. An important step would be to harmonize insurance programmes and improve insurance portability. This is critical for reducing the disparity in health across regions and areas.

Appendix

Table 1.A1: Summary of medical insurance programmes

Insurance programme	Premium	Insurance fund	Medical account	Enrolment unit	Main benefits	User fee
Urban employee basic medical insurance	Employer Employee	Pool at city level	The individual	Employee (the individual)	Inpatient Outpatient	Deductible Co-payment
Urban resident basic medical insurance	Subsidy of central and local govt The individual	Pool at city level	–	The individual	Inpatient	Co-payment
New CMS	Subsidy of central and local govt Household	Pool at county level	–	Household	Inpatient	Co-payment

Notes: Author's compilation based on information from *Decision of the Establishment of the Urban Employee Basic Medical Insurance Programme* (1998), *The View on the Pilot Programmes on the Urban Resident Basic Medical Insurance Programme* (2007), and *The Notice of the Establishment of New Cooperative Medical Scheme* (2003).

There are arguments for abolishing the medical account of the urban employee basic medical insurance programme because it does not contribute to controlling the financial risks associated with uncertain illness. However, as of March 2008, any notice or decision related to its abolition has not been released.

Notes

1. The source of Japan's MMR is Millennium Development Goals Indicators. The official United Nations site for the MDG Indicators is: http://mdgs.un.org/unsd/mdg/Default.aspx
2. This scheme of health service provision was known as the labour insurance system (LIS). In addition, health service provision was financed publicly for personnel of government organs and institutions, and this was known as the publicly funded health system (Zhang 2001; Wong et al. 2006).
3. The household responsibility system was introduced in rural areas in the late 1970s. In this system, an individual farmer (family) rather than a collective farm group directly contracts the government to manage the agricultural business. This change weakened and finally resulted in the disbanding of people's communes, which were up to then the collective basis for agricultural production, administration and social services in rural areas. In line with the disbandment of people's communes, the cooperative medical scheme in rural areas also went into decline.
4. The government imposes a price regulation on services provided by publicly owned health institutions in order to control user charges (World Bank 1997, 2002; Blumenthal and Hsiao 2005). However, it should be pointed out that controlling healthcare costs has been a serious challenge in China due to overprescription, excess provision of health services, or preference for expensive services.
5. In the conventional health system, the urban population obtained healthcare services that were basically free of charge, whereas the rural population had to pay user fees as well as the insurance premium of the CMS.
6. China's registration system (*hukou*) segments the population into urban population and rural population. There hence exist two types of registration, urban registration and rural registration. In recent times, population mobility has increased in China, and the *hukou* system has gradually become more flexible. In addition, in line with urbanization, some of the rural population has become urban population (urban registration). However, the social security system, including health insurance, still reflects the distinction between urban and rural registration based on the *hukou* system.
7. Referring to other countries' experiences, dependent family members can obtain insurance benefits without paying an additional premium in the Philippine insurance programme (see Chapter 2). The treatment of dependent family members differs among insurance programmes in Japan's current social insurance system (see Chapter 3).
8. This new urban medical insurance is funded by individual premiums and subsidies from central and local governments. The subsidy from central government mainly targets central-western regions.
9. In the central and western provinces, the individual annual premium was 10 RMB, and the subsidy from the central and local government was 20 RMB, in 2007. The central government plans to raise its subsidy to 40 RMB per person per year in the two years from 2008.
10. Note that the fiscal health expenditure shown in Table 1.2 is the operating expense for health, which does not reflect all of the fiscal expenditure on health.

11. The province own revenue includes all tiers of government revenues below the provincial level, namely provinces, prefectures and counties. The fiscal transfer from the central to local governments includes the fiscal transfer to all tiers of local government below the provincial level.

12. For details of the tax-sharing system, see Naito (2004) and OECD (2006). Details for calculating of tax refunds are on page 96 of OECD (2006).

13. Data on the fiscal transfer at prefectural level is not available. However, the difference between local (prefecture) own revenue and local (prefecture) total expenditure can be assumed to be a fiscal transfer from the upper tiers of government. We hence use the data of local (prefecture) total expenditure as a proxy for the data of local (prefecture) total revenue that includes local own revenue and fiscal transfer from the upper tiers of government.

14. The fiscal transfer from central government to local government in Tibet is exceptionally high compared to its own fiscal revenue. Due to such exceptionality, the sample of Tibet is excluded from the data set used for the empirical analysis.

15. Fiscal data are from the *Finance Yearbook of China* (Ministry of Finance, China), and health data are from the *Health Statistical Yearbook of China* (Ministry of Health, China).

16. The model is tested by the Hausman test, which also supports a fixed-effect model.

17. As indicated in Table 1.5, both dependent and independent variables are defined in logs in the estimation model. Coefficients of the variables can be interpreted as elasticity through a log transformation. Therefore, the coefficient of per capita local own revenue is interpreted as the elasticity of per capita local own revenue with respect to per capita hospital beds.

18. As expressed in the equation, the impact discussed here includes the effect of transfer itself (β_2) and the proportion of the transfer allocated for health purposes to total transfer (γ).

19. Since fiscal transfer is a key factor that influences the incentive as well as the capacity of local governments in decentralized countries, other literatures also study the role of fiscal transfer in decentralization. For instance, Bird and Smart (2002) review the issues of intergovernmental transfer design, in relation to efficient service provision. Ahmad et al. (2005) provide the framework for evaluating decentralization by focusing on the incentives and accountability of service providers in decentralized conditions. Smart (2007) focuses on the effects of fiscal transfer on allocative efficiency by particularly focusing on the incentives built into transfer systems.

20. Governance is seen as an important factor for improving priority health interventions not only in the decentralization context, but also in general conditions (Hanson et al. 2003).

21. Note that in some cities, local enterprises as well as local governments (city-level) cooperate in enabling rural migrants who work in local enterprises to enrol in the urban employee insurance programme (*urban employee basic medical insurance programme*). According to the field research in Suzhou city conducted by Yamaguchi (Institute of Developing Economies, Japan), some local enterprises attempt to provide better welfare conditions for rural migrants in order to attract them. This is because local enterprises face a tight supply of labour (rural migrant), and local governments (city-level) encourage

enterprises to provide rural migrants with better welfare conditions. Besides health system reforms, the government has attempted to improve the working and living conditions of rural migrants in recent years, and this also includes improving healthcare for migrants. The Ministry of Labour and Social Security released 'Notice to improve the enrolment of rural migrants in medical insurance' in 2006. It indicates an attempt to increase the enrolment of rural migrants in medical insurance, especially in capital cities of provinces, in large and medium-sized cities and in enterprises that employ large numbers of rural migrants (Ministry of Labour and Social Security 2005; Yamaguchi 2008).

References

Ahmad, Junaid, Shantayanan Devarajan, Stui Khemani, and Shekhar Shah (2005) 'Decentralization and Service Delivery,' *World Bank Policy Research Working Paper*, No. 3630.

Bird, Richard M. and Michael Smart (2002) 'Intergovernmental Fiscal Transfers: International Lessons for Developing Countries', *World Development*, Vol. 30, No. 6: 899–912.

Blumenthal, David and William Hsiao (2005) 'Privatization and its Discontents – The Evolving Chinese Health Care System', *The New England Journal of Medicine*, Vol. 15: 1165–70.

Chalkely, Martin and James M. Malcomson (2000) 'Government Purchasing of Health Services', in Anthony. J. Culyer and Joseph P. Newhouse (eds), *Handbook of Health Economics*, Volume 1B: 848-890, Elsevier Science BV.

China National Health Economic Institute (2006) *China National Health Accounts Report 2006*.

Dabla-Norris, Era (2005) 'Issues in Intergovernmental Fiscal Relations in China', *IMF Working Paper*, IMF Institute, International Monetary Fund.

Department of Comprehensive Statistics, National Bureau of Statistics, China. *China Statistical Yearbook for Regional Economy*, China Statistics Press.

Gertler, Paul J. (1998) 'On the Road to Social Health Insurance: the Asian Experience', *World Development*, Vol. 26, No. 4: 717–32.

Hanson, Kara, M. Kent Ranson, Valeria Oliveira-Cruz and Anne Mills (2003) 'Expanding Access to Priority Health Interventions: A Framework for Understanding the Constraints to Scaling-up', *Journal of International Development*, Vol. 15: 1–14.

Jinno, Naohiko (2007) *Zaiseigaku, dai ni han* (in Japanese) (Public Finance, second edition), Tokyo: Yuhikaku.

Li, Lian Hua (2004) 'Iryo Hoken Kaikaku (in Japanese) (Medical Insurance Reforms)', in Hidenori Tada (ed.) *Gendai Chugoku no Shakai Hosho Seido* (in Japanese) (The Social Security System in China), Ibaraki, Japan: Ryutsu Keizai Daigaku Syuppankai.

Liu, Yuanli (2004) 'China's Public Healthcare System: Facing the Challenges', *Bulletin of the World Health Organization*, Vol. 82, No. 7: 532–38, WHO.

Liu, Xiao Mei (2002) *Chugoku no Kaikaku Kaihou to Shakai Hosho* (in Japanese) (The Economic Reforms and Social Security Systems in China), Tokyo: Shoubun Sya.

Lundberg, Mattias and Limin Wang (2006) 'Health Sector Reforms', in Aline Coudouel and Stefano Paternostro (eds) *Analyzing the Distributional Impact of Reforms,* Volume 2, Washington: World Bank.

Mei, Hong and Xiaolin Wang (2006) *China's Budget System and the Financing Education and Health Services for Children,* Paris: United Nations Children's Fund (UNICEF).

de Mello, J. R. Luiz, R. (2000) 'Fiscal Decentralization and Intergovernmental Fiscal Relations: A Cross-Country Analysis', *World Development,* Vol. 28, No. 2: 365–80.

Ministry of Finance, China *Finance Yearbook of China,* China Finance Press.

Ministry of Health, China *Health Statistical Yearbook of China,* Peking Union Medical College Press.

Ministry of Health, China *Health Yearbook of China.* The People's Health Press (Renmin Weisheng Chubanshe)

Ministry of Health, China (2003) *The Notice of the Establishment of New Cooperative Medical Scheme,* Ministry of Health, PRC.

Ministry of Health, China (2008) *The Report on Health Development in 2007,* Ministry of Health, PRC.

Ministry of Health, Foreign Loan Office (2002) *Basic Health Service Project (Health VIII & Health VIII Support Project): Report on Phase One Review,* Foreign Loan Office, Ministry of Health, PRC.

Ministry of Labour and Social Security (1998) *Decision of the Establishment of the Urban Employee Basic Medical Insurance Program.* Ministry of Labor and Social Security, PRC.

Ministry of Labour and Social Security (2005) *Blue Book of the Chinese Employment 2005,* Labor Science Research Institution, Ministry of Labour and Social Security, PRC, 2005, China Labour and Social Security Press.

Ministry of Labour and Social Security (2007) *The View on the Pilot Programs on the Urban Resident Basic Medical Insurance Program,* Ministry of Labour and Social Security, PRC.

Musgrove, Philip (1996) *Public and Private Roles in Health: Theory and Financing Patterns,* Health, Nutrition and Population (HNP) Discussion Paper, July 1996, Washington: World Bank.

Naito, Jiro (2004) *Chugoku no Seihukan Zaisei Kankei no Jittai to Taiou* (in Japanese) (The Present State and Handling of Intergovernmental Fiscal Relations in China), Nihon Tosho Center, Japan.

Nakagane, Katsuji (1999) *Chugoku Keizai Hattenron* (in Japanese) (Economic Development in China), Yuhikaku, Japan.

National Bureau of Statistics, China. *China Statistical Yearbook.* China Statistics Press.

Oates, E. Wallace (1972) *Fiscal Federalism,* New York: Harcourt Brace Jovanovich.

OECD (2006) *Challenges for China's Public Spending – Toward Greater Effectiveness and Equity,* Paris: OECD.

Roemer, Milton I. (1993) *National Health Systems of The World, Volume II: The Issues,* New York: Oxford University Press.

Smart, Michael (2007) 'The Incentive Effects of Grants', in Robin Boardway and Anwar Shah (eds) *Intergovernmental Fiscal Transfers: Principles and Practice,* Washington: World Bank.

Uchimura, Hiroko and Johannes Jütting (2007) 'Fiscal Decentralization, Chinese Style: Good for Health Outcomes?', *IDE Discussion Paper* No.111, Institute of Developing Economies, IDE-JETRO, Japan.

Wang, Wen Liang (2006a) *Kakusa de Yomi Toku Gendai Chugoku* (in Japanese) (Analysis on China from the Viewpoint of Inequality), Kyoto: Minerva shobou.

Wang, Xiaoling. 2006b. 'Public Expenditure in the Education and Health Sectors', in Hong Mei and Xiaoling Wang (eds) *China's Budget System and the Financing of Education and Health Services for Children*, Paris: United Nations Children's Fund (UNICEF).

Wong, Chack-kei, Vai lo Lo and Kwong-leung Tang (2006) *China's Urban Health Care Reform*, Lanham: Lexington Books.

WHO (World Health Organization) (2004a) *The World Medicine Situation*, Geneva: World Health Organization.

WHO (2004b). *Implementing the New Cooperative Medical Schemes in Rapidly Changing China*, Office of the World Health Organization Representative in China.

WHO (2005a) *The World Health Report 2005: Make Every Mother and Child Count*, Geneva: World Health Organization.

WHO (2005b) *China: Health, Poverty and Economic Development*, Office of the World Health Organization Representative in China and Social Development Department of China State Council Development Research Centre.

World Bank (1997) *China 2020: Financing Health Care*, Washington: World Bank.

World Bank (2002) *China National Development and Sub-National Finance: A Review of Provincial Expenditures*, Report No. 22951-CHN, April 2002, Washington: World Bank.

World Bank (2005) *Public Expenditure and the Role of Government in the Chinese Health Sector*, Briefing Note No. 5, May 2005, Washington: World Bank.

World Bank (2006) *Health Financing Revisited*, Washington: World Bank.

Yamaguchi, Mami (2008) 'Noson Rodoryoku no Chiikikan Idou wo Meguru Seisaku no Hensen,' (in Japanese) (Transition of Policies on Mobility of Rural Migrants Across Regions) in Akihide Ikegami and Hisatoshi Hoken (eds) *Chugoku Noson Kaikaku to Nogyo-Sangyoka Seisaku ni yoru Nogyo-Seisan Kozo no Henyo* (in Japanese) (Structural Reform of the Rural Economy and Change of the Agricultural System Through Agro-industrialization Policy in Rural China), Institute of Developing Economies, IDE-JETRO, Japan.

Zhang, Jixun (2001) *Gendai Chugoku Shakai Hosyo Ron* (in Japanese) (Social Security in China), Japan: Soseisya.

Zhu, Si Lin (2004) 'Zaisei Kaikaku to Chuou Seihu no Aratana Yakuwari (in Japanese) (Reforms of Public Finance and New Role of Central Government)', in Hidenori Tada (ed.) *Gendai Chugoku no Shakai Hosho Seido* (in Japanese) (The Social Security System in China), Ibaraki, Japan: Ryutsu Keizai Daigaku Syuppankai.

2
Health Financing For Accessible Services: A Study of the Philippines

Hiroko Uchimura

Introduction

Developing countries face an insufficiency of financial resources for providing accessible and affordable healthcare services. A health financing system can be a mechanism for mobilizing resources for health and utilizing limited resources effectively in the health sector. Collecting revenue, pooling resources, and purchasing health services are the basic functions of health financing (WHO 2000; World Bank 2006). Myriad ways exist to combine these three functions which comprise a health financing system. The three functions are interrelated (WHO 2000) so that not only each of the functions but also the interaction between the functions will critically affect the performance of health financing systems. The design of health financing systems will hence strongly influence the scale of resources for health and the effectiveness of resource utilization.

Due to the lack of health financing systems or malfunction of the systems, developing countries tend to suffer from inadequate resource mobilization and inefficient or inequitable resource allocation in the health sector. As a result, a large share of the total health expenditure in developing countries is covered by out-of-pocket payments (OOP). Although OOP financed less than 20 per cent of total health expenditure in high-income countries, it financed more than 65 per cent of total health expenditure in low-income countries in 2002.[1] The high OOP impedes people, in particular the poor, from accessing healthcare services (WHO 2000; Commission on Macroeconomics and Health; WHO 2001). Moreover, the high OOP is a major factor causing the vicious circle between ill-health and impoverishment in developing countries.

In this context, this chapter focuses on health financing systems and examines the Philippines as a case study. The Philippines has continued to reform the health sector since the late 1990s. One of the focal issues has been the reform of its health financing system, with the aim of improving financial accessibility to needed healthcare services for Filipinos through mobilizing resources and reducing OOP.

Have the reforms actually reduced the financial burdens on patients for obtaining healthcare services in the Philippines? Does the health financing system function so as to provide people with financial protection against uncertain health risks? More precisely, the concern is whether the reforms have led to a decrease in OOP for health expenditures. To address the concern, this chapter clarifies the mechanism of the health financing system in the Philippines and examines the design and function of the system. In addition, we consider the essential factors in designing the health financing system to improve financial accessibility to needed healthcare services.

The next section presents an overview of the health sector reforms in the Philippines and summarizes the mechanism of health financing and health service provision. We examine the transition in the health expenditure structure and the population's financial burden for accessing healthcare services in section 2.2. We find that the health service price has inflated and OOP have not decreased in the Philippines. By examining the health financing mechanism, section 2.3 investigates the background of price inflation and looks at who bears the financial risks associated with uncertain illness. Moreover, section 2.4 considers further policy actions to improve the financial accessibility of the services. The final section summarizes the lessons learned from our study.

2.1   Health financing in the Philippines

2.1.1   Reforms in the health sector

The focus of the development of the health sector in the Philippines shifted in the late 1960s from attempts to provide broad social protection for the population to attempts to improve the financial access of the population to healthcare services (WHO 2005). The original Medicare programme was initiated in 1969 with the approval of the Philippines Medical Care Commission. However, this insurance programme only covered a limited population, that is, formal employees in the private and public sectors (Jowett and Hsiao 2007). There was no substantial progress for nearly three decades after the original Medicare programme was initiated. It has been pointed out that the Philippine health sector was a highly marketized system (Roemer 1993). Major reforms in the

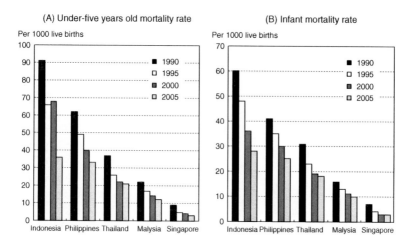

Figure 2.1: Health outcomes in ASEAN five original member countries
Source: Author's compilation based on data from *Millennium Development Goals Indicators*,
United Nations: http://mdgs.un.org/unsd/mdg/Default.aspx.

health sector had to wait until the Philippines embarked on its health
sector reform agenda in the late 1990s (WHO 2005).

The first steps to improve health sector performance took place from
1999 to 2004 and were known as HSRA (the Health Sector Reform
Agenda).[2] Health outcomes, such as the infant mortality rate (IMR) or
under-five-years-old mortality rate (U5MR), have been improving in the
Philippines; however, the level is not much better than other major
ASEAN countries. IMR and U5MR in the Philippines were much lower
than those of Indonesia in 1990. However, the pace of the improvement decelerated in the Philippines, so that both these mortality rates
became nearly equal to those of Indonesia by 2005 (Figure 2.1). A challenge is the large differentials in health outcomes among regions, areas
and socioeconomic groups in the Philippines (Table 2.1). The physical
and financial accessibility of healthcare services strongly depends on the
patients' geographical locations or socioeconomic positions. Improvement of the financial and physical accessibility of healthcare services
has been a challenge in the Philippines.

In this light, HSRA, aiming at improvement in health sector performance, devoted special attention to the issues of finance, regulation
and healthcare service delivery. As a packaged reform programme, HSRA
comprised five major components: local health system development;
public health programme reforms; health regulatory reforms; hospital

Table 2.1:   Health outcomes in the Philippines (per 1000 live births)

	Infant mortality rate		Under-five mortality rate	
	1999	2003	1999	2003
Residence				
Urban	31	24	46	30
Rural	40	36	63	52
Education				
No education	79	65	136	105
Elementary	45	43	73	62
High school	31	26	46	35
College or higher	23	15	28	18
Wealth index quintile				
Lowest		42		66
Second		32		47
Middle		26		32
Fourth		22		26
Highest		19		21

Source: *Philippines National Demographic and Health Survey 1998* (Department of Health 1999), *Philippines National Demographic and Health Survey 2003* (National Statistical Office 2004).

reforms; and social health insurance reforms. In the context of decentralization in the Philippines, the first component was intended to improve local health services by facilitating cooperative networking as well as cost sharing among local government units (LGUs).[3] A challenging issue in the Philippines has been regulatory mandate, or an enforcement capacity to ensure that affordable and safe health services and goods are available. The last component, social health insurance reforms, was intended to reduce Filipinos' financial burden by expanding the coverage of social health insurance and enhancing the insurance benefit package. All components, which are interrelated with each other, were adopted to improve the financial and physical accessibility of Filipinos to needed healthcare services.

Following HSRA, the second step, known as *FOUR*mula *One* for Health,[4] began in 2005 and will go on to 2010 (Department of Health 2005). *FOUR*mula *One* for Health is an implementation framework for health sector reforms, the end goals of which are a more responsive health system, more equitable healthcare financing, and better health outcomes. Reflecting the issues of HSRA, *FOUR*mula *One* for Health comprises four implementation components: financing; regulation; service delivery; and governance. Governance involves the coordination across local health systems, private-public partnerships and national health sector management. Health service delivery focuses on the availability of essential services in localities, whereas the purpose of regulation is to address the issues of affordability and quality of health services and goods. The financing reforms aim to mobilize adequate and sustainable resources and to allocate those resources efficiently through expanding social health insurance programmes. The fundamental agenda is to improve healthcare service provision and to reduce financial burdens on patients for obtaining the services.

Regarding social health insurance, the reform of the social health insurance system was initiated in the middle of the 1990s, just before HSRA was launched. An act establishing the National Health Insurance Program (NHIP) for all Filipinos as well as the Philippine Health Insurance Corporation (PhilHealth) was enacted in 1995 (Act No. 7875). The aim of the act was to provide universal coverage of social health insurance. PhilHealth was created in place of the Philippine Medical Care Commission, that had implemented the Medicare programme. As mentioned above, the Medicare programme only covered a limited range of people, that is, formal employees in the private and public sectors. PhilHealth is the agency administrating the National Health Insurance Program that aims to provide all Filipinos with the financial tools to access healthcare services.

PhilHealth administers five social health insurance programmes for different employment statuses: the employed sector (formally employed) programme; the non-paying programme; the indigent (sponsored) programme (since 1997); the individually paying programme (since 1999), and the overseas workers' programme (since 2006). The individually paying programme covers the self-employed informal sector, the agricultural sector, and freelance professionals, while the non-paying programme is for retired persons who have paid at least 120 monthly contributions (premiums).

The indigent programme targets the poor who are exempted from premium payment; instead of having insured persons pay the enrolee premium, the national and local governments subsidize the indigent programme. In other words, both national and local governments are *sponsors* of the programme. Local governments (cities or municipalities) are responsible for the identification of indigent persons. In practice, the City/Municipal Social Welfare and Development Office administers the Community-Based Information System-Minimum Basic Needs (CBIS-MBN) approach at the barangay level. It is a social research survey, or a sort of means test, designed to determine the socioeconomic and health profile of the indigent in each LGU (Philippine Health Insurance Corporation 2004; Jowett and Hsiao 2007). The indigent programme, tailored for the poor, is intended to provide the poor with a financial tool for accessing healthcare services.

PhilHealth unified the insurance benefits for all members of the insurance programmes, effectively from the end of 1999 (WHO 2005). The benefits include both inpatient and outpatient care, but comparatively speaking, they are more inpatient-oriented (Jowett and Hsiao 2007). The benefits for inpatient hospital care include room and board, professional healthcare services, diagnostics and other medical examination services, use of surgical or medical equipment, and prescription drugs and biologicals, whereas the benefits for outpatient care include professional healthcare services, diagnostic and other medical services, use of surgical or medical equipment, personal preventive services, and prescription drugs and biologicals (Philippine Health Insurance Corporation 2004).

The benefits are portable nationwide, but a ceiling is placed on them by PhilHealth according to hospital category and services. In addition to these benefits, PhilHealth introduced new packages of benefits, such as the maternity care package and the outpatient package for the Directly Observed Treatment Short Course (DOTS) for tuberculosis, in 2003. PhilHealth also introduced an additional benefit for the indigent programme in which PhilHealth applies the capitation payment scheme for accredited rural health units (RHUs); hence, members of the indigent programme are entitled to obtain free services, included in the benefit, at accredited RHUs (WHO 2005). Under a capitation payment scheme, an insurer funds the accredited health institutions prospectively, based on the number of insured members. Therefore, the accredited RHUs are prospectively funded for this benefit package by PhilHealth, based on the number of the indigent programme members in their localities.

2.1.2   Health financing and service provision

Flow of funds and health services

How do the continuous reforms work? In the following sub-section, we will summarize the mechanism of the health fund and service flows in the Philippines, and examine the progress of the reforms. Figure 2.2 briefly summarizes the flow of funds and health service provision. Healthcare services are provided by public or private providers in the Philippines. Public providers, financed by the government, basically provide free healthcare services, including essential drugs (see Table 2.A1 in the Appendix for the structure of public health institutions).[5] Patients

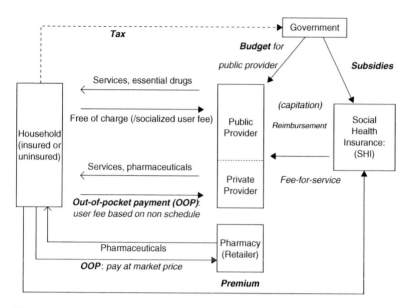

Figure 2.2: Flow of funds and health services in the Philippines
Source: Author's compilation.

therefore are not required to bear financial costs to obtain basic health-care services at public health institutions; however, appropriate health-care services are not always available. A lack of medical supplies and personnel at public health institutions is a common problem in developing countries. The quality of service is another critical issue in the provision of appropriate healthcare services. In addition, limited deployment is a physical barrier to accessing public health institutions.

Private providers supply healthcare services, including prescribed pharmaceuticals, by charging user fees. Patients who are not insured have to pay the full costs to access the services. If the patients are insured, PhilHealth will partially reimburse providers for the services provided, and the insured patient will be required to pay the remaining part of the cost. Since the user fees, borne by patients, are not on schedule in the Philippines, the financial costs incurred by the patients are unpredictable even if patients are insured.

People have several routes to accessing pharmaceuticals in the Philippines. Drugs listed on the essential drug list are supposed to be available at public health institutions, including rural health units (RHUs), the public health institutions that are the closest to the people.[6]

Table 2.2:   Fund source and risk pooling level

Source	Risk pooling level	Source goes to
Govt	National/Local level	Public provider
SHI	Insurance fund level (cross-subsidies between insurance programmes)	Public/Private provider
OOP (household)	None	(basically) Private provider

Notes: 'Govt' refers to both central and local governments.
'SHI' refers to social health insurance, and 'OOP' refers to out-of-pocket payments.
Source: Author's compilation.

If the needed drugs are available at public health institutions, they will be provided free of charge. However, if the drugs are not available there, patients have to purchase the drugs at retailers at varying market prices. Meanwhile, private medical providers prescribe medicines, and patients purchase them, at private medical institutions or at retailers at varying market prices. Spending on pharmaceuticals is a heavy financial burden for Filipinos. As we will see below (Table 2.5), nearly half of family expenditure on medical care is spent on drugs and medicines.[7]

Resource mobilizing and risk pooling

A focus of the health financing reforms in the Philippines is to expand social health insurance coverage. What role does social health insurance play in the health financing system? One of the roles is to mobilize funds for health. As we saw in Figure 2.2, social health insurance (SHI) collects contributions (subsidies/premiums) from the government and from individuals.[8] Its other important role is to control financial risks of the insured members associated with uncertain illness by pooling funds and spreading the risks among the pooling members. The pooling level depends on the funding sources (Table 2.2). The national government or local government units finance the public health institutions under their jurisdiction to provide free services (Table 2.A1). The financial risks are hence pooled throughout the nation or each locality. Social health insurance categorizes the enrollees into five insurance programmes, while funds of the five programmes practically subsidize each other; that is, there is cross-subsidization. Therefore, the financial risks are spread across all members of the five insurance programmes. Out-of-pocket payments are directly paid by each individual patient, so that the individual patient has to bear all financial risks for OOP. Uninsured Filipinos then have to bear the overall financial burdens to access private healthcare services. The most vulnerable are the uninsured poor.

Progress of social health insurance

Insurance enrolment has expanded substantially since the establishment of PhilHealth. Formal employees in the private and public sectors have been the most stable members since the time of Medicare. The enrolment of the poor has accelerated since the indigent programme was initiated in 1999, and membership surged particularly in 2004 in connection with the national elections (Table 2.3)[9] The indigent programme involves several implementation problems; the identification of the poor, the sustainability of the membership, and treatment for the poor who are not entitled to be members of the indigent programme. Nevertheless, it is an significant achievement that a social health insurance programme has reached out to a substantial number of poor families under the sponsorship of the national and local governments. The other significant feature is that PhilHealth programmes provide insurance benefits to dependent family members; spouses, children, or disabled family members are frequently excluded from insurance programmes in developing countries (Carrin et al. 1999). Under the PhilHealth insurance scheme, such dependent family members are eligible to receive insurance benefits without paying an additional premium.

The most critical challenge to attaining universal coverage is how to extend insurance coverage to the self-employed informal sector and the agricultural sector.[10] The enrolment of the self-employed sector is far less developed, compared with other programmes. The difficulties lie in identifying individuals in the self-employed sector and collecting the contributions (premiums). People do not always understand the mechanism and the lure of social health insurance; hence, they are not always willing to enrol in the insurance programme. To extend insurance coverage to the informal sector, PhilHealth launched an attempt, called *Kalusugang Sigurado at Abot-Kaya sa PhilHealth Insurance* (KaSAPI),[11] which is a strategic initiative to expand and sustain the enrolment of the informal sector in the social health insurance programme. Under the KaSAPI initiative, PhilHealth has entered into partnership with key organizations such as microfinance institutions and NGOs which provide financial services for informal workers, to collaboratively expand informal workers' enrolment and collect their premiums. In addition, the inpatient-oriented benefit is less attractive to ordinary people; hence, as listed above, PhilHealth attempts to expand

Table 2.3: Progress of PhilHealth insurance programmes

	Collection: Million pesos	Benefit payments: Million pesos	Claims: No. of paid	Membership: families				
				Employees (private)	Sponsored (indigent)	Individually paying	Non-paying	Overseas workers
1998	5,518	2,999	503,324	–	47,290	32,944	–	–
1999	5,367	4,218	957,606	–	86,827	494,462	–	–
2000	8,557	6,764	1,309,768	–	347,016	929,589	–	–
2001	10,515	7,672	1,417,124	–	619,014	1,364,387	–	–
2002	12,749	8,832	1,574,954	–	1,260,864	1,768,175	–	–
2003	13,152	10,957	1,831,786	–	1,762,116	2,151,225	–	–
2004	16,516	12,925	2,148,633	–	6,258,150	2,839,455	–	–
2005	18,736	17,511	2,646,352	–	2,492,356	2,597,335	–	–
2006	22,580	17,201	2,419,682	–	4,946,433		–	–
March 2007				Million families				
				6.45	3.98	2.62	0.28	1.26

Source: Author's compilation base on the data from Stats & Chart: January–March 2007, PhilHealth (2007), Stats & Chart 2003, PhilHealth (2004).

the benefits to some outpatient services, as well as to supply prescribed drugs.

Although there are still miles to go to achieving universal coverage, the contribution (premium) has risen substantially since extended social health insurance was initiated under PhilHealth (Table 2.3). New resources are being mobilized from all members in society – individuals, employers, and the government. Given these new resources, benefit payments by PhilHealth have surged. Whereas the benefit payment was 66.3 million pesos in 1997, it reached 17,511.4 million pesos in 2005 (PhilHealth 2007).

2.2 Has the patient financial burden been reduced?

2.2.1 The transition of OOP

By translating a portion of out-of-pocket payments into insurance benefit payment, the reform is expected to improve people's financial accessibility to healthcare services and to provide people with financial protection against uncertain illness. Reflecting the continuous reforms, how has the health expenditure structure changed? Has the financial burden to Filipinos for obtaining healthcare services lessened?

The increase in total health expenditure has accelerated since 2003, following a slight slowdown in 2002 (Figure 2.3). Expenditure reached 182 billion pesos in 2005, a figure nearly triple that of 1995. Despite the increase in social health insurance contributions, out-of-pocket payments expanded much more than the social health insurance contribution over the period. In fact, nearly half of the expansion in total health expenditure has been covered by the expansion of out-of-pocket payments.

Table 2.4 presents each source as a percentage of total health expenditure. The government contribution gradually increased in the latter 1990s, peaked in 2000, and then entered a downtrend. Part of the government expenditures may have come to flow indirectly to the health sector as subsidies for the social health insurance's indigent programme. While the percentage share of social health insurance has gradually increased, that of out-of-pocket payments does not appear to have decreased accordingly. The share of out-of-pocket payments got back on the expansion track after slowing down in the latter 1990s, after which it expanded at nearly the same pace as total health expenditure.

2.2.2 Health cost inflation

Total health expenditure is expanding in the Philippines, and a large part of the expansion is still being borne by out-of-pocket payments.

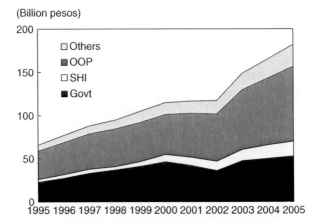

(Billion pesos)

Figure 2.3:   Changes in the Philippine health expenditure structure
Source: Author's compilation based on the following data. Data for 1995 to 2004 is from *Philippine National Health Accounts 2004*, National Statistical Coordination Board (2006). Data for 2005 is from WHO Core Health Indicators: www.who.int/whosis/database/core/core_select.cfm

Table 2.4:   Health expenditure by source (per cent)

	1995	1996	1997	1998	1999	2000	2001	2002	2003	2004	2005
Government	35.0	36.0	38.0	39.1	39.2	40.6	36.2	31.0	31.9	30.3	29.1
Social health insurance	4.5	5.0	5.1	3.8	5.0	7.0	7.9	9.0	8.7	9.5	9.2
Out-of-pocket payment	50.0	48.3	46.5	46.3	43.3	40.5	43.9	46.8	46.6	46.9	47.7
Others	10.5	10.8	10.5	10.8	12.5	11.9	12.0	13.2	12.8	13.3	14.0

Source: Author's compilation based on the following data. Data for 1995 to 2004 is from *Philippine National Health Accounts 2004*, National Statistical Coordination Board (2006). Data for 2005 is from WHO Core Health Indicators: www.who.int/whosis/database/core/core_select.cfm

Does the health expenditure expansion mean that Filipinos obtain more actual healthcare services? Per capita health expenditure in terms of current prices increased by 106 per cent between 1995 and 2004, whereas the expenditure in terms of real prices (1985 constant prices) increased only by 20 per cent (Figure 2.4). This suggests that the health service price level has substantially inflated over the period. The health service price level surged by 71.3 per cent between 1995 and 2004, a more rapid rise than the climb of the CPI over the same period (64.8 per cent).[12]

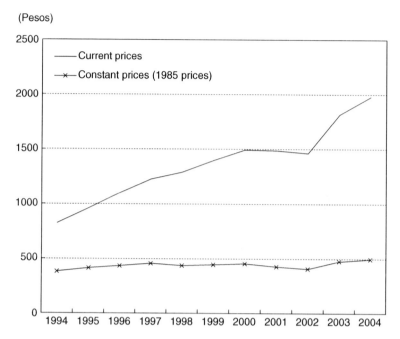

Figure 2.4: Per capita health expenditure at current and constant prices
Source: Author's compilation based on the data in *Philippine National Health Accounts 2004*, National Statistical Coordination Board (2006).

Inflation is also confirmed by demand-side data. The change in family expenditure on medical care in terms of current prices presents a significant contrast to the same expenditure in terms of real prices. Family expenditure at current prices increased by 13.7 per cent between 1997 and 2000, while the expenditure at real prices (constant prices) decreased by 6.8 per cent over the same period (Table 2.5). This suggests that, despite the increase in family medical care expenditure, families' actual consumption of medical care services decreased over the period.

Although total health expenditure rose in the Philippines, this did not necessarily mean that Filipinos obtained more actual healthcare services. Health expenditure expansion was led by health service price inflation in the Philippines. The health service prices increased due to markup charging for the insured patients in the case of the Philippines (Gertler 1998). The inflated health service cost has been heavily borne by individuals (through out-of-pocket payments). In contrast to the purpose of the reforms, out-of-pocket payments have not been substituted

Table 2.5:   Family expenditure on medical care

1000 pesos	Current prices			% Share		Constant prices (1997 prices)		
	1997	2000	% Growth	1997	2000	1997	2000	% Growth
Total	30,449	34,631	13.7	100.0	100.0	30,449	28,386	−6.8
Drugs and medicines	14,900	16,085	8.0	48.9	46.4	14,900	13,185	−11.5
Hospital room charges	6,893	8,344	21.1	22.6	24.1	6,893	6,840	−0.8
Medical charges	6,230	7,522	20.7	20.5	21.7	6,230	6,165	−1.0
Dental charges	754	760	0.7	2.5	2.2	754	623	−17.4
Other medical goods and supplies	1,193	1,204	0.9	3.9	3.5	1,193	987	−17.3
Other medical and health services	479	629	31.4	1.6	1.8	479	516	7.7

Note: The sum of each column may not equal the total due to rounding of figures.
Source: Author's compilation based on the data in *1997 and 2000 Family Income and Expenditures Survey*, National Statistical Office (2002).

by social health insurance; in addition, people's actual health service consumption does not appear to have increased.

As mentioned above, the aim of the act that established NHIP for all Filipinos and for PhiHealth itself was to attain universal coverage by social health insurance. Such coverage is essential to ensure the access of the people to healthcare services and protect them in case of illness (Carrin et al. 1999; WHO 2006). The case of the Philippines, however, poses a question about the effectiveness of universal coverage. Below, we highlight the mechanism of the health financing system and examine the factors behind the persistent heavy burden of out-of-pocket payments in the Philippines.

2.3   Why have OOP not reduced?

2.3.1   Payment and pricing mechanism

The payment mechanism

Despite the endeavour to do so, why have out-of-pocket payments not fallen? Based on the mechanism of flows of funds and health services

Insured patient   **Uninsured patient**

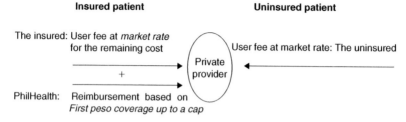

Figure 2.5: Payment mechanism for private providers
Source: Author's compilation.

presented in sub-section 2.1.2, the majority of out-of-pocket payments are supposed to flow to private providers in the Philippines.[13] Figure 2.5 summarizes the payment mechanism for private providers. If providers are accredited by PhilHealth, the accredited providers will be reimbursed for services provided to insured patients. The remuneration is generally based on the fee-for-service (FFS) method, with a payment ceiling that caps the insurance benefit payment.[14] The insurance benefit covers from the first peso up to a cap, and the insured patient is required to pay the remainder as a user fee.[15] The remaining cost is based on market rates, which means that the healthcare service price (user fee) is not set according to a schedule; that is, this scheme allows providers to set their own rates, and providers can discriminate between insured and uninsured patients on healthcare service prices. Providers can consequently capture the insurance benefits by not reducing the user fees of insured patients; in other words, by raising the total service prices for insured patients, which include both user fees and insurance reimbursement.

Price discrimination

Figure 2.6 illustrates three distinctive cases of insured and uninsured patient payments for healthcare services with *possible* price discrimination. If a patient is not insured, the patient has to pay the full charge (by out-of-pocket payment). If a patient is insured, a part of the total healthcare cost is covered by insurance benefits under the scheme of first peso coverage with a capped benefit. As pointed out earlier, the patient is liable for payment of the remainder of the cost at market rates. Case (A) presents the case in which social health insurance functions as expected. A part of the insured out-of-pocket payment is decreased by transferring a part of OOP to social health insurance benefit payment.

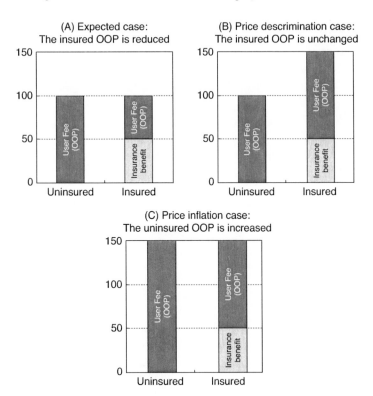

Figure 2.6:   Distinctive cases of insured and uninsured payment for services
Source: Author's compilation.

Meanwhile, Cases (B) and (C) show examples where the insured OOP does not decrease as it should.

The service price is different for the insured and the uninsured patients in Case (B). The insurance benefit covers from the first peso up to a ceiling (light shaded area in the right bar of Case (B)). Because the healthcare service price (user fee) is not on a schedule, providers can charge the patient basically what they want. A provider therefore does not necessarily reduce the user fee for the insured patient even though the provider is reimbursed for a part of the service costs by the insurance. In this case, the insurance benefit is captured by the provider, and the insured user fee (OOP) consequently does not differ from that of the uninsured (dark shaded area). Case (B) presents a case in which 100 per cent of the insurance benefits are captured by providers. Note that the total healthcare cost, the sum of the light shaded area (insurance benefits) and dark shaded area (OOP), rises without an increase in the actual services provided.

Case (C) shows how health service prices can inflate even further. The total service price does not differ for the insured and the uninsured patients in this case. Moreover, a part of the insured payment (OOP) is translated to the insurance benefits. The realized outcome, however, is opposite to the expected outcome. Because the healthcare price (user fee) is not on a schedule, providers can raise the user fees both for the insured and the uninsured, which results in further inflation of health-care service prices. As presented in the figure, the share of the patient payment (OOP) in the total healthcare service cost will hardly change in this case. In both Cases (B) and (C), total healthcare cost expands without increasing the actual healthcare service consumption.

Gertler and Solon (2002) point out that the combination of first dol-lar coverage up to a cap, fee-for-service payment, and fee at market rate (no schedule) provides a desirable condition for providers wherein they can capture the insurance benefits by raising the service prices for insured patients that include a user fee as well as insurance reimburse-ment. The current health service pricing and payment mechanism in the Philippines creates this condition, and so the real consumption of medical care services did not increase despite an increase in the nominal expenditure on medical care (Table 2.5). In other words, social health insurance benefits appear to be eroded by the provider capturing, which is a critical barrier to reducing out-of-pocket payments.

By using sample survey data of patients from 132 hospitals, Gertler and Solon (2002) examined the capture of the insurance benefits of the Medicare programme (the former social health insurance programme covering formal employees and their dependent family members). They found that about 84 per cent of insurance benefits were extracted by hospitals (providers). Obermann et al. (2006) suggest that insur-ance payments continue to be captured by providers. Although the insurance system was amended in the transition from the Medicare programme to the National Health Insurance Program administrated by PhilHealth, the principle of the payment mechanism has not been changed. Although insurance coverage has been extended, the insur-ance benefits are still likely to be captured by providers. The WHO (2005) has noted that the support value of the insurance has declined with the increase in the cost of healthcare services under the current financing systems in the Philippines.[16] It has also been pointed out that Phil-Health controls its own financial risk under the current insurance scheme (Jowett and Hsiao 2007). Although we need a more detailed data analysis to provide conclusive results, the most important issue is that the current *design* of the health financing system in the Philippines appears to facilitate price discrimination, that is, provider capturing of insurance benefits.

The flaws in the design of the health financing system hinder the healthcare system from functioning as it should. The critical factors in the design are price regulation and the social health insurance scheme. At present, healthcare service prices (user fees) are not on schedule in the Philippines, and this allows providers to charge what they want. Critically, this obstructs the reduction of insured out-of-pocket payments and lead to healthcare cost inflation. In addition, the scheme of first peso coverage with a benefit cap also facilitates price discrimination and the fee-for-service payment method is considered to fuel an expansion in health expenditure. Fee-for-service payment is recognized as a payment method that tends to cause an excess provision of healthcare services (World Bank 2006); however, in the case of the Philippines price inflation appears to be more serious problem than supply expansion.

2.3.2   Who bears financial risks?

Controlling the financial risks associated with unpredictable catastrophic illness is another essential challenge, because the financial burden associated with such illness will tend to impoverish people in developing countries. Public providers offer free healthcare services in the Philippines; however, in practice, due to financial or physical limitations on public service provision, people cannot always obtain such free services. Moreover, as free healthcare services are generally basic services, they do not necessarily cover treatment for catastrophic illness. The general problems in the provision of public healthcare in developing countries, such as limited quality of care and informal payments, are also barriers to making necessary care accessible. Against such limitations on public provision, social health insurance can be established to mobilize resources and to spread the financial risks of uncertain serious illness across all insured members.

The Philippine social health insurance, which aims at mandated universal coverage, can potentially provide all Filipinos with financial protection against uncertain serious illness. The present social health insurance, however, does not appear to function as expected. This is not only because of the limited coverage of the insurance, but also because of its mechanism. As pointed out earlier, the current social health insurance mechanism is based on a system of first peso coverage up to a ceiling. This

Table 2.6: Who bears the financial risks?

Source	Provider	Payment			Fee schedule	Who bears
		for provider	by patient	ceiling		
Govt						
	Public	Budget/Salary	Free[2]	–	–	*
SHI		FFS[1]	User fee	On insurance benefit	Not for patient	Patient (insured)
	Private					
OOP		FFS	Full user fee	No	No	Patient (uninsured)

Notes: 1. A case-based or capitation payment method is also applied in some cases.
2. A socialized user fee is required for some cases.
* The services provided will be limited in line with the financial or physical capacity of the public providers.
'FFS' refers to the fee-for-service payment method.
Source: Author's compilation.

system caps the payment of insurance benefits but not payments made by patients to providers. Moreover, this latter payment is not capped even in the case of catastrophic illness. Contrary to its expected function, the current system of social health insurance does not succeed in controlling the insured members' financial risks.[17] In addition, any remaining cost incurred by the patients beyond the cap is not set according to a schedule, which aggravates their financial burdens and uncertainty.

Therefore it is not only the uninsured but also the insured who have to bear the financial risks associated with uncertain illness under the present Philippine health financing system (Table 2.6). Establishment of a scheme to control patients' financial risks in cases of catastrophic illness is commonly a challenge for developing countries. The financial capacity of the health financing system is crucial to the establishment of a scheme that can cap patients' payments in catastrophic cases. In addition, the fund scale, the fund-pooling level and service cost containment are matters crucial to the design of the scheme.

2.3.3 Flaws in the design of the health financing system

The reforms in the Philippine health financing system appear to have led to mixed results. Social health insurance expanded its target from a limited number of people (formal employees) to all Filipinos, aiming at mandated universal coverage. In line with that, it also expanded the contributors. Individuals contribute the insurance premium, and both the national government and local governments subsidize the indigent insurance programme. The reforms strengthened a fundamental function of the health financing system – mobilization of resources. The financing system, however, appears to have flaws in its other functions. The present health service (user fee) pricing mechanism, the market rates, allows providers to capture insurance benefits by raising service prices for the insured without increasing the services provided. The insurance scheme of first peso with a capped benefit facilitates provider capturing, and the fee-for-service payment method fuels the expansion of health expenditure. It appears that the present scheme does not effectively offer people financial protection against the risks associated with uncertain illness.

The flaws in the *design* of the health financing system cause the malfunction of the systems and undermine government efforts to reduce the financial burdens on Filipinos for obtaining necessary healthcare services. The reforms provide the poor with a financial tool for accessing healthcare services; however, the present system also allows mobilized resources to leak in unintended ways. Unless the flaws are amended, the effectiveness of the reforms will remain considerably reduced.

2.4   Policy actions

A fundamental agenda is to reduce the financial burden on patients for accessing healthcare services. To this end, the problems discussed above need to be ameliorated. The primary policy option might be to establish price regulations in the health financing system. This, however, may not be a realistic option in the Philippines, at least in the short-term, due to implementation, enforcement and legislation obstacles. Nonetheless, in order to secure adequate resources and to make the insurance system function better, measures to contain health service price should be set up. This is in fact a general challenge for developing countries that suffer a rise in health service prices (Carrin et al. 1999).

2.4.1   A possible measure

Will it be possible to indirectly deal with the issue by using the resources mobilized by the social health insurance scheme? Figure 2.7 summarizes a *possible* indirect mechanism for controlling price inflation. Currently, the social health insurance scheme is also applied to public providers in the Philippines, although public providers are funded by the government and essentially provide free services. The accredited public providers

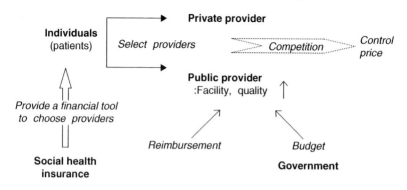

Figure 2.7:   A *possible* mechanism to control price inflation
Source: Author's compilation.

will hence be reimbursed for services provided to insured patients. Public health institutions, in particular RHUs, rural health facilities at the municipal level, generally lack funding to ensure adequate medical equipment or drugs (Schneider and Racelis 2004). The reimbursement will hence provide additional funds for public providers. They can invest the additional funds in equipment for their health facilities and medical supplies, which means that public providers will be able to afford to improve their insufficient facilities and low quality of care.

Meanwhile, social health insurance will provide the individuals (patients) with a financial tool which will enable them to select providers. Both private and public providers would have incentives to treat the insured patients who have certain compensation – insurance benefits.[18] This will induce competition between providers, and the public providers that provide free or low-price services with improved facilities and quality of care would be expected to become reasonably competitive against private providers. The competition between providers would consequently contribute to price containment.

We need detailed data, such as health service prices before/after reforms, the price difference between insured and uninsured patients, and data on the utilization of public institutions before/after reforms, to conclusively evaluate the function of this *possible* mechanism. Several features of the healthcare market, however, pose questions about the impact of this *possible* mechanism on price inflation. Features in the healthcare market suggest that physicians (providers) have some market power to set the price as well as the quantity of care in the health economics context (Dranove and Satterthwaite 2000; McGuire 2000).

For instance, even though patients may have a choice of physicians, the physicians are not perfect substitutes for each other due to, for example, geographical issues (location/distribution), or their clinical specialty. Collusion among physicians may obstruct reduction in service prices so that they would continue to maximize their return (Kessel 1958). Demand for healthcare will not rise in response to price cuts, that is, low-price elasticity of demand, which would reduce the providers' motivation to lower the prices. Uncertainty and information asymmetries have been identified as important elements of the physician-patient relationship in healthcare (Arrow 1963; Lundberg and Wang 2006). The asymmetries of information between patients and physicians would allow physicians to influence the choice of medical services by patients. In addition, the nonretradability of physician service has been identified as an important factor in price discrimination.[19]

A positive effect of the indirect mechanism would be to improve the quality of care supplied by public providers by channelling additional funds (insurance benefits) to public providers as well as motivating them to improve their quality of care. In fact, Schneider and Racelis (2004) reported that RHUs utilized the additional funds from PhilHealth (the insurance benefits) mainly for purchasing medicines and other medical equipment, which resulted in the better availability of drugs at RHUs. In addition, the function of accreditation by PhilHealth contributes to improvement in the quality of services provided by public health institutions and ensures the quality of their services (WHO 2005; Jowett and Hsiao 2007). Public providers supply free or low-price services. Therefore, improving their quality of care will contribute to reducing the financial burden on patients.

Based on the abovementioned features of the healthcare market, private providers are, however, not price-takers. The limited deployment of public health institutions reduces patients' choices. It has also been pointed out that deployment of public health institutions does not necessarily reduce the utilization of private services; or rather, they may either compete against or complement each other (World Bank 1994; Schneider and Racelis 2004). Private providers would retain market power to set prices and quantity of care. The impact of the indirect mechanism on price inflation accordingly may not be clear.

In addition, over-reliance on patients' decisions would not be appropriate in the healthcare market because of their insufficient knowledge of healthcare. Patients will choose providers depending on their personal preference and other information, but they do not necessarily know what medical services are necessary for them or who will provide those services adequately. Because health and medical care knowledge is generally too limited among consumers (patients) for them to make decisions that maximize their welfare, a mechanism that is overly dependent on patients' decisions may not lead them to obtain appropriate healthcare services.

An important step in working on the problems and evaluating the likely impact of the *possible* mechanism on controlling price inflation is to collect data on health service prices that include patient user fees as well as insurance benefits. Because user fees are at market rates, they differ among patients and among areas/regions. In order to evaluate the functions of the present insurance scheme and the *possible* indirect mechanism, data needs to be systematically collected on health service costs for the insured and the uninsured in various regions/areas.

2.4.2 A possible alternative

The overall insurance support value was estimated at about 62 per cent in 2004 (Department of Health 2005), but a more precise number should be estimated based on detailed price data.[20] By taking the estimated support value as the baseline, a possible alternative would be to modify social health insurance from the present scheme to a coinsurance scheme. Patients would pay a certain percentage of the total costs, for instance 40 per cent of service costs, and insurance benefits would cover the remaining proportion of under a coinsurance scheme (Hsiao 2004).

Jowett and Hsiao (2007) also proposed an option to amend the current flaws. Their suggestion is to reverse the design of the insurance benefit packages; that is, the patient pays for an initial deductible payment, and PhilHealth covers the 'second peso', which caps the amount of payment by the insured patient. Their suggestion is to fix the amount of the patient payment depending on the services provided, whereas a possible alternative, the coinsurance option discussed here, is to fix the patient payment at certain percentage of the total cost of services provided. In either option, the important point is to control the financial risks of patients by making the patient payment prospectively. That is the function of social health insurance.

Under the current scheme, patients have to bear the financial risks of uncertain illness. The most significant difference between the coinsurance scheme and the current scheme is that the former controls the financial risks faced by the individual patient, but the latter not. Under the coinsurance scheme, the patients' financial risks are controlled; in addition, the insurer would be strongly motivated to control total healthcare service prices that will directly affect the balance of the insurance fund. Patient moral hazard, physician-induced demand and excess care provision would then become issues to face in the control of the expansion of total healthcare expenditure. These are common problems relating to health insurance. Payment methods other than fee-for-service, such as case-based, capitation, or deductible, are worth applying to restrain the moral hazard of both the supply and demand side. Each method, however, has both positive and negative aspects (Carrin and Hanvoravongchai 2003; Hsiao 2004). Any single method will not be perfect, so that a combination of several methods is a realistic option.[21]

Another important challenge that needs to be dealt with is the financial risk associated with catastrophic illness. The financial risk is particularly critical because the heavy health expenses tend to impoverish patients in developing countries. A benefit schedule for catastrophic illness is prepared under the current social health insurance programmes of the Philippines; however, the first peso coverage with a capped benefit scheme is also applied. Even though the scale of the insurance benefit is higher in catastrophic cases than in regular cases, the insurance benefit covers expenses only up to a certain ceiling and then the patient is liable for payment of the remaining costs. Moreover, the cost borne by the patient is neither based on a schedule nor capped. A more desirable scheme for catastrophic cases would be to cap the patient payment. However, the actual cost of the care would need to be known in order to examine the feasibility of establishing such measures, given the overall limited financial capacity of the Philippine health financing system.

2.5   Lessons learned

Reforms of the health sector in the Philippines have continued since the late 1990s, which indicates that the government pays high attention to health issues. A focal issue of the reforms has been and continues to be health financing, which aims to mobilize financial resources for healthcare and to reduce the financial burden on patients. However, despite the continuous reforms, the share of out-of-pocket payments in total health expenditure has not decreased significantly since the mid-1990s.

We found three major factors behind the situation. The first is the fee-schedule for healthcare services (user fees). Healthcare services are not on schedule in the Philippines. In other words, providers can charge user fees at market rates. This allows providers to capture the insurance benefits by setting different service prices (user fees) for the insured and the uninsured. This would be the most critical factor in keeping the out-of-pocket payments high. In addition, the social health insurance scheme makes it easy for providers to set service prices. The present scheme consists of first peso coverage up to a cap. Under this scheme, health insurance covers a part of the health service costs up to a cap, but the remaining costs need to be covered by the patient. Because the health service cost borne by patients is not on schedule, the total service costs are not managed by the insurer or the government, and are not predictable. Therefore, even though a patient is insured, the patient still has to bear uncertain financial risks. Another factor is the payment method for providers. In general, the fee-for-service payment method tends to cause an excessive provision of healthcare services, which increases not only the financial burden of patients but also total health expenditure.

The problem is that healthcare pricing depends on the market. As we have discussed, elements such as information asymmetries and uncertainty distinguish health services from ordinary goods and services, and would cause market failure. Enforcement of the appropriate regulations is frequently a difficult challenge in developing countries. The essential issues are the setting of appropriate legal and regulation frameworks in the healthcare-pricing mechanism and the strengthening of enforcement capacity.

Establishing the health financing system is important for the mobilization of financial resources for health. A critical factor in making the system function adequately and utilizing mobilized resources efficiently is the *design* of the health financing system. A flaw in the system will cause resources to leak in unintended ways and will obstruct attainment of the expected results. Several factors within the health financing system, such as price regulation, payment method and the social health insurance scheme, interact with each other. The interaction influences the behaviour of the actors in the health sector – providers, patients and insurer – by changing their incentives for healthcare service provision, consumption and management.

In addition to the function of each factor in the health financing system, one needs to comprehend the effect of the interaction among the factors in order to design a functioning system. It should be noted that a provider is not a price-taker but has some market power in the healthcare market; in addition, patients do not necessarily have appropriate or sufficient information about the healthcare services that they need. This feature distinguishes healthcare services from other regular goods and services. One needs to take account of the effects of interaction of factors within the health financing system as well as the specific features of healthcare services in order to design a functioning health financing system.

Appendix

Table 2.A1:   Structure of public health institutions

Government	Health Administrative Institution	Health Institution
Central Government:		
National	Department of Health (DOH)	DOH hospital
Regional	Regional DOH (CHDs: Center for Health Developments)	
Local Government Units (LGUs)		
Province	Provincial Health Office	District Hospital
Municipality/City	Municipalty Health Office/City Health Office	Rural Health Units (RHUs)/City Health Center
Barangay	Barangay Health Office	Barangay Health Station

Source: Author's compilation.

Notes

1. Data from the World Bank (2006: 41) indicates that the ratio of private expenditure as a percentage of total health expenditure is 34.85, of which 55.78 per cent was covered by OOP in high-income countries in 2002, whereas the ratio was 70.86, of which 92.84 per cent was covered by OOP, in low-income countries.
2. Details are available from the Philippines Department of Health (DOH) website: www.doh.gov.ph/hsra/hsra-convergence.htm.
3. Local government units (LGUs) comprise the province, city, municipality, and barangay. The LGUs, which have autonomy, are the primary units for local healthcare service provision.
4. Details are available from the DOH website: www.doh.gov.ph/f1primer/F1-Page.htm.
5. A user fee, which is known as socialized user fee that is adjusted according to patients' income level, is sometimes required to obtain services at a DOH hospital or district hospital. And, a 'donation', which is a sort of informal payment, seems to be needed to access services sometimes.

6. A barangay health station is also a public health institution, which is on a lower tier than RHUs. Doctors or nurses are not stationed at a barangay health station but midwives are.

7. The average family expenditure for medical services was about 2.3% of the average annual expenditure of families in 2000 (National Statistical Office 2002).

8. In addition, employers also contribute a part of the premium for their employees' insurance programme (employed sector insurance programme).

9. Plan 2/25, launched by President Arroyo, aimed to enroll five million poor families into the PhilHealth programme (the indigent/sponsored insurance programme).

10. Expansion of the health insurance mechanism to cover the informal and the agricultural sectors is a commonly faced challenge in developing countries. Chapter 3 in this volume retraces Japan's experiences in this regard.

11. This means 'surely good health and reachable PhilHealth'.

12. The price level of health expenditure is calculated by using data on health expenditures in nominal terms and in real terms from the Philippine National Health Accounts 2004 (NSCB 2006). The CPI increase rate is calculated based on data from the Economic Indices and Indications Division, Industry and Trade Statistics Department, National Statistics Office.

13. Private hospitals make up a large proportion of health institutions in the Philippines. The number of DOH-licensed hospitals was 1761 in 2005, of which 1066 hospitals were private, while the number of RHUs was 2322 in 2002 (PhilHealth 2007). PhilHealth accredited hospitals total 1569, of which 61 per cent are private hospitals (PhilHealth 2007).

14. In addition, the capitation method and the case based method are applied to some cases.

15. The indigent insurance programme provides some free benefits, such as free primary consultation with the physician and free laboratory examination for complete blood count, which the enrollees can obtain without paying user fees.

16. The support valued is defined as the percentage ratio of the insurance benefits to the total cost of health services provided.

17. Jowett and Hsiao (2007) also suggest that the current Philippine insurance scheme does not limit the financial risks of insured members but those of the insurer.

18. Note that this would cause discrimination against patients. Providers would prefer to treat the insured patients rather than the uninsured.

19. McGuire (2000) reviews healthcare market and physician behaviour in detail. Regarding the price elasticity of demand for medical services, Gertler (1998) points out that the elasticity seems to be greater in developing countries than in developed countries. In that case, lowering medical service prices will lead to more demand for medical services in developing countries. Focusing on the incentives and their influence on physician behavior, Kutzin (2001) summarizes the incentives generated by payment methods, which are important elements of the analytical framework for healthcare financing systems.

20. Jowett and Hsiao (2007) indicate that the insurance support value is not clear in the Philippines due to the combination of the first peso coverage with

a insurance benefit cap scheme and market-based health service (user fee) pricing (no fee-schedule).
21. Jegers et al. (2002) particularly focus on types of provider payment method in relation to incentives that would affect provider behaviours. They provide a typology to classify the payment methods.

References

Arrow, Kenneth J. (1963) 'Uncertainty and the Welfare Economics of Medical Care,' *The American Economic Review*, Vol. 53, No. 5: 941–73.

Carrin, Guy, Diana de Graeve and Leo Devillé (1999) 'Introduction to Special Issue on the Economics of Health Insurance in Low and Middle-Income Countries', *Social Science & Medicine*, Vol. 48: 859–64.

Carrin, Guy and Piya Hanvoravongchai (2003) 'Provider Payments and Patient Charges as Policy Tools for Cost-Containment: How Successful Are They in High-income Countries?', *Human Resources for Health*, Vol. 1, No. 6, at: www.human-resources-health.com/content/1/1/6/.

Commission on Macroeconomics and Health: WHO (2001) *Macroeconomics and Health: Investing in Health for Economic Development*, Geneva: World Health Organization.

Department of Health (1999) *National Demographic and Health Survey 1998*, National Statistics Office (NSO), Department of Health, Philippines.

Department of Health (2005) *National Objectives for Health Philippines*, 2005–2010, Department of Health, Republic of the Philippines.

Dranove, David and Mark A. Satterthwaite (2000) 'Industrial Organization of Health Care Markets', in Anthony. J. Culyer and Joseph P. Newhouse (eds) *Handbook of Health Economics*, Volume 1B: 1093–1139, Elsevier Science BV.

Gertler, Paul J. (1998) 'On the Road to Social Health Insurance: the Asian Experience,' *World Development*, Vol. 26, No. 4: 717–32.

Gertler, Paul and Orville Solon (2002) 'Who Benefits From Social Health Insurance? Evidence from the Philippines', *World Development*, Vol. 26, No. 4: 717–32.

Hsiao, William (2004) 'Payment', in Marc J. Roberts, William Hsiao, Peter Berman and Michael R. Reich (eds) *Getting Health Reform Right*, Oxford: Oxford University Press.

Jegers, Marc, Katrien Kesteloot, Diana De Graeve and Willem Gilles (2002) 'A Typology for Provider Payment Systems in Health Care', *Health Policy*, Vol. 60: 255–73.

Jowett, Matthew and William C. Hsiao (2007) 'The Philippines: Extending Coverage Beyond the Formal Sector', in William C. Hsiao and R. Paul Shaw (eds) *Social Health Insurance for Developing Nations*, WBI Development Studies, Washington: World Bank.

Kessel, Reuben A. (1958) 'Price Discrimination in Medicine', *Journal of Law and Economics*, Vol. 1: 20–53.

Kutzin, Joseph (2001) 'A Descriptive Framework for Country-level Analysis of Health Care Financing Arrangements', *Health Policy*, Vol. 56: 171–204.

Lundberg, Mattias and Limin Wang (2006) 'Health Sector Reforms', in Aline Coudouel and Stefano Paternostro (eds) *Analyzing the Distributional Impact of Reforms*, Volume Two, Washington: World Bank.

McGuire, Thomas G. (2000) 'Physician Agency', in Anthony J. Culyer and Joseph P. Newhouse (eds) *Handbook of Health Economics*, Volume 1A: 461–536, Elsevier Science BV.

National Statistical Coordination Board (2006) *Philippine National Health Accounts 2004*, Republic of the Philippines.

National Statistics Office (2002) *1997 and 2000 Family Income and Expenditures Survey*, Household Statistics Department, National Statistics Office, Republic of the Philippines.

National Statistics Office (2004) *Philippine National Demographical and Health Survey 2003*, Republic of the Philippines.

Obermann, Konrad, Matthew R. Jowett, Maria Ofelia O. Alcantara, Eduardo P. Banzon and Claude Bodart (2006) 'Social Health Insurance in a Developing Country: The Case of the Philippines', *Social Science and Medicine* Vol. 62: 3177–85.

PhilHealth (2004) *Stats & Charts 2003*: www.philhealth.gov.ph/stats&charts.htm

PhilHealth (2005) *Stats & Charts 2006*: www.philhealth.gov.ph/stats&charts.htm

PhilHealth (2007) *Stats & Charts: January–March 2007*, June 2007.

Philippine Health Insurance Corporation (2004) *The Implementing Rules and Regulations of the National Health Insurance Act (R.A. 7875) as Amended by R.A. 9241*, 2004 Edition, PhilHealth.

Roemer, Milton I. (1993) 'National Health Systems Throughout the World', *Annual Review of Public Health*, Vol. 14: 335–53.

Schneider, Pia and Rachel Racelis (2004) *The Impact of PhilHealth Indigent Insurance on Utilization, Cost, and Finances in Health Facilities in the Philippines*, Bethesda MD: The Partners for Health Reform*plus* Project, Abt Associates Inc.

WHO (World Health Organization) (2000) *The World Health Report 2000*, Geneva: World Health Organization.

WHO (2005) *Social Health Insurance: Selected Case Studies from Asia and the Pacific*, SEARO Regional Publication No. 42, Geneva: World Health Organization.

WHO (2006) *Health Financing: A Basic Guide*, Geneva: World Health Organization.

World Bank (1994) *Philippines Devolution and Health Services: Managing Risks and Opportunities*. Report No. 12343-PH, Washington: World Bank.

World Bank (2006) *Health Financing Revisited*, Washington: World Bank.

3
Development of Social Health Insurance Systems: Retracing Japan's Experience

Masako Ii

Introduction

Since the Second World War, many developing countries have tried to introduce a healthcare system similar to those already established in developed countries. However, such a system has often tended to aim at people living in urban areas and not those in rural areas. Unlike many of these developing countries, Japan had already introduced a kind of universal health insurance system at the end of the 1930s and a more genuine universal insurance system in the early 1960s. Developing countries that are currently in the process of moving from a partial to a universal healthcare system would benefit significantly by drawing lessons from the Japanese experience.

In light of the above, this chapter reviews the evolution of the Japanese healthcare systems from the Meiji era to the present. The events that led to the introduction of the Factories Act, a law that was designed to protect workers during modernization law is discussed. Then, the Health Insurance Law, a full-scale piece of legislation, and the National Health Insurance Law, which was hastily prepared during the war, will be reviewed.

The Japanese health insurance system after the establishment of universal insurance is also discussed, focusing on the following four points: 1) national health insurance issues – the system's institutional rigidity that severely limits its ability to adapt to changing economic situations and an aging population, and its complex financing structure; 2) unequal obligations on the part of the insurer and the insured; 3) the coverage of public medical insurance for the elderly; and 4) the role of the insurers.

3.1   From Meiji to Showa: from none/nil to universal[1]

3.1.1   Predecessor to the Health Insurance Law: the Factories Act

Meiji era: the rise of modern industries

Guided by the policy of 'increasing production and promoting industry (*shokusan kogyo*)', the Meiji Government (1868–1912) embarked on state undertakings in key industries such as railways, marine transport, shipbuilding, textiles and manufacturing. They were sold mostly to private entrepreneurs in 1880s who took advantage of the government's generous protective policies. With the establishment of the government-run Yawata Iron and Steel Works in 1897, steel production – which underpins heavy industries – reached full swing, and gave rise to modern industries under the capitalist economic system in the 1890s. The main industry at that time was the textile industry, which includes spinning and silk reeling. The focal point of the spinning business had shifted from households to factories by the early 1900s.

Cotton exports exceeded imports, and cotton spinning accounted for some 70 per cent of Japan's factory production. Cotton yarn and raw silk accounted for about half of Japan's exports in the last decade of the 19th century. Raw cotton accounted for a third of Japan's imports (Flath 2000). In 1909, Japan surpassed China in being the world's largest raw-silk exporter.

With the rise in modern industries came an influx in the number of factory workers and wage-earners. The majority of these workers were women and children employed in textile mills. Around 1897, female labourers accounted for two-thirds of the approximately half million workers in factories with ten or more employees. Male workers were involved primarily in mining and railway work, while the number of skilled male workers in heavy industries such as shipbuilding and steel was limited.

These labourers worked under extremely poor conditions where they were forced to work long hours at low wages. The textile industry's poor working environment led to diseases such as tuberculosis, beriberi and eye problems among the female and child labourers. Even worse, since the (silk) spinning industry workers were sent back to their home villages when dismissed, tuberculosis also spread throughout rural communities.

These exploited workers spontaneously resorted to resistance movements and uprisings. Riots and strikes of various magnitudes broke out, and labour unions were organized. Studies and campaigns for socialism began, resulting in the establishment of the Society for the Study of Socialism. In response, the government established the Public Order and Police Law in 1900, and socialist movements were severely suppressed by the government. However, the opinion that it was necessary to protect workers and improve labour-management relations, rather than forcibly oppress labour movements and socialist movements, began to gain prevalence within the government.

Accordingly, the Factories Act was enacted in 1911 as the first legislation for the protection of workers in Japan. This law prohibited the employment of underage workers and late-night work by female labourers and obligated business owners to provide care for workers' illnesses and injuries incurred during work. This law contained many exemptions however, and was criticized as being essentially ineffectual (JICA 2004). For example, this law only applied to factories with 15 or more employees, but most of the factories at that time employed fewer than 15 people.

When the government first drafted the Factories Act in the late 1890s, the proposed legislation provoked strong opposition from the business owners, therefore postponing its enactment. Even after it was passed into law, the owners succeeded in postponing its enforcement for another five years.

In the 1890s, while studying in Germany, Shinpei Goto of the Ministry of Home Affairs became aware of the 1882 enactment of the Sickness Insurance Law in that country. In 1895, Goto advised then Prime Minister Hirobumi Ito to appropriate the indemnity received after the First Sino-Japanese War to finance sickness insurance, but this advice was neglected. In 1898, Goto drafted a sickness insurance bill, which unfortunately was not enacted.

Meanwhile, mutual-aid associations and relief funds began forming at both private and government factories and mines. In 1905, the Kanebo Mutual Aid Association and the Yawata Mutual Aid Association were formed. The Railway Workers Mutual Aid Association of the Imperial Government Railways (Japan National Railways Mutual Aid Association) was formed in 1907. In the early 20th century, mutual-aid associations were established in monopolistic enterprises and other government undertakings in the fields of printing, marine transport, land transport and forestry.

3.1.2   Enactment of the Health Insurance Law

Background to the establishment of the health system

In 1919, the International Labour Organization (ILO) was founded in accordance with the Treaty of Versailles. With this, the working day was limited to eight hours, a minimum age for workers was set, and a treaty concerning unemployment was signed. The exemptions in the Factories Act proved to be an obstacle to Japan's admission as a permanent member of the ILO. These exemptions were phased out gradually, expanding the protection of workers. In 1923 the Factories Act was revised, expanding the scope of application to include factories with ten or more workers and raising the minimum age for employment to 14.

Movements both inside and outside of Japan had a significant effect on labour administration. In 1922, the Ministry of Home Affairs promulgated the Health Insurance Law, which had been enacted by the Ministry of Agriculture and Commerce.

In contrast to the Factories Act, the Health Insurance Law – Japan's first social-insurance legislation – was passed only about ten days after the bill was submitted to the Diet. The speedy passage was due to three reasons; first, the Health Insurance Law was designed to protect workers at factories or mines with 15 or more employees covered by the Factories Act and the Mines Law, with the exception of staff members whose annual income was over 1200 yen (following the German example); second, the law was also designed to create cooperation and harmony between capital and labour; and third, the law was modelled on the sickness insurance systems of Germany and other countries. As Shimazaki (2005) pointed out, the Health Insurance Law contributed greatly to the successful enactment of the National Health Insurance Law in 1938 that targeted farmers who normally do not adapt to social insurance, and this played an important role in the establishment of the later public health system in Japan.

Workers at small-scale factories with fewer than 15 employees, government officials, bank employees, and a few others such as farmers and the self-employed were not covered by the Health Insurance Law. There were some arguments regarding the treatment of the then-existing mutual-aid associations such as the association at Kanebo. Eventually, it was decided that only mutual-aid associations for public servants were exempted from the application of the law, and private organizations were not allowed to continue the operation of their health insurance programmes. This meant that health insurance programmes were no longer managed by autonomous private organizations and the government was compelled to become the insurer.

Amendments to the Health Insurance Law were made several times in order to expand its coverage. The Law, in 1923, covered workers at factories that engaged more than nine workers and, in 1934, it covered workers at factories that engaged more than four workers. Furthermore, in 1947 the exclusion from coverage based on income was removed.

Salient points of the Health Insurance Law

When the Health Insurance Law was first established, the insurer (government or health insurance association) could directly negotiate a contract with physicians. Each insurer could freely determine the unit price and the calculation method used to pay the physicians' service fees in the contract with medical institutions. However, the direct contract system was not carefully formulated (Fukuda 2003). The government or health insurance association simply did not see the relationship between the insurers and medical institutions as a serious problem. The reality was that the content of the contract was believed to be a matter of common sense. Insurers signed contracts with the Japan Medical Association (JMA) that included a clause on service fees, and insurers could select health insurance doctors (physicians who belonged to the JMA and could provide health insurance treatment) based on the contract. However, the JMA actually selected the health insurance doctors.

The healthcare package

The Health Insurance Law covered only the insured's illnesses, injuries, death and childbirth incurred both on and off the job but did not cover disabilities of aged people. The maximum period to receive benefits was 180 days. There were various restrictions on medical benefits. In principle, the insured were not allowed to change their doctor when being treated for the same disease, and changing to another doctor in other circumstances still required an approval from the insurer.[2] Cash benefits included disability allowances, funeral-rite benefits, childbirth expenses and maternity allowances.

The Health Insurance Law was enforced, in the case of government-managed health insurance, using a contract between the government and the JMA. The government – the insurer of government-managed health insurance – and the JMA signed a comprehensive service contract, wherein the government paid the JMA a lump-sum remuneration for medical treatment according to the number of insured persons, and the JMA then distributed this money to individual doctors via prefectural medical associations. Insurance payment was, therefore, based on capitation. Guidance and supervision of doctors was also left to the JMA.

Responsibility for the cost

The cost of operating health insurance was defrayed by the premiums paid by employees and business owners as well as by contributions from the Japanese government. It was determined that the maximum premium to be paid by the employees would be set at 3 per cent of the daily wage,[3] and any excess amount was to be paid by the business owners. Additionally, the Japanese government paid 10 per cent of the insurance benefit up to 2 yen per insured person, which was approximately same as the administrative cost.

The Health Insurance Law in Japan was modelled on the medical insurance law in Germany, which grew out of a long history of mutual-help organizations for people in the same trade that had existed since medieval times (guilds for merchant associations and *Zunft* for artisans' trade unions). Self-governing organizations (mutual-benefit funds) based on these were well developed from the mid-19th century, and they served as parent bodies for the insurers (health insurance funds). Each insurer (health insurance fund) in Germany has autonomy and is responsible for managing the insurance. Each insurer is independent of government management. In Japan, there were two insurers, the government and health insurance associations subsidized by the Japanese government.[4]

Enforcement of the Health Insurance Law

The Great Kanto Earthquake in 1923 caused the enforcement of the Health Insurance Law to be postponed until 1927. The law gave rise to considerable complaints and dissatisfaction. Those complaints came from: 1) workers who then had to pay their insurance premiums at least partially, a departure from the provisions of the Factories Act and the Mining Law;[5] 2) owners of small-to-medium-size businesses who had to face completely new obligations; 3) physicians who had to treat many patients for relatively small fees; and 4) the insured, who faced a low quality of healthcare, the unkindness of health insurance doctors, and discrimination based on their insurance status. The operating cost was more than what the government had expected, and it did not have legal power to forcibly collect premiums. In 1929, the Health Insurance Law was amended. One change was to grant the government the right to forcibly collect premiums from delinquents. Another change related to the provision concerning state liability; the provision stipulating that 'one-tenth of insurance benefits shall be funded by the general account' was revised to 'insurance benefits shall be funded as required by the budget'. On this basis, state liability began to decline steadily over time. In the same year, a health insurance administration was placed under the police department of each prefectural government. Thus, the health insurance system was administered by the police and security corps.

3.1.3   Maintenance of the health insurance system: rapid expansion during the war

Healthcare in rural communities

In the 1920s and the 1930s, agricultural areas suffered from severe poverty caused by economic depression and natural disasters. Medical expenses were a tremendous burden on poor farmers, making medical consultations a problem,[6] resulting in an extremely high infant mortality rate and a high prevalence of parasitic diseases, trachoma and tuberculosis.

In 1932, the government began providing outreach diagnostic and treatment services as well as mobile consultation services. Charitable organizations such as the Imperial Gift Foundation Saisei Association, established in 1911 under the Imperial aegis, and other private organizations began to extend these services and sent public health nurses to remote areas without doctors.

Other initiatives in this regard included the formation of mutual support associations that were jointly funded by residents. These associations resembled health insurance cooperatives that had existed as mutual-aid organizations in rural villages since the Meiji Era.

In 1932, the infant mortality rate in urban areas was 13.78 per 1000 live births, and 19.40 in rural areas. In agricultural areas, the infant mortality was particularly high, and there were many cases of trachoma, parasitic diseases and tuberculosis. Since these farming villages were a source of recruitment for the military, a decline in the physical strength

Table 3.1:   History of Japanese healthcare insurance

	National health insurance	Government-managed health insurance	Society-managed health insurance
Related law	National Health Insurance Law	Health Insurance Law	Health Insurance Law
Pre-war	1938	1927	1927
Post-war	1958		
Target		(formal) Employee	(formal) Employee
Initial	Self-employed/ farmer	(in relatively small enterprises)	(in relatively large enterprises)
Present	Self-/part-time employee (informal employee)/farmer		

Note: The Health Insurance Law was promulgated in 1922.

of farmers and peasants raised concern from a national defence point of view. Healthcare improvement measures in farming villages were thus fervently requested by the government.

Foundation of the national health insurance system

In 1933, the government began studying an insurance system that would cover the general public in rural areas. Following more than a year's investigation and research, the government announced in 1934 a draft outline of the national health insurance system, wherein an association would be formed in each municipality, and each association would serve as an insurer.

This draft garnered a generally favourable response from the public. However, the JMA raised concerns that it might lead to poor-quality medical services as doctors would have to live with small remuneration for medical treatment and work in medical institutions directly under the associations. Moreover, general practitioners would lose patients to a small number of commissioned doctors.

The most important issue in the implementation of the National Health Insurance Law was the question on who would be the insurer – or, in other words, the chief operator of the system. This issue was resolved by having the municipalities form the National Health Insurance Associations and as a result, the municipalities became the de facto insurers.

The establishment of and participation in an association were voluntary. The association had autonomous and discretionary powers and benefit rates, and some of the co-payment amounts were determined by each association. There was a contractual relationship between an association and its insured. The original system was very different from the basic characteristics of the current National Health Insurance, and much closer to that of a private insurance scheme. With the local authority's permission, physicians and insurers could directly sign contracts.

One of the reasons why a municipality-based association was adopted was that many people in rural areas already had a sense of community through irrigation and rice-farming activities in each village, and therefore a strong sense of community and mutual assistance already existed. Many rural areas traditionally had mutual financing associations as well, and the national health insurance system reflected these social realities (Shimazaki 2005).[7]

However, as soon as the plan for the National Health Insurance Law was announced, controversies were raised, and the law was not passed at the first deliberation by the Diet. The law was eventually enacted in 1938. There were significant differences between the Health Insurance Law of 1922, which passed without major controversies, and the National Health Insurance Law of 1938. First, the earlier Health Insurance Law was aimed at protecting workers, stabilizing their lives and improving capital-labour relations, which were strained at that time. The law therefore helped enhance the work environment. In addition, the law aimed at improving the physical strength of the people by boosting national defence capabilities and easing the burden of medical expenses for the general public in rural areas. Second, while the Health Insurance Law was applicable to approximately two to three million factory workers, the National Health Insurance Law applied to several tens of millions, which was about 60 per cent of the total population (which at that time was an unprecedented proportion in global terms).

The National Health Insurance Law was developed and implemented without difficulty due to the enactment of the National Mobilization Law in the same year, and the wartime 'healthy people – stronger soldiers' policy. The National Mobilization Law allowed the government to direct orders on the mobilization of labour power, determine wages and other working conditions, and give directives on the production and distribution of goods. Under this law, all resources and materials came under government control (Nakamura 1995). This was also the first time that Japan had unified all aspects of the administration of public health and medical services under a single authority (JICA 2005).

The National Health Insurance Law of 1938 was closer to the basic idea of insurance than the next-generation National Health Insurance Law, enacted in 1958. The latter was significant because it marked the beginning of health insurance in Japan becoming more than just labour insurance. The eventual result was that the insurance was also extended to the general public, which paved the way for a universal health insurance.

Consolidation of various health insurance laws and
the first universal insurance

In 1939, Employees' Health Insurance was inaugurated. Unlike the Health Insurance Law, which was only applicable to labourers at factories and other similar workplaces, this insurance covered office workers as well. Under this system, the insured bore a partial out-of-pocket contribution. Ordinances concerning mutual-aid associations of government employees and school personnel were also enacted because they were excluded from the Health Insurance Law.

In 1939, the Health Insurance Law was amended. Changes included providing dependents' benefits and extending the payment period of medical expenses for treatment of tuberculosis. Then, in 1942, the Health Insurance Law and the Employees' Health Insurance Law were integrated. In order to prevent unnecessary medical consultations, the out-of-pocket contribution system was fully introduced.

It was decided that remunerations for medical services, which had been paid to doctors via the JMA in line with the group contract between the government and the JMA, would be paid directly from the Ministry of Health and Welfare to doctors based on a medical fee table devised by the Ministry. This amendment was possible because only about half of all doctors in the country were willing to accept health insurance patients.

Physicians' fees were determined by the unit price and a points system, which were used both for employees' insurance and National Health Insurance. At that time, only half of the physicians in Japan were interested in rendering their services under the health insurance programme. Originally, the reimbursement formula paid lower unit prices the higher the number of patients. However, at the request of JMA, this method was subsequently corrected under wartime regulations. Also, the health insurance system, which was managed by the government at that time, had a large surplus, and the government wanted to use the surplus to make the insurance more popular. All of these eventually led to the current fee-for-service system which does not have a ceiling on the maximum total service fee. The amendment in 1942 introduced a mandatory designation system administered by the prefectural governors. On behalf of the insurers, the government, without undergoing consultation, put healthcare providers in charge of all the insurers (employees' insurances, the National Health Insurance, seaman's insurance), and physicians could not refuse to cooperate without a legitimate reason. The purpose was to control health insurance doctors in order to ensure their cooperation with the 'healthy people – stronger soldiers' policy during wartime. For health insurance, the insurers' right to select health insurance doctors was ended, and the system of appointing insurance doctors by the government still remains in effect today (Fukuda 2003).

In 1942, the National Health Insurance Law was amended. The most significant amendment was the mandatory establishment of national health associations imposed by the provincial governors on municipalities; the establishment of associations had, until then, been optional. By 1942 or 1943, the General National Health Insurance Association was established in 95 per cent of municipalities. This can be considered the accomplishment of the first universal insurance system (Yoshihara and Wada 1999); however, some of the municipal associations were created only for number-crunching, and the reality was far from universal coverage.

The integration of the Health Insurance Law and the Employees' Health Insurance Law, as well as the amendment of the National Health Insurance Law, represented a milestone reform: it was the first time that social health insurance systems within a country had been consolidated; the idea of a universal health insurance system was explicitly spelled out; an out-of-pocket contribution system was partially introduced; health insurance doctors were forcibly designated; and the government was given a great amount of power over the operation of the system. These amendments provided a basic framework for the current health insurance system in Japan.

With the exception of pension schemes for the farming-sector population and the self-employed, a social system that covered almost all citizens was completed during the Second World War. Although most of the social systems were on the verge of breaking down toward the end of the war, these social insurance systems survived and were reconstructed while many of the pre-war institutions and laws were being abolished. It can truly be said that Japan's social insurance systems were a legacy created and fostered by recessions and wars during the early 20th century.

3.1.4   The post-war health insurance system: from the reorganization after the war to the establishment of universal insurance

By the end of the Second World War, 98 per cent of all towns and villages and 63 per cent of the cities, other than the six major metropolitan cities, had established a national health insurance association, covering over 40 million people. In the years immediately after the war, however, the majority of these associations were either poorly operated or inactive. The services rendered by doctors to health insurance-covered patients were inferior, and the system remunerated doctors poorly. They grew increasingly negative towards and distrustful of the health insurance system, an attitude that carried over from the pre-war period.

Over several years following the end of the war, as related laws were amended, the medical fee schedule was revised and the level of fees was increased; a medical fee payment fund was established; health insurance hospitals were established; and the national health insurance system gradually regained its intended function as well as the confidence of the people.

A free appointment system (although the government still appointed doctors, but with doctors' consent) was introduced in 1948, but the selection of doctors was still done by the government and not the insurers (Fukuda 2003). When the Health Insurance Law first became effective, each insurer could determine the rate of the insurance premium and benefits as well as the collection of the premium, but the maximum amount of the premium was regulated in 1948. In its first enactment, the National Health Insurance Law dictated that the insurers would determine the premium, but the amendment to the law in 1948 transferred the responsibility from national health associations to municipalities, and premiums were to be determined by administrators. The Health Insurance Law and the National Health Insurance Law mandated the range and the level of benefits. Insurance premiums and the delivery of the benefits were regulated, and there was almost no opportunity for the insurer to calculate the premiums and benefits.

Other major changes that took place immediately after the war included: 1) the Labour Union Act, the Labour Standards Act and the Industrial Accident Insurance Act were enacted, which excluded identified industrial diseases from the jurisdiction of the Health Insurance Law, and transferred jurisdiction over them to the Ministry of Labour, which was established in 1947; 2) the National Health Insurance (NHI) Law was amended in 1948 to ensure that the NHI became the responsibility of municipalities, with the aim of promoting NHI programmes across the country.[8] Since the method of implemention of the law was similar to that of the municipality's routine tasks, the municipality took over the administration of NHI, in principle, and; 3) not only the heads of households but all members of households were required to be insured.

However, forcibly insuring everyone regardless of his/her individual will or ability to pay the premium and spreading understanding of the principle of insurance basically are mutually exclusive. The term universal health insurance is rather peculiar. Insurance dictates payment of a certain premium and it is possible that not all people can afford to pay. But Japan used government subsidies to pay the premiums of those who could not pay, thereby making the insurance, in practice, universal. An amendment to the Local Tax Law in 1951 created the National Health Insurance Tax, and the method of collecting National Health Insurance premiums became the same as that for municipal taxes. The purpose was to increase the collection rate; as about 90 per cent of municipalities chose the National Health Insurance Tax as the method of collection, people then tended to deviate from the idea of the National Health Insurance as an insurance system, and began to see it as a tax. As well, after the establishment of universal health insurance, the national health insurance system, as a group of insurance societies, gradually lost its homogeneity as the significance of traditional local communities declined over time.

Even so, in the mid-1950s, about one-third of the Japanese population, being largely engaged in agriculture and other self-owned businesses, still was not covered by health insurance. Uninsured people numbered approximately 30 million, of which 10 million low-income earners had no choice but to go on social welfare once they became ill.

In 1953, the government finally introduced subsidies equivalent to 20 per cent of medical care benefits. This established a universal financial base for health insurance, and a comprehensive foundation for universal insurance was laid.

A new National Health Insurance Law was enacted in December 1958, went into effect in 1959, and was enforced all over the country in 1961. The National Pension Law was also enacted in 1959. Universal health insurance and pension schemes were thus fully achieved in April 1961.[9]

3.2   Issues of public health insurance in Japan in the universal insurance era

3.2.1   The current organizational structure of health insurance programmes in Japan

Discussion of issues related to the current health insurance system can be best conducted by looking into its organizational structure. Japan's universal health insurance system is composed of three main insurance systems – employees' health insurance (Government-managed health insurance and Society-managed health insurance); community health insurance for the self-employed and unemployed (national health insurance, NHI), and a cross-financing system for the elderly. Each system comprises multiple insurance plans or sub-schemes with differing premium rates. Insurance premiums are calculated based on the insured person's income (ability-to-pay) regardless of their risks and the amount of benefits paid out to them. The method of calculating the premium rate for each system is different, depending on its insurers. The number of such insurers in Japan now exceeds 3000 (Table 3.2).

Employees' health insurance programmes have relatively high ratios of healthy and wealthy enrollees. Society-managed health insurance is a programme for employees of large corporations and their dependents (1561 associations). Employers deduct the employees' premiums directly from their paychecks and bonuses. Premium contributions are typically borne equally by employers and employees, although many companies pay more than half their employees' premiums. In 2005, premium rates for Society-managed health insurance ranged from 3.0 per cent to 9.5 per cent of employee (indexed) monthly earnings, and the average

Table 3.2: Japanese healthcare insurance programmes

	NHI	Government-managed health insurance	Society-managed health insurance
Number of insurers (2006)	1835 insurers	1 insurer	1561 insurers
Number of enrollees (2006)	47.7 million	35.7 million	30 million
Average age (excluding those older than 70 years) (2004)	53.7 (44.0)	37.2 (34.8)	34.2 (33.0)
Percentage of population 70 years or older (2005)	24.2%	4.6%	2.1%
Average monthly income (2004)	–	¥283,000	¥371,000
Annual household income (estimate)	¥1.6 million	¥2.4 million	¥3.8 million
Annual premium per household (2004)	¥152,000	¥169,000	¥190,000
Public contribution (% of the medical benefit expenditures)	43%	13%	–
Government budget (2007)	¥3.3 trillion	¥0.8 trillion	¥4.7 billion
Annual medical expenditure per capita (2006)	167,000	115,000	101,000

Source: Ministry of Health, Labour and Welfare, Japan.

premium rate was 7.28 per cent. Employers paid 55 per cent of the total contributions. In the same year, the premium rate for Government-managed health insurance, covering employees of small-and-medium-sized firms and their dependents, was 8.2 per cent of an employee's monthly salary, with half the contributions paid by employers.

NHI covers the self-employed, the unemployed, workers in companies with fewer than five employees, and retirees. This programme is managed by municipalities and 1835 associations all over Japan. NHI has a relatively high ratio of ill and poor enrollees. Most of the self-employed declare their own earnings, and the NHI premiums are collected on

Table 3.3: The distribution of financial resources in each system (FY 2004)

	NHI	Government-managed health insurance	Society-managed health insurance
Premium	34.1%	88.1%	97.6%
Public contributions	46.5%	11.6%	0.1%
Other	2.1% (prefectural disbursement) 10.1% (transferred from general accounts)	0.2%	2.3%

Source: Ministry of Health, Labour and Welfare, Japan.

the basis of household income, fixed assets and other wealth. Premium rates vary among insurers.[10] On average, NHI enrollees have the lowest incomes, followed by Government-managed enrollees and Society-managed enrollees, respectively. Taking into account employer contributions, the household premium rates for NHI, Government-managed, and Society-managed enrollees in 2001 were 10.2 per cent, 6.7 per cent, and 4.6 per cent of their annual income, respectively. Therefore, NHI enrollees, with the exemption of the poorest reprieve recipients, pay the highest rates. The government subsidizes 13 per cent of Government-managed health insurance benefit expenditures and 43 per cent of NHI benefit expenditures.

Upon retirement, employees leave their health insurance scheme and join NHI. Three-quarters of the elderly are members of the NHI. A pooling fund was created in 1983 so that costs would be shared equally by all insurers. Contributions to the pooling fund increase with age, and amount to 40 per cent of premiums.[11]

All the insurance programmes are similar in terms of the range of medical services covered, the procedures for obtaining medical care, and the system of reimbursing medical providers. However, there are significant differences in eligibility, administration, cost-sharing, cash benefits, financing and the level of government subsidy provided to fund administrative costs and to recover deficits (Tables 3.2 and 3.3). In recent years, the differences have become larger and more diversified.

The percent distribution of the total healthcare expenditure by financial resource is as follows: 36.4 per cent for public contribution,

41.9 per cent for insurance premiums (employers 20.2 per cent, employees 28.9 per cent), and 14.4 per cent for patients. The share of insurance premiums in the total insurance cost has been decreasing in recent years; the slumping economy and a decreasing population that pays the insurance premiums are causing this decrease.

3.2.2   Various current issues facing the Japanese health insurance system

Since the national universal insurance system was introduced, medical expenditure has expanded rapidly due to increased access to medical care, lifting of restrictions on the period for receiving treatments, maintenance of healthcare facilities, provision of benefits for high-cost medical care, and free medical care for the elderly (1973). This has increased pressure on the country's finances. It took almost 30 years to correct the 1973 policy which provided for medical care to the elderly; since 2002, the elderly have been required to pay 10 per cent of their medical costs.

In this subsection, the current issues facing the Japanese health insurance system will be discussed, focusing on the following four points: 1) the institutional rigidity of National Health Insurance caused by the system's failure to accommodate various societal changes after the establishment of universal insurance; 2) unequal obligations on the part of the insurer and the insured; 3) the coverage of public medical insurance for the elderly and; 4) the role of the insured.

Institutional rigidity

Unlike in the United States, people in Japan keep their health insurance after they lose their jobs. Insurance also serves as a safety net to reduce the risks people face during their lifetime. It is not easy to carry out the principle of insurance in the form of a mandatory insurance policy for everyone.

Japan's health insurance system has increased its importance as a provider of both occupational insurance and regional insurance. The premiums for and benefits from the social insurance do not correspond. In order to establish public insurance societies, it is rational to consider groups with an established sense of belonging (solidarity) among its members. In Japan there are two strong communities: occupational communities such as companies and agencies, and regional communities such as villages. Insurance societies were created with the social realities in mind.

After universal insurance was introduced, insurance associations lost their homogeneity as traditional villages and corporations were dissolved. Conflict of interest between employees' health insurance and local insurance regarding contributions to the health insurance system for the elderly, as discussed above, as well as the conflict within the national health insurance system due to the gaps in the financial strength of and medical expenses in each municipality, have tended to increase expenditure by the national government.

The NHI system's coverage has changed dramatically since 1961. NHI was targeted at farmers when universal insurance was introduced. In 1965, two-thirds of the workforce was either self-employed or in the agriculture, forestry or fishery industries. Further, lifetime employment and seniority-based corporate structures were a norm, and an employee's health insurance could be established with the corporation as a unit. However, the aging of the population and changes in the industrial structure fundamentally altered the situation in subsequent years. Currently, more than half the people insured by NHI are unemployed, 24 per cent are employees of offices with fewer than five employees or part-time workers, and 19.3 per cent are self-employed or farmers.[12] The aging of the population, which started around the time when the universal insurance system was established, also placed increased pressure on the finances of the NHI system. Those who are insured under the employees' health insurance are then turned over to NHI upon retirement, and this entails a decrease in income and increase in medical expenses for retirees. Government subsidy has become available, but it will be impossible to cover the medical expenses of everyone. A rapid decrease of rural population led to a decrease in the number of insurers after the universal insurance system was instituted.

Ad hoc financial support

For national health insurance, each municipality operates as the insurer. Since 2000, mergers have led to a decrease in the number of municipalities from over 3200 to 1835 in 2006, and gaps have developed in the capacity of public finance. Every time a financial crisis rises, new financial support measures are adopted in order for the system to keep up with the changes. With NHI and health insurance for the elderly combined, the insurance premiums cover only one-third of operating costs, and only a small amount of municipal financing is used to cover the revenue shortages created by NHI. This trend is more pronounced in rural compared to urban areas (Tajika and Yui 1999).

Since 1988, the National Health Insurance Law has been amended several times, and various ad hoc financial assistance measures have been introduced. As a result, the mechanism for financing the costs of the

NHI system has become extremely complicated and involves joint sub-sidies between national and local governments. This system includes an insurance-based stability system for people with low incomes, a joint project to mitigate the effect of high medical expenses, and financial measures to stabilize municipal finances.

Because of the practice of being provided with new financial support measures, municipalities now expect such measures to be implemented whenever new crises arise, therefore creating moral hazard for the NHI system. Overly supportive financial measures have reduced the incentives for municipalities to ensure the collection of insurance premiums and to improve the efficiency of healthcare services. As a result, the municipalities' responsibility as insurers remains ambiguous. Also, people have accepted the system without clearly understanding who actually pays for their medical expenses. As a result, government's share of medical expenditure has continued to increase over the years.

The fairness of the burden

Japan's medical care system has often been called 'equal and fair' (OECD 2004). Under the universal public insurance system, people can receive universal medical service at any time, anywhere in the country at a relatively low cost. In addition, when the Health Insurance Law was amended in 1997, the coinsurance rate for primary policyholders of employees' health insurance was increased. The Health Insurance Law reform of 2002 stated that as a general rule, primary policyholders of employee health insurance pay 30 per cent and insurers pay 70 per cent of medical costs. Benefits are distributed almost equally.

However, there are large regional differences in the actual amount of healthcare services that people receive, which are reflected in medical expenses, as well as differences in the amount of public insurance premiums. Unequal contributions have been one of the serious issues in the healthcare insurance system. Specifically, the amount of insurance premiums for employees' health insurance is determined by ability-to-pay (indexed monthly earnings) only. The rate of insurance premium is 3 per cent to 9.5 per cent of income (indexed monthly earnings) depending on health insurance unions, and the ratio of split between employees and employers varies from each employer to another. The rate is 8.2 per cent for Government-managed health insurance, and the premium is split between the employee and the employer. In employees' health insurance, both Government- and Society-managed, family members who are dependents of the primary policyholders can receive healthcare without paying separate insurance premiums. Unlike employ-ees' insurance, each individual is insured under the NHI system, but the head of the household is responsible for paying premiums (or insurance taxes) for all members of the household. Municipalities can freely set the amount of insurance premiums (or insurance taxes). They can also set the rules for determining insurance premiums and the ratio of the premium payments. Thus, premiums are calculated using a combina-tion of the following factors: income rate or asset rate (ability-to-pay); and per capita basis or per household basis (pay-for-benefit). As long as the income-rate and per-capita basis are included, each municipality can decide how many factors to combine.

Approximately half the benefits paid by NHI are covered by the national government. Nine per cent of this is a subsidy which is based on the differentials between the financial capacities of municipali-ties. Even with this subsidy, there are large gaps in medical expenses among the approximately 2531 municipalities. The highest premium, in Rausu-cho, Hokkaido (117,940 yen), is about five times as much as that of the lowest, in Aguni-son, Okinawa Prefecture (22,840 yen).

The health insurance system for the elderly – background and purpose of changes in the system

Japan's health insurance system not only retains the original function of health insurance, which is to cover the risk of illnesses in society as a whole, but also serves as a mechanism for transferring income from the young to the elderly. In 1983, over 90 per cent of the financial resources of the health insurance system created for the elderly were contributions from insurance and public expenditure. Since many of the elderly are covered by NHI, contributions from the working population covered by employees' health insurance decrease NHI's financial burden. In other words, the majority of the cost is covered by transferring money from the working population to the elderly. Many elderly suffer from chronic illnesses or, if they do not, pose a high risk of falling ill. Income redis-tribution to some extent will then be unavoidable. However, in the case of NHI, Government-managed health insurance and Society-managed health insurance, more than 20 per cent of their expenditure is paid into the health insurance system for the elderly. Additionally, this contribu-tion has been increasing every year since the introduction of the health insurance system for the elderly. It has been a major factor in the deteri-oration of the financial standing of each sector of the health insurance system.

The health insurance system for the elderly – design of the system and its responsibilities

The Law of Health and Medical Services for the Aged was amended in 2002, raising the target age from over 70 to over 75 and changing the proportion of public contribution from 30 per cent to 50 per cent of medical benefit expenditures. Elderly patients also became responsible for paying 10 per cent of their medical costs. The current health insurance system for the elderly is therefore a joint undertaking by all insurers. Municipalities provide the benefits, but they are not insurers. Therefore, they are not financially responsible, and they are not entitled to receive any incentive for efficiently using the funds to cover medical expenses for the elderly. It is necessary to delineate the responsibilities in the operation of the system by clearly stating which entities are responsible for providing benefits and which for finances (Shimazaki 2005).

A new healthcare system for old-old population (75 years or older) was established in April 2008. The insurers in this new medical insurance system for the old-old population are designated as an extended association of prefectural governments. Although financial responsibility is still unclear, prefectural governments are expected to formulate various plans, including healthcare plans and the rationalization of medical expenses. Accordingly, prefectural governments will become more important. The problem is that the gaps between premiums and medical expenses within the prefectures (that is, among municipalities) are larger than the gaps among prefectures. Currently, municipal governments have their own methods of determining NHI premiums, but standardization of assessment plans will become an important issue.

3.2.3 The role of the insurers

As previously discussed, when the Health Insurance Law was first enacted, insurers could directly sign contracts with physicians, and according to the rules, a patient had to secure permission from the insurer before being admitted to a hospital. Under the National Health Insurance, the establishment of and participation in an association was optional, and the benefit rate and co-payment was left to the discretion of the association. This was formalized into a contract, signed by the association and its participants. When compared with the pre-war period, the post-war period saw the government's role as an insurer increased while that of associations decreased.[13] The government still functions as an insurer today.

However, many of the problems facing the Japanese healthcare system today are due to the incapacity of the insurers to act as 'insurers'. These problems include excessive outpatient visits (because of the ease of outpatient visits), long hospital stays, a large number of hospital beds in the wards, social hospitalization, sizable regional gaps in the numbers of hospital beds and the number of physicians, and excess investment in expensive medical equipment. Other problems include differentials in premiums for the same insurance among different insurers and a lack of fairness due to universal physicians' service fees which do not take the level of their skills into consideration.

However, it is impossible for insurers to selectively sign contracts with specific physicians and hospitals in the free-access system, wherein anyone can receive necessary healthcare service anywhere in the country. The government both appoints physicians (health insurance doctors) and selects hospitals (health insurance hospitals). Those covered by insurance cannot select their insurers, and insurers cannot select their insured, either.[14]

Insurers and healthcare providers should act as the main actors in insurance contracts which involve the delivery of healthcare, in matters such as the determination of the insurance premium and benefit package, the review and approval of benefits, and the selection of healthcare facilities. However, in the current system, the government selects health insurance hospitals and appoints health insurance doctors without adequate evaluations; physician service fees are determined in line with administrative guidance, and the original purpose of the insurance contract is ignored. It should be possible for insurers to exclude inefficient healthcare providers individually from the list of health insurance service providers, such as occurs in Germany. However, the Japanese system makes that impossible, and German-style systems are rare in the world (Fukuda 2003). It is difficult to encourage competition between healthcare providers and to evaluate them under the Japanese system.

The strong correlation between the number of hospital beds and inpatient healthcare cost has been repeatedly pointed out in materials prepared by the Ministry of Health, Labour and Welfare. Many of the insurers designated by the national health insurance system as 'municipalities with high healthcare cost' that still remain on the list even after creating plans and working to solve the problem are located in regions with an excess number of beds (Ogata 2003). Ogata pointed out that the medical equipment in each hospital was not standardized, and explained how this led to excess investment in expensive medical equipment. It is important that insurers, as a responsive party, should become more than just the payers and become involved in responding to their area's medical needs.

Over 40 years have passed since the establishment of universal insurance in 1961. The aging of society is more pronounced, and both the economic structure and the disease structure has significantly changed. The roles that the government has traditionally played should be transferred to the insurers, and the system should be modified so that insurers can carry out their original role. If healthcare continues to be provided by public insurance, it may be necessary to consider a unified health insurance system. Current financial support for national health insurance comes from national and local governments as well as from employee funds. As an alternative, people with low incomes should receive a fixed amount from national or local government using the payment to finance their insurance premiums. In other words, individuals with low incomes could pay lower insurance premiums, or pay nothing at all, instead of insurers receiving reductions or exemptions. Insurers could then concentrate on the collection of insurance premiums that correspond to benefits, which is the principle of insurance.

The most important healthcare policy in postwar Japan was the establishment of equality, through free healthcare access for all Japanese. Under the universal health insurance system, the differences in benefit or out-of-pocket payment are relatively small from insurer to insurer. When looking at the GDP-healthcare expenditure ratio, Japan has a high level of efficiency compared to other countries. However, it has been over 40 years since universal insurance was implemented in Japan and, in the light of current institutional fatigue, today's Japanese health insurance system needs drastic reform. Changing and enhancing the role of the insurer would be a core task in such a reform.

3.3 Conclusion

The Japanese health insurance system started in the early 1900s when mutual-aid associations began to form at both private and government factories and mines. The first legislation for the protection of workers in Japan, the Factories Act, was enacted in 1911. In 1922, the Ministry of Home Affairs promulgated the Health Insurance Law, which had been enacted by the Ministry of Agriculture and Commerce. However, this law was applicable only to workers in the manufacturing and mining industries, and labourers at factories or mines with 15 or more employees. Workers at small-scale factories with fewer than

15 employees, government officials, bank employees, and some others were not covered.

In rural villages in Japan, organizations resembling health insurance cooperatives had existed as mutual-aid organizations since the Meiji Era. The government introduced the National Health Insurance Law in 1938 to expand it into a national system to cover those not formally employed, particularly farmers. In 1939, Employees' Health Insurance was inaugurated, covering salaried workers in the cities. By the end of 1943, the national health insurance system already covered 95 per cent of municipalities throughout Japan. This period was considered to be the first 'universal health insurance era'.

When universal national health insurance was created, the majority of Japanese people were farmers or self-employed, and urbanization had not progressed to a great degree. Lifetime employment and seniority-based corporate management did exist in large companies, and employees' health insurance, which utilized a company as a unit, covered this sector. However, as the industrial structure changed significantly, the number of self-employed and agricultural workers experienced a sharp decline, and employers' liquidity also steadily rose. The need to maintain separate insurance systems for the self-employed and the employed therefore began to decline.

If healthcare is to be provided by public insurance, it may be necessary to consider a unified health insurance system, in which case the insurers need to be reorganized at the prefectural level. Healthcare in Japan has traditionally considered quantity and equality of benefits as more important than quality of care and level of competition. As long as reforms improve social security, equality and fairness in benefits, and the discharging of care responsibilities, it will be necessary to explain to the public that the transfer of income is to some degree unavoidable. And in order to explain to the public how much tax and insurance premium they are paying and how much they are receiving as benefits, it will be necessary to come up with easy-to-understand, publicly available statistics.

In light of the foregoing account of the development of social health insurance systems in Japan, there are two important implications for developing countries. One is the active inclusion of people in the informal sector (such as farmers and self-employed workers) into the public health insurance system by the government, even if their population is relatively large.[15] The treatment of non-employed workers is the most critical issue in designing a social security system in a developing country. Western developed countries did not have much experience in tackling this difficult challenge. These countries were already industrialized by the time they established their social security systems from the late 19th century to the middle of the 20th century, by which time the proportion of non-employed workers in these countries was comparatively small. Japan, having achieved industrialization later than others, was the first country to make considerable efforts to include those in the informal sector, such as farmers and fishermen, in the public health insurance system.

The second is strengthening a role of the insurer. For Japan's unique health insurance framework, the government acts as the insurer. Japan has about 3400 insurers and they are under strict government control, which in part reflects paternalism. As discussed in this chapter, premiums and benefits in the Japanese public health insurance system are not designed to balance each other. Each time municipalities, the insurers for NHI, face a new financial crisis, they expect the national government to provide new financial support measures. These overly supportive financial measures have reduced incentives for the municipalities to ensure financial discipline and to improve the efficiency of their healthcare services.

In Western developed countries, insurers have improved their functioning by competing with each other, while in Asia, the governments of countries such as South Korea and Taiwan are sole insurers. Governments of most Asian countries, including Australia, play an influential and significant role as insurer, especially through maintaining financial discipline.[16] The Japanese government should also become aware of its responsibilities as an insurer in order to operate a financially secure public health insurance system.

Having gone through the pains of development later than Western countries but earlier than other Asian countries, Japan's experience in designing its health insurance system could also provide important guidance for the setting up of social security systems in developing countries.

Notes

1. This section heavily draws on Yoshihara and Wada (1999) and Shimazaki (2005).
2. This requirement was abolished in 1940.
3. According to a household budget survey of labourers in 1921, 3 to 5 per cent of their total living expenses was used for healthcare.
4. Shimazaki (2005) pointed out two other differences, namely that the Health Insurance Law also applied to work-related accidents and sicknesses in Japan

and that payment of the insurance premium was split in half by the employer and the employee, as a general rule.

5. When the Health Insurance Law was enacted, the targeted population was limited to those who were covered by the Factories Act or the Mining Law. Other blue-collar workers were included in 1935, and the families of the insured as well as white-collar workers in sales and finance were also included in 1939 with the enactment of the Employees' Health Insurance Law. This law was replaced by the Health Insurance Law of 1942, as will be discussed later, when the Employees' Health Insurance system and Health Insurance Law became unified.

6. The insured paid medical expenses twice per year (mid-August and year-end), and three times per year in silk districts (according to the seasonal patterns of silkworm-raising). Usually, payments were made in cash, but sometimes in rice. Some had to borrow money from informal money lenders or make use of pawnbrokers' services.

7. There was a national health insurance system in Fukuoka Prefecture dating from the Edo period called *Johrei*. Rice was collected from the residents as association dues and a pre-determined amount was paid to physicians based on the services they provided. The system enabled residents to seek medical care at minimal cost when they became sick. The association dues were calculated using a combination of ability-to-pay and the ratio of contribution and benefit. The reason why public health insurance was not created in the United States at the beginning of the 20th century was that funds for sick people and private insurance were not fully developed in the 19th century.

8. As a result, by 1961, all municipalities throughout the country had NHI programmes.

9. This achievement is attributable to Prime Minister Kishi – a strong advocate of constitutional revision – and his cabinet, which amended the Execution of Police Duties Law and the Japan-US Security Treaty.

10. Details are discussed in sub-section 'The Fairness of the Burden' below.

11. Details are discussed in sub-section 'Health Insurance System for the Elderly' below.

12. All these numbers are from the Ministry of Health, Labour and Welfare

13. It was almost impossible for insurers of different sizes and capabilities to negotiate with each healthcare facility and insured person. Accordingly, the decision to have the government act as an insurer was practical in order to establish and spread universal insurance.

14. The only exception is National Health Insurance Societies.

15. See JICA (2004) for a detailed discussion.

16. These insurers analyse the health-cost data and clinical indicators and provide the insured with the information on issues such as the quality of health or disease management.

References

Flath, David (2000) *The Japanese Economy*, Oxford: Oxford University Press.

Fukuda, Motoo (2003) *Hokensha to iryou kyokyuu shutai no Kannkei* (Relation between Insurer and Health Provider), in Yasuhiko Yamazaki and Hiroya Ogata (eds) *Iryouseidokaikaku to hokennsha kino* (Health System Reform and the Role of the Insurer), Toyo Keizai Shimposha.

JICA (2004) *Development of Japan's Social Security System – An Evaluation and Implications for Developing Countries*, Tokyo: Institute for International Cooperation, Japan International Cooperation Agency.

JICA (2005) *Japan's Experiences in Public Health and Medical Systems*. Tokyo: Institute for International Cooperation, Japan International Cooperation Agency.

Nakamura, Takafusa (1995) *The Postwar Japanese Economy: Its Development and Structure*, 2nd ed., Tokyo: University of Tokyo Press.

OECD (2004) *The OECD Health Project: Towards High-Performing Health Systems*, Paris: Organization fro Economic Co-operation and Development.

Shimazaki, Kenji (2005) *Wagakuni no iryouhoken seido no rekishi to tennkai* (History of Japanese Health Insurance and Its Development). In Hisao Endo and Naoki Ikegami (eds) *Iryouhoken/sinnryouhoshuseido* (Health Insurance and the System of Fee Schedules), Tokyo.

Tajika, Eiji and Yui Yuji (1999) *Koureika to kokuimin kenkou hoken kaigo hoken* (Aging and National Health Insurance/Long-term Nursing Insurance), *Kikan Shakai Hosho Kenkyu* (*Quarterly of Social Security Research*).

Ogata, Hiroya (2003) *Dougakutekina hokensha kino nojyujitu niyoru iryoukyokyu no kaikaku* (Reform of Health Provider by Introducing a Dynamic Role for the Insurer), in Yasuhiko Yamazaki and Hiroya Ogata (eds) *Iryouseidokaikaku to hokennsha kino* (Health System Reform and the Role of the Insurer), Toyo Keizai Shimposha.

Yoshihara, Kenji and Masaru Wada (1999) *Nihon iryohoken seidoshi* (History of the Japanese Medical Insurance System), Toyo Keizai Shinposha.

4
Emerging External Funds for Health: A Study of Global Health Partnerships

Banri Ito

Introduction

This chapter focuses on global funds which are attracting attention as an important external fund resource for the health sectors of developing countries in recent years. In order to increase access to health services in developing countries, there must be debate on how to secure and efficiently use fund resources. The Commission on Macroeconomics and Health (henceforth CMH), which the World Health Organization (henceforth WHO) established in January 2000, indicated that it is possible to raise the economic growth rate by injecting funds into the health sector of developing countries, and it was shown that the investment effect exceeds the expense (WHO 2001a). The CMH pointed out that the biggest problem caused by the financial deficit of the health sector is the fact that health and medical services are not fully accessible to people living in poverty, who are the beneficiaries of the service. For a developing country that suffers from financial deficiency, the role of the external donor, which can close the financing gap, is presumed to be important. The WHO (2001a) has argued strongly concerning the necessity for financial support and expansion of it in low-income countries, emphasizing that it is essential to increase financial support to a US$27 billion level per year by 2007 and a US$38 billion level per year by 2015.

Meanwhile, a number of Global Health Partnerships (henceforth GHPs)[1] which aim to solve health problems of significance for developing countries have been established successively in recent decades. The number already amounts to approximately 100, and the presence of GHPs is increasing globally. On the other hand, there is no clear grasp of fundamental information on how the GHPs' activities, which focus on different diseases and carry out different functions, are distributed globally. Although the nature of the tendency of GHPs to rapidly increase is a very interesting research subject, there is little study clearly focusing on this point. Further, analysis concerning whether the partnerships are supporting a country and what those countries' attributes are may also bring to light interesting issues that could reveal factors that determine external fund resources.

In this chapter, fundamental situations, such as that global distribution situation, are examined first, using comprehensive information regarding GHPs. Via empirical analysis, this chapter attempts to clearly illustrate whether GHPs are carried out among recipient countries and with what kind of attributes by using cross-country data from 111 developing countries. The questions of whether to proceed with deployment according to the situation of the recipient country and whether the partnership suits the needs of the recipient country are analysed empirically. Furthermore, the Global Fund to Fight AIDS, Tuberculosis and Malaria (henceforth the Global Fund), which has an especially large fund scale, is taken up as a case study. The Global Fund was launched in 2002 to disburse funds to support aggressive interventions against these diseases. By the end of 2007, it had committed US$9.9 billion in 136 countries to fight these diseases. The Global Fund has approved 586 grants and has already disbursed US$4.6 billion in grants. In order to function efficiently and sustainably to provide the financial support that will lead to improvement of access to necessary health services and medical supplies and the like, it is necessary to show clearly what is important. The second subject of this chapter is to examine what kinds of factors have acted to raise grant performance. To reply to this question, a second empirical examination is conducted, using information on grant rating undertaken by the Global Fund as a proxy for an index which shows whether funds were used efficiently to improve access to health services.

The conclusions of this chapter can be summarized as follows: 1) the neglected diseases are covered by at least one or more partnership(s) while a large number of GHPs concentrate on three major diseases, such as HIV/AIDS, tuberculosis and malaria; 2) the contribution of the Gates Foundation is significantly high in terms of fund scale and coverage of diseases; 3) the GHPs are implemented in countries where there is low performance of governance, and there is a strong positive correlation between the presence of GHPs and the burden of diseases, and 4) contrary to the findings in 3), the performance of grant programmes is strongly affected by the capacity of the health sector and by governance performance in the recipient country. In particular, the three dimensions of governance – effectiveness of government, rule of law and control of corruption – are positively correlated with grant performance.

This chapter is organized as follows. The next section presents general facts regarding the distribution of GHPs and an empirical examination of the determinants of the number of GHPs across countries. Considering the outstanding nature of the Global Fund as a global fund, Section 3 focuses on the funding system of the Global Fund and explores the factors determining the performance of grant programmes. Section 4 presents the conclusions.

4.1   Global distribution of global health partnerships

4.1.1   General facts about GHPs' distribution

The trends and the typology

In a series of reports about the partnerships undertaken by the health centre of the British government's Department for International Development (DFID), 'Global Health Partnerships (GHP)' is adopted as the basic general term based on the following three definitions. The first key criterion is related to 'Partnerships'. It is defined as a collaborative relationship among multiple organizations, in which risks and benefits are shared in pursuit of a shared goal. The focus is on more formal collaborative ventures and not exclusively on public-private partnerships, although these latter constitute the majority. The second criterion is related to 'Health'. The purpose of partnership establishment aims to solve health problems of significance for developing countries. The final criterion, 'Global' indicates that partnerships must be the framework to cross borders (Caines et al. 2004). In the above point, GHPs have this feature, unlike conventional assistance cooperation.

In the number of GHPs established annually, a remarkable climb is evident, especially from the second half of the 1990s, and establishment peaked in 2000 with 17 new entities. Although Richter (2004) pointed out that the importance of partnerships was already recognized in the United Nations in 1990, the year 1997 is shown to have been another turning point in the relationship between the United Nations and the business community, as evidenced by the statement by the former Secretary-General of the United Nations, Kofi Annan, that the UN's relationship with the business community is particularly important. USAIDS was established in 1996 as a collaborative organization, comprising many UN organizations concerned with HIV/AIDS problems, including the WHO, UNICEF, UNESCO, the ILO, and UNHCR.

Table 4.1:   Distribution of GHPs over objective, 2003

Approach	No. of GHPs
1. Product Development	35
2. Improvement of Access to Health Products	26
3. Global Coordination Mechanism	12
4. Strengthening of Health Services	9
5. Public Advocacy, Education and Research	15
6. Regulation and Quality Assurance	3
7. Other	1

Source: The data are from The Partnerships Database by the Initiative on Public-Private Partnerships for Health (IPPPH).

In response to the multi-sector approach, it seems that the number of GHPs increased rapidly in 1996 and thereafter.

This section analyses GHPs from various angles. In order to understand the actual conditions, the nature of the purpose for which the partnership is being developed must be mapped out. Table 4.1 shows the cumulative number of partnerships for each given objective as of 2003, as presented by the Partnerships Database which was originally created by the Initiative on Public-Private Partnerships for Health (IPPPH).[2] This database classifies the objectives of partnerships into the following seven categories: 1) Product Development; 2) Improvement of Access to Health Products; 3) Global Coordination Mechanism; 4) Strengthening of Health Services; 5) Public Advocacy, Education and Research; 6) Regulation and Quality Assurance; and 7) Other. According to these classifications, the majority of partnerships, 35, target the development of new medicines ((1) Product Development), and when partnerships aiming to improve access to existing medicine ((2) Improvement of Access to Health Products) are added, these two objectives focusing on the development and distribution of medicines represent 60 per cent or more of the overall total.

Another interesting consideration is whether specific partnerships are targeting specific diseases. Table 4.2 shows the cumulative number of GHPs by target disease or condition as of 2003. The majority of partnerships, 20, are for HIV/AIDS, reflecting the degree of attention and the seriousness of the plight of people with this condition. There are also many partnerships for other major damaging diseases, such as malaria (18) and tuberculosis (10). The partnerships for these three diseases amount to half of all partnerships. Since the coverage and seriousness of such three infectious diseases are large compared with other infectious

Table 4.2: Distribution of GHPs over disease or condition, 2003

Disease/Condition	No. of GHPs
All human diseases and medical conditions	1
Blindness	3
Cataract	1
Chagas	2
Chemical safety information	1
Communicable diseases	2
Counterfeit and substandard drugs	2
Dengue	2
Diarrhoea dehydration	1
Digital divide	1
Diseases of the poor	1
Guinea worm (dracunculiasis) disease	1
Harmonization of drug applications	1
Health policies and health systems	1
HIV/AIDS	20
Human African trypanosomiasis	4
Human hookworm infection	1
Injection safety, syringes	2
Lassa fever	1
Leishmaniasis	3
Leprosy	2
Lymphatic filariasis (LF)	2
Malaria	18
Meningitis	2
Micronutrient deficiency	2
Neglected diseases	1
Onchocerciasis (river blindness)	4
Parasitic and other neglected infectious diseases	1
Pneumococcal vaccines	1
Polio	1
Reproductive health	5
Schistosomiasis	1
Sexually transmitted infections	7
Tetanus, maternal and neonatal	1
Trachoma	3
Tuberculosis (TB)	10
Vaccine vial monitors	1
Vaccine-preventable diseases of the poor	5
Vitamin A deficiency	1

Source: The data are from The Partnerships Database by the Initiative on Public-Private Partnerships for Health (IPPPH).

Table 4.3:   Major participants in GHPs

	Participants	Number
1	World Health Organization (WHO)	43
2	United Nations Children's Fund (UNICEF)	21
3	World Bank	18
4	Bill & Melinda Gates Foundation	16
5	US Centers for Disease Control & Prevention (CDC)	15
6	GlaxoSmithKline (UK)	13
7	UNDP/WB/WHO Special Programme for Research & Training in Tropical Diseases (TDR)	13
8	US Agency for International Development (USAID)	12
9	Merck & Co., Inc.	11
10	Sanofi-Pasteur (merger of Aventis-Pasteur and Sanofi)	9
11	UK Department for International Development (DFID)	9
12	Joint United Nations Programme on HIV/AIDS (UNAIDS)	8
13	London School of Hygiene & Tropical Medicine	8
14	Pfizer Inc.	8
15	Medecins Sans Frontieres (MSF)	7
16	Novartis	7
17	Bristol-Myers Squibb Company	6
18	Canadian International Development Agency (CIDA)	6
19	Carter Center	6
20	Program for Appropriate Technology in Health (PATH)	6

Source: The data are from The Partnerships Database by the Initiative on Public-Private Partnerships for Health (IPPPH).

diseases and the public degree of attention and the necessity for assistance are high, many GHPs will concentrate on these. As for 'neglected diseases'[3] such as Chagas, human African trypanosomiasis (alias sleeping sickness), leishmaniasis and meningitis, the table shows that they were covered by one or more partnership(s).[4] This indicates that the stance adopted by the public and private sectors to cope with these diseases via a market mechanism does not function.

Participants and founders of GHPs

Although GHPs target various diseases with various approaches, the questions as to the nature of the organization remain for the subjects who participate in such partnerships. Table 4.3 shows what kind of organizations have played the major role in GHPs participating in the health sector. The WHO has participated in many partnerships as expected, while the other top ten rankings include four international organizations, two US government organizations, three pharmaceutical

Table 4.4:   Major funders of GHPs

Funder	Number	Contribution (US million)
1 Bill & Melinda Gates Foundation	31	4,646
2 United Kingdom, Government of	2	2,929
3 France, Government of	3	2,665
4 US Agency for International Development (USAID)	5	1,540
5 Italy, Government of	3	1,000
6 Norway, Government of	6	808
7 United States, Government of	2	566
8 European Commission	5	564
9 Canada, Government of	2	324
10 UK Department for International Development (DFID)	6	299
11 Netherlands, Government of	6	266
12 Spain, Government of	2	240
13 Japan, Government of	1	200
14 Canadian International Development Agency (CIDA)	5	137
15 Bristol-Myers Squibb Company	1	115
16 Sweden, Government of	2	107
17 Bill & Melinda Gates Foundation Challenge Grant	1	100
18 Swedish International Development Agency (SIDA)	4	73
19 Eli Lilly and Co.	1	70
20 Merck & Co., Inc.	1	50

Source: The data are from The Partnerships Database by the Initiative on Public-Private Partnerships for Health (IPPPH).
Note: The table is arranged in order of the fund scale.

companies and a private foundation. This table demonstrates how various organizations have cooperatively participated in GHPs.

It is also interesting to investigate issues concerning the fund donor organizations. As shown in Table 4.4, a famous private foundation, the Bill & Melinda Gates Foundation, has subscribed an overwhelming proportion of funds to many partnerships. Further, while the government of each country occupies a higher rank within a fund scale, the contributions of the Gates Foundation turn out to be the largest, as shown in the far right column.[5] It is clear that the Gates Foundation is contributing significantly to the development of GHPs from the perspectives of the scale and coverage of funding. The partnerships to which the Gates Foundation is donating funds should be investigated in further detail. As for the coverage, the Gates Foundation donates to partnerships covering various diseases, including neglected diseases such as leishmaniasis, malaria, human African trypanosomiasis and meningitis. Further, there exists a frequent tendency for the amount contributed to each partnership by the Gates Foundation to make up the vast majority of that partnership's total funds in many cases. Of the partnerships receiving donations from the Gates Foundation, 17 out of 29 saw the foundation contribute over 80 per cent of their total funds. Moreover, the management of a further 11 partnerships is solely based on contributions from the Gates Foundation. It emerged that in the case of large-scale partnerships such as GAVI or the Global Fund, the majority of funds were provided by donations from national government, while the Gates Foundation was a significant presence in other partnerships.

4.1.2   The determinants of GHPs' distribution

Analytical framework

The CMH report has clamed that the donor should insist on stringent conditions for the fund offer and withhold large-scale aid to countries with inefficient fund management (WHO 2001a). On the other hand, although GHPs are actually increasing their presence in various developing countries, little analysis has been conducted concerning the actual circumstances of GHPs. An interesting subject for investigation is what country-specific factors determine the entry of GHPs. In this section, the type of attributes of recipient countries capable of affecting the volume of partnership activities is shown. According to the CMH report, leadership, accountability and transparency as well as the ability to manage the investments of the fund are considered important factors when receiving the external funding support. Thus, those country-specific factors can be established as characteristics that explain the volume of GHPs within a country. As a hypothesis, the good governance of a recipient country is expected to have a positive relation with GHPs' entry. The demand factor is also important as a determinant for GHPs' entry. Intuitively, it is presumed that GHPs represent viable support in countries with considerable disease burdens as well as in those with insufficient funds for the health sector. Thus, the burden of diseases is expected to be positively related to GHPs' activities in the recipient country, while a negative correlation between GHPs' activities and financial capacity in the health sector is expected.

The aim of this section is to investigate the association between GHPs' activities and the abovementioned characteristics in recipient countries using a method of regression analysis. More precisely, this section examines whether the coefficient of the governance indicator is significantly positive or not, after controlling the country size, the financial capacity of the health systems, and the burden of diseases. Since the number of GHPs in each country is set as a dependent variable representing the extent of GHPs' activities in recipient countries, the Poisson regression model, which is appropriate for count regression, is used in the estimation.[6]

GHPs' data and summary statistics

The data used in the estimation regarding the determinants of partnerships was obtained from data on the partnerships investigated by Carlson (2004) on a specific-country basis. Carlson provides a table detailing the partnerships that have entered each country, based on the information on the website of each GHP as of 2003. Looking at the table, the number of partnerships in each country can be used as a measurement of GHPs' volume by individually counting them. It must be noted that this measurement of the number of GHPs may be inappropriate because the scale of funding is a better proxy variable than it, but it is difficult to collect such data for each GHP and country, due to limited data. Thus, in this section, the number of partnerships is assumed to have a strong correlation with the funding scale. In this analysis, 111 nations where data on the country characteristics was successfully collected were selected from the 127 nations studied by Carlson (2004).

The data on the nature of each country is compiled from various data sources. As a proxy measurement of the key variable, namely the measure of governance in a recipient country, global governance indicators in 2003, provided by the World Bank Institute, have been adopted. These indicators cover 213 countries and territories and assess six dimensions of governance, namely: voice and accountability; political stability and the absence of violence; government effectiveness; regulatory quality; rule of law; and the control of corruption. The indicators are based on hundreds of variables and reflect the views of thousands of citizen and survey respondents and experts worldwide (Kaufmann et al. 2006).[7] This study uses the sum of six indices for these dimensions as the governance index in the estimated equation. For the burdens of diseases, a measure called Disability Adjusted Life Years (DALY) has been developed by the WHO. This measure incorporates various kinds of damage imposed by diseases and injuries, such as death and disability, and is hence more suitable than using the number of deaths or the number of infected persons as an index, to illustrate the various burdens of the disease more precisely. In this analysis, DALY aggregated within the field of 'infectious

Table 4.5: Summary statistics

Variables	Mean	Std Dev	Min	Max
The number of GHPs	5.18	4.41	0	19
Sum of 6 governance indices (−10 ~ 10)	−2.83	3.60	−9.67	7.15
Burden of infectious diseases (1,000 DALY)	2.92	7.56	0	63.93
Helath expenditure by public (% of GDP)	2.79	1.46	0.65	9.73
GDP current US dollars in log	22.73	1.90	17.80	27.87

and parasitic diseases' in each country in 2002 is used as a proxy for the magnitude of burdens caused by infectious diseases in the country.[8] The other national characteristics are compiled from the World Development Indicators 2003. The country size is measured by GDP, converted to US dollars at current rates, and the health expenditure of the public sector (percentage of GDP) is included in the estimation as a proxy for the maturity degree of the health sector in the country. Summary statistics of these variables are presented in Table 4.5.

Estimation result on GHPs' distribution

The estimation results are presented in Table 4.6. Column (1) presents the estimates from a specification of the Poisson regression model, and column (2) presents the results for the negative binomial model. Both models include the same set of explanatory variables. The samples are a cross-sectional 111 countries in 2003. The likelihood-ratio test of the over-dispersion parameter of the Neg-bin model indicates the existence of over-dispersion, suggesting that the negative binomial model is presumed to be more appropriate than the Poisson model for the data set. Figure 4.1 shows the relationship between the cumulative number of GHPs as of 2002 and the sum of six indices of governance. Each plot presents one of the 111 countries. It seems that GHPs are established in countries where performance of governance is low, to the extent revealed by these figures.

In fact, contrary to expectations, the estimated coefficients for the governance index are significant and negative in both the Poisson and negative binomial models.[9] In both models, the calculated marginal effect of governance on GHP entry was approximately −0.25, implying that a decrease in four units of the governance score is associated with one GHP entry in the recipient country on average, with all other factors held constant.[10] However, this result may be distorted by other country variables in the estimated equation. Therefore, the sensitivity

Table 4.6: Estimation results (dependent variable: number of GHPs in a country)

	(1) Poisson	(2) Neg-bin
Governance index (−10 ~ 10)	−0.054	−0.050
	[0.014]**	[0.024]*
Burden of infectious diseases (1,000 DALY)	0.031	0.055
	[0.004]**	[0.014]**
Health expenditure by public (% of GDP)	−0.083	−0.094
	[0.036]*	[0.059]
ln (GDP)	−0.078	−0.101
	[0.027]**	[0.046]*
Constant	3.312	3.782
	[0.658]**	[1.104]**
Over-dispersion parameter		0.352
		[0.080]**
Observations	111	111
Pseudo R-squared	0.15	0.07
Log likelihood	−318.7	−280.3

Note: Standard errors in parentheses. * Statistically significant at the 5% level, ** at the 1% level. Over-dispersion parameter is tested by a likelihood-ratio test.

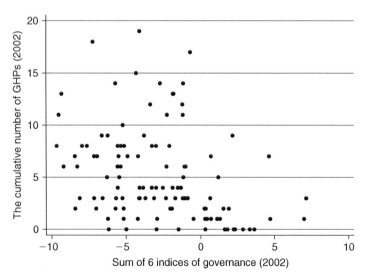

Figure 4.1: The relationship between GHPs and the governance of the recipient country

Source: The data on GHPs are from Carlson (2004), while the governance indicators are from the World Bank Institute.

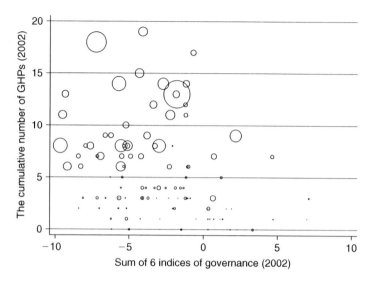

Figure 4.2: The relationship between GHPs and the governance weighted by DALY

Source: The data on GHPs are from Carlson (2004), while the governance indicators are from the World Bank Institute.

Note: The symbols' size represents the DALY aggregated within the field of 'infectious and parasitic diseases' in each country as of 2002.

analysis was conducted in spite of coefficient of governance changes by omitting other country variables such as GDP per capita, DALY and public health expenditures. The result of sensitivity analysis shows that the magnitude of governance was not changeable and was significantly negative. Although this result is an interesting finding, it is inconsistent with the assertion of the CMH report, namely that the performance of governance and management should be noted as a factor to determine financial support for the country.

The coefficient of the burden of infectious diseases is strongly significant and positive as expected, indicating that the greater the burden of infectious diseases, the higher the number of GHPs. Figure 4.2 also demonstrates the scatter plot of GHPs against the governance, but the size of the symbols is proportional to the volume of DALY aggregated within the field of 'infectious and parasitic diseases' in each country by the frequency weight. Each circle displays one of the 111 countries (as in Figure 4.1). Since the symbol size reflects the burden of diseases, the symbol with large (small) size shows that the burden of infectious and parasitic diseases in the country is large (small). The figure suggests that

GHPs target the burden of diseases significantly. It may be reasonable to presume that these results are linked to the fact that almost all GHPs have been carrying out activities suited to their purpose.

Public expenditure in the health sector shows a negative correlation with the number of GHPs, as expected, while the result of the negative binomial model reveals insignificance. This result is acceptable because it suggests that GHPs help support countries that have insufficient funding for their health sector. The marginal effect of health expenditure in the Poisson model is computed as -0.4, which means a 1 per cent increase in public health expenditure, with the ratio for GDP decreasing by 0.4 following the GHPs' entry. The estimation equation also includes GDP in natural logarithms to control the size effect of the country involved, while the GDP coefficient is also negative and significant in both models. This result suggests that GHPs may enter a country even if the country scale is small.

4.1.3 Discussion

The empirical analysis attempts to clearly show why GHPs are implemented in recipient countries in terms of those countries' attributes. Although the CMH report claimed that support by a partnership is only offered to countries where the performance of leadership, accountability and transparency and where fund management ability is high, there is nothing in the report that analysed the reality of what actually happened. An earlier study by Carlson (2004), meanwhile, examined the single correlation coefficient between GHPs numbers and country characteristics and concluded that there is moderate correlation between the prevalence rate or case number of a disease and the GHPs' presence, but no correlation between governance and the GHPs' presence. The analysis in this section that controls multiple factors simultaneously is the first comprehensive empirical study on the determinants of GHPs' entry.

The empirical result reveals that GHPs are indeed implemented in countries where the performance of governance is low, contrary to the assertions of the CMH report and the previous study. The model also takes into account the burden of diseases as a demand factor and shows that there is a strong and positive correlation between the presence of GHPs and the burden of diseases. One possible explanation for these results is that the target conditions for GHPs exclusively exist in countries where the burden of diseases is high, even in those countries with weak governance. In order to evaluate the financial support administered via the GHPs to such countries, this section covers another controversial issue, namely the difference in the effects of the GHPs' presence on countries' health sectors. Further research should focus on this issue.

Moreover, to evaluate the activity of GHPs, it will be necessary to collect information on the output produced by GHPs' support. Although these issues remain unsolved and require further examination, it should be noted that the findings on the determinants of GHP prevalence contribute to the deepening of our understanding of the GHPs' deployment situation and suggest the importance of investigating the possible inefficiency of GHPs in countries with low governance. The empirical analysis in the next section will attempt to reply to this issue by using the available information on the grant programme of the Global Fund.

4.2   A case study of the Global Fund

4.2.1   The grant system of the Global Fund[11]

Henceforth in this chapter, the Global Fund, which has an especially large fund scale among GHPs, is taken up as a case study. The Global Fund was launched in 2002 to disburse funds to support aggressive interventions against three major diseases, HIV/AIDS, malaria and tuberculosis. By the end of 2007, it had committed US$9.9 billion in 136 countries to fight these diseases. The Global Fund has approved 586 grants and has already disbursed US$4.6 billion in grants.

Grant applications are coordinated by the Country Coordinating Mechanism (henceforth CCM) which is established in each country. Generally, CCM consists of various stakeholders: government, international multilateral and bilateral aid agencies, and private organizations (non-governmental organizations, faith-based organizations, and civil society organizations, for example). CCM nominates one or more principal recipients in an application, which it submits as a proposal to the Global Fund. The proposal is reviewed by the Global Fund's Technical Review Panel (henceforth TRP) which is installed independently of the executive board and the secretariat of the Global Fund. Next, the TRP examines whether the submitted application is technically appropriate and whether the cost addition is appropriate, and it recommends action to be taken by the executive board, as follows: 1) fund; 2) fund if certain clarifications are provided; 3) encourage resubmission; or 4) do not fund. Based on this evaluation, the executive board decides how to award grants.

The grant is typically for five years, and a portion of the funds are disbursed for two years at the beginning, which is called Phase I. Twenty months after receiving the first disbursement, CCM requests funding for an additional three years, called Phase II. In order to check the financial status and management capabilities of the principal recipient and to monitor the progress of the programme, the CCM secretariat requests the relevant data from the Local Fund Agency (henceforth LFA). Usually, the LFA is an international accounting firm such as Pricewaterhouse-Coopers (henceforth PwC) or KPMG which has established a branch office in the given country.

The secretariat and the principal recipient agree in advance on grant conditions, subjective indicators and milestones that will be used to evaluate the grant.[12] Funds disbursed to the principal recipient are then allocated to sub-recipients in the country. The principal recipients must periodically report the degree of progress and accounting information through the LFA. The progress report submitted by the principal recipient is verified by the LFA and, based on the project performance reports, the LFA makes recommendations to the secretariat concerning disbursements.

Near the end of Phase I, grants are evaluated and given an explicit performance rating. An 'A' rating is given to programmes that have achieved more than 80 per cent of their targets, a 'B1' rating for 50 per cent to 79 per cent, a 'B2' rating for 30 per cent to 49 per cent, and a 'C' rating for less than 30 per cent. Contextual and qualitative information such as natural disasters and the political situation is also taken into consideration in the final evaluation. Based on this information, a panel in the secretariat evaluates the performance of each project and assigns one of following four ratings: 'A' rating – the programme meets or exceeds expectations; 'B1' – the programme shows adequate performance; 'B2' – the programme shows inadequate performance but demonstrates potential; and 'C' – the programme shows unacceptable performance. Finally, the executive board decides whether to continue funding the programme unconditionally, continue funding with conditions, or discontinue funding. This performance-based funding system is the main system under the Global Fund funding framework.

4.2.2 General facts relating to grant rating

It is interesting to examine what the important factors are in grant performance. Knowledge of what kinds of factors raise grant performance will have policy implications for the efficient operation of external funds that aim to improve access to necessary health services. Although whether or not funds were used efficiently to improve access to health services cannot be directly observed from the outside, it is possible to examine information on grant ratings undertaken by the secretariat of the Global

Table 4.7: Distribution of grant rate over regions

Region	Rate after Phase 1				Total number of grants
	A	B1	B2	C	
East Asia & the Pacific	27.7%	59.6%	12.8%	0%	*47*
Eastern Europe & Central Asia	63.2%	28.9%	7.9%	0%	*38*
Latin America & the Caribbean	33.3%	54.2%	8.3%	4.2%	*48*
North Africa & the Middle East	13.3%	66.7%	20.0%	0%	*30*
South Asia	26.7%	66.7%	6.7%	0%	*30*
Sub-Saharan Africa: East Africa	21.3%	63.8%	12.8%	2.1%	*47*
Sub-Saharan Africa: Southern Africa	9.8%	73.2%	17.1%	0%	*41*
Sub-Saharan Africa: West & Central Africa	27.0%	44.4%	28.6%	0%	*63*
Total number of grants	*96*	*193*	*52*	*3*	*344*

Source: The data are from the Global Fund website: www.theglobalfund.org.

Fund after Phase I. As a proxy for an index that shows the amount of funds used efficiently to improve access to health services, this section focuses on the grant rate.[13]

Applications for grants have been made according to rounds – one round per year. Although the Global Fund funding is now at Round 7 starting from November 2007, the only grants that have completed evaluation after Phase I are those in Rounds 1 to 5. So, there exist 344 grants with rating data, including the grants for multi-country recipients. Table 4.7 shows the distribution of grant ratings by region. As shown in the 'Totals' row, C-rated grants account for only 3 (1 per cent), and while B1-rated grants constitute the most, at 193 grants (56 per cent), A-rated grants number 96 (28 per cent), and B2-rated grants number 52 (15 per cent). The grant evaluations differ in distribution by region, and the regions with a particularly high number of A-rated grants are Eastern Europe and Central Asia (63.2 per cent). Conversely, the regions where ratings are low, with many B2-rated grants, are North Africa and the Middle East (20 per cent) and Sub-Saharan Africa: West & Central Africa (28.6 per cent). The difference in the distribution of ratings indicates that country characteristics, such as the capacity of health sectors, may affect grant performance.

Table 4.8 shows the distribution of grant rating *vis-à-vis* targeted diseases. The grants for HIV/AIDS programmes claim a large share (44 per cent), while the share of grants for both malaria and tuberculosis

Table 4.8:   Distribution of grant rate over target diseases

Disease	Rate after Phase 1				Total number of grants
	A	B1	B2	C	
HIV/AIDS	30.0%	54.0%	15.3%	0.7%	*150*
Malaria	28.6%	57.1%	14.3%	0%	*92*
TB	27.2%	58.7%	14.1%	0%	*92*
Multi	30.0%	50.0%	20%	0%	*10*
Total number of grants	*96*	*193*	*52*	*3*	*344*

Source: The data are from the Global Fund website: www.theglobalfund.org.

Table 4.9:   Distribution of grant rate over principal recipients

PR Type	Rate after Phase 1				Total number of grants
	A	B1	B2	C	
CS/PS: FBO	14.3%	71.4%	14.3%	0%	*7*
CS/PS: NGO	38.1%	46.0%	12.7%	3.2%	*63*
CS/PS: PS	15.4%	76.9%	7.7%	0%	*13*
Gov: MOF	9.1%	59.1%	27.3%	4.5%	*22*
Gov: MOH	32.3%	52.0%	15.7%	0%	*127*
Gov: Oth	28.6%	61.2%	10.2%	0%	*49*
MO: Oth	14.3%	85.7%	0%	0%	*7*
MO: UNDP	19.6%	60.7%	19.6%	0%	*56*
Total number of grants	*96*	*193*	*52*	*3*	*344*

Note: Civil Society/Private Sector, CS/PS: FBO (Faith-Based Organization), CS/PS: NGO (Non-Governmental Organization), CS/PS: PS (Private Sector), CS/PS. Government: Gov: MOH (Ministry of Health), Gov: MOF (Ministry of Finance), Gov: Oth (Other). Multilateral Organization: MO: UNDP (United Nations Development Programme), MO: Oth (Other).
Source: The data are from the Global Fund website: www.theglobalfund.org.

is 27 per cent. Although it was predicted that the difficulty of achieving project goals varies depending on the disease, a difference in rating by diseases is seldom seen, as shown in the table.

The principal recipient receiving the disbursement from the Global Fund is responsible not only for implementation of the grant in the country, but also for monitoring sub-recipients and maintaining good communications with the CCM regarding programme progress. Table 4.9 tabulates the number of grants rated according to principal recipients. There are eight types of principal recipients. Those classified as Civil Society/Private Sector (CS/PS) are faith-based rganizations (FBOs), non-governmental organizations (NGOs), and the private sector (PS). Those classified as government (Gov) are the Ministry of Health (MOH), Ministry of Finance (MOF), and other governmental organizations (Oth). Those classified as multilateral organizations (MO) are the United Nations Development Programme (UNDP) and other multilateral organizations (Oth). The cases in which the governmental organizations have been the principal recipient account for approximately 60 per cent of the total, and the Ministry of Health in particular is the principal recipient in an overwhelming number of cases. NGOs are also major principal recipients, while the UNDP has a significant share as a multilateral organization. The table indicates that the distribution of grant ratings differs greatly according to types of principal recipients. Many of the grants that are A-rated are those where an NGO or the MOH acted as the principal recipient, while there exists a tendency for performance to be poor when the MOF is the principal recipient. This tendency suggests that the management capacity of the principal recipient may affect the grant performance.

4.2.3   An empirical analysis of grant rating

Method and estimation equation

This section examines what types of factors have contributed to improvement of grant performance using econometric methods. The answers will help in the design of schemes for efficient and sustainable financial support that will enhance access to needed health services, medical supplies and so forth. Radelet and Siddiqi (2007) analysed the determinants of grant rating using data on 134 grants by the Global Fund. Following this study, this analysis uses grant rating data after Phase I as a proxy for a performance index of grants because it is difficult to observe whether funds were used efficiently to improve access to health services in general. Therefore, the dependent variable is grant rating, and categorical choice variables are A-ratings, B1-ratings, B2-ratings and C-ratings. In the estimation, the effect of grant characteristics (for example, grant size, principal recipient) on the grant rating and the effect of country characteristics (income level, capacity in health sector, governance performance and so on) on the grant rating are examined, respectively. In short, the empirical examination uses the data set constructed by matching the grant-level data of the Global Fund with the statistics of the host countries. The grants used in the estimation are the 273 grants out of the 344 grants displayed in Table 4.7 which could be successfully matched with all explanatory variables. The distribution of grant ratings is as follows: 71 A-rated, 158 B1-rated, 41 B2-rated, and 3 C-rated. In this analysis, the B2-rated and C-rated grants are combined because the C-rated grants are too few to be significant.

Since the categorical variable is ordinal and has more than two levels, an ordered logit model or ordered probit model is appropriate for the estimation. However, it is difficult to interpret the estimated coefficients in the cases of these models, and so the ordinary least squares (OLS) method is also used.[14] In the OLS estimation, the values of 100 points, 50 points, and the zero point are assigned to A-rated grants, B1-rated grants and B2/C-rated grants, respectively.

Grant attributes and country attributes – grant attributes

The data used for the estimation consists of grant-level data and country-level data. Regarding grant characteristics, various factors are controlled. First, as a measure of grant size, the total grant amount per capita (US$100) is included in the equation to identify the scale effect of the grant on the performance. Second, to express the management capacity in each project, the number of days from grant signing date to programme start date (10 days) is adopted. Although a delay in a programme's start may also be attributed to the Global Fund secretariat, it is supposed that the influence of the Global Fund is constant for all grants and it is predicted that there is a correlation between the grant management capability and the delays in programme starts. The management capability in the case of grants with a long duration is expected to be inferior. Hence, a negative sign for the duration from signature date to programme start date is predicted.

As shown in Table 4.9, the subject that acts as the principal recipient may also influence the grant performance. Considering the fact that the principal recipient plays an important role, it is interesting to analyse whether the selection of principal recipient affects the grant performance after taking other factors into consideration. The dummy variables for principal recipients of six organizations (FBO, NGO, PS, MOF, Gov:Oth and MO) are included and the Ministry of Health (MOH) is set as the benchmark. In order to control other grant-specific factors, the type of targeted diseases (HIV/AIDS, TB, malaria and multi), the type of Local Fund Agency (PwC, KPMG, UNOPS and others) and the disbursement round (1 to 5) are taken into account, respectively, as dummy variables.

Country attributes

The performance of grants may also depend on various country attributes. For example, countries where the health sector is well established would be expected to efficiently promote grant programmes. Therefore, the capacity of health sector is expected to have a positive effect on the grant performance. Two measures of the capacity of the health sector are adopted: public health expenditure as a percentage of GDP and the infant mortality rate per 1000 live births. The income level of the country may also affect the grant performance. GDP per capita (US$100) is used to control income level. These country characteristics are compiled from World Development Indicators. Although the grant data is pooled over disbursement rounds, all measures of country attributes used are as of 2002.

The burden of the target diseases may also affect the difficulty of a grant programme. To present the burden of the target diseases, Disability Adjusted Life Years (DALY) for three diseases in 2002 estimates by the WHO[15] is included in the model so that it might correspond with the target diseases of each grant programme. Further, experience in receiving similar external funds may contribute to efficient use of a grant. Since it is difficult to know the amount of external funds received for health, the cumulative number of Global Health Partnerships as of 2003, which was used in the analysis in Section 2, is included as an explanatory variable.

Another interesting issue is how the governance in a recipient country influences the grant performance. As a proxy measurement of governance in a recipient country, global governance indicators in 2003, provided by the World Bank Institute, were used in Section 2 also.[16] It is predicted that the governance indicators are positively related to grant performance. The indicators cover six dimensions of governance: voice and accountability; political stability and the absence of violence; government effectiveness; regulatory quality; rule of law; and the control of corruption. Together with analysis using the sum of the six indices for these dimensions, estimation was also carried out regarding each of the six indices. This analysis shows clearly the dimension out of the six in which the performance is sensitive. CCMs – which consist of various stakeholders, including government and international multilateral and bilateral aid agencies as well as private organizations – are key organizations in recipient countries and are responsible for local ownership and participatory decision-making. Hence the quality of a CCM may influence the performance of each grant programme. The Technical Evaluation Reference Group (henceforth TERG) conducted an assessment study on CCMs in 2005. This assessment covered 107 countries and evaluated CCMs from various aspects. Since each result of the evaluation criteria is unobservable, whether or not a CCM completely replied to the investigation can be used as a dummy variable. According to TERG (2005), 83 CCMs replied to the survey. Table 4.10 shows the data descriptions and the summary of the statistics for each variable.

Results of estimation of grant rating

The results of the estimation of grant rating are presented in Table 4.11 (robust standard errors are given in parenthesis). Column (1) presents the OLS estimates, column (2) presents the results for the ordered probit model, and column (3) presents the results for the ordered logit model. The three models include the same set of explanatory variables. The number of observations, namely the number of grants, is 273 from Rounds 1 to 5. Although the ordered choice models are appropriate for this case, the result of OLS estimates is useful for interpreting the coefficients. The statistical significance of explanatory variables is almost the same in all three models.

The grant size is not correlated with grant performance at all, while the duration from grant-signing date to programme-start date is negatively related to the grant rating, as expected, but the relation is not so robust. The coefficient of the duration by OLS estimates is 0.5. This result means that the probability of obtaining an A-rating falls 0.5 per cent when the programme-start date is 10 days behind and implies that efforts to accelerate the commencement of a programme are useful for improvement in performance. The result of the principal recipient dummy shows that performance differs depending on which organization undertakes the grant programme. The coefficient of dummy for the Ministry of Finance (MOF) is strongly significant and negative, while other dummy variables for the principal recipient are not significantly different from zero. With the Ministry of Health (MOH) set as the benchmark, the probability of obtaining an A-rating decreases 25 per cent when MOF is the principal recipient instead of MOH. The target disease was found to have no influence on performance, and the signs of coefficients for malaria and tuberculosis are negative. For the dummy variables for LFA, PwC is set as the benchmark. Only the UNOPS dummy is positive and statistically significant, at the 10 per cent level. Although the statistical significance is not robust, this result indicates that the probability that UNOPS gains an A-rating increases approximately 13 per cent compared to PwC. In order to control-round-specific factors, round dummy variables are included in the model. The Round 2 dummy shows a significant negative sign. On the whole, the coefficients of round dummy variables are negative and imply that there exists a tendency for evaluations to worsen.

The country-specific variables are not significantly different from zero except for the infant mortality rate and the sum of the six governance

Table 4.10: Summary statistics

Variables	Obs	Mean	Std Dev	Min	Max
Grant rate score (A = 100, B1 = 50, B2/C = 0)	273	54.95	32.13	0	100
Grant rate category (A = 3, B1 = 2, B2/C = 1)	273	2.10	0.64	1	3
Grant amount per capita (US$100)	273	2.49	5.28	0.005	53.032
Duration from signing date to programme start date (10 days)	273	6.80	7.15	−5.20	45.40
PR type dummy (Civil Society/Private Sector: FBO)	273	0.07	0.25	0	1
PR type dummy (Civil Society/Private Sector: NGO)	273	0.04	0.21	0	1
PR type dummy (Civil Society/Private Sector: PS)	273	0.25	0.43	0	1
PR type dummy (Government: MOF)	273	0.06	0.24	0	1
PR type dummy (Government: Other)	273	0.14	0.35	0	1
PR type dummy (Multilateral Organization)	273	0.17	0.38	0	1
Disease dummy (Malaria)	273	0.27	0.45	0	1
Disease dummy (Tuberculosis)	273	0.29	0.45	0	1
LFA dummy (KPMG)	273	0.25	0.43	0	1
LFA dummy (UNOPS)	273	0.07	0.26	0	1
LFA dummy (Other)	273	0.12	0.33	0	1
Round 2 dummy	273	0.29	0.45	0	1
Round 3 dummy	273	0.20	0.40	0	1
Round 4 dummy	273	0.21	0.40	0	1
Round 5 dummy	273	0.15	0.35	0	1
GDP per capita (US$100)	273	25.50	21.26	5.16	110.86
DALY of the targeted disease	273	1082.86	2148.77	0	10421.67
The cumulative number of Global Health Partnerships	273	7.86	4.59	0	19
Public health expenditures/ GDP (%)	273	2.35	1.17	0.65	6.71
Infact mortality rate (per 1000 live births)	273	7.28	3.73	0.8	16.6
Sum of 6 governance indices (−10 to 10)	273	−3.66	2.86	−9.67	7.15
CCM evaluation dummy	273	0.68	0.47	0	1

128

Table 4.11: Estimation results for grant rate of the Global Fund

	(1) OLS	(2) Ordered Probit	(3) Ordered Logit
Grant amount per capita (US$100)	0.430	0.017	0.024
	[0.404]	[0.015]	[0.026]
Duration from signing date to	−0.537	−0.021	−0.042
programme start date (10 days)	[0.292]*	[0.011]*	[0.021]**
PR type dummy (Civil Society/	−16.174	−0.653	−1.108
Private Sector: FBO)	[13.451]	[0.525]	[0.858]
PR type dummy (Civil Society/	−0.175	−0.004	−0.042
Private Sector: NGO)	[5.881]	[0.226]	[0.404]
PR type dummy (Civil Society/	8.102	0.341	0.492
Private Sector: PS)	[16.088]	[0.626]	[1.031]
PR type dummy (Government:	−25.564	−1.029	−1.709
MOF)	[8.612]***	[0.341]***	[0.574]***
PR type dummy (Government:	−5.420	−0.217	−0.403
Other)	[6.610]	[0.254]	[0.456]
PR type dummy (Multilateral	0.526	0.025	−0.008
Organization)	[6.063]	[0.233]	[0.404]
Disease dummy (Malaria)	−5.161	−0.207	−0.419
	[4.829]	[0.186]	[0.327]
Disease dummy (Tuberculosis)	−2.209	−0.093	−0.190
	[4.735]	[0.183]	[0.318]
LFA dummy (KPMG)	−0.584	−0.025	−0.033
	[4.990]	[0.192]	[0.334]
LFA dummy (UNOPS)	13.749	0.584	1.023
	[8.840]*	[0.353]*	[0.598]*
LFA dummy (Other)	7.848	0.317	0.590
	[6.072]	[0.235]	[0.414]
Round 2 dummy	−12.012	−0.494	−0.845
	[5.951]**	[0.234]**	[0.400]**
Round 3 dummy	−8.915	−0.369	−0.587
	[6.580]	[0.257]	[0.445]
Round 4 dummy	−9.936	−0.410	−0.748
	[6.484]	[0.253]	[0.432]*
Round 5 dummy	−10.484	−0.434	−0.711
	[6.897]	[0.270]	[0.466]
GDP per capita (US$100)	−0.249	−0.010	−0.018
	[0.156]	[0.006]*	[0.010]*
DALY of the targeted disease	0.001	0.000	0.000
	[0.001]	[0.000]	[0.000]
The cumulative number of Global	−0.139	−0.006	−0.010
Health Partnerships	[0.663]	[0.026]	[0.045]
Public health expenditures/	−2.063	−0.082	−0.139
GDP (%)	[1.951]	[0.075]	[0.136]

(Continued)

Table 4.11: Continued

	(1) OLS	(2) Ordered Probit	(3) Ordered Logit
Infant mortality rate (per 1000 live births)	−2.523 [0.814]***	−0.100 [0.032]***	−0.173 [0.055]***
Sum of 6 governance indices (−10 to 10)	2.065 [1.039]**	0.083 [0.041]**	0.142 [0.072]**
CCM evaluation dummy	−3.241 [4.375]	−0.127 [0.169]	−0.268 [0.298]
Constant	109.393 [14.732]***	–	–
Cut 1		−3.318	−5.829
Cut 2		−1.436	−2.624
Number of observations	273	273	273
R-squared	0.19		
Root MSE	30.2		
Pseudo R-squared		0.112	0.112
Log likelihood		−232.938	−232.963
LR chi2		58.8	58.75

Note: Robust standard errors in parentheses. * Statistically significant at the 10% level, ** at the 5% level, *** at the 1% level.

indices. Estimates of the coefficient for GDP per capita of a recipient country are negative but statistically insignificant for OLS specifications, while they are significant at a 10 per cent level for ordered choice models. Income level has no effect on the grant performance, or if an effect exists, income level seems to negatively influence grant performance. The results were totally insignificant for the cumulative number of Global Health Partnerships, which is used as a proxy for an experience effect on performance, and for the DALY of target disease, which is a proxy for the difficulty of programme in a recipient country. The capacity of the health sector in a recipient country is incorporated into two variables: public health expenditures in terms of GDP and the infant mortality rate. Although the former variable is not significant, the latter variable is strongly and negatively significant.[17] The estimate of the coefficient on the infant mortality rate is −2.5, suggesting that a 1 per cent increase in the infant mortality rate reduces the probability of winning an A-rating by 2.5 per cent. This result implies that the capacity of the health system measured by the infant mortality rate contributes to the grant performance.

Table 4.12:   Estimation results for six governance indicators

(1) Voice and Accountability	(2) Political Stability/No Violence	(3) Government Effectiveness	(4) Regulatory Quality	(5) Rule of Law	(6) Control of Corruption
2.482	4.889	12.033	7.544	13.991	14.015
[3.475]	[3.572]	[6.738]*	[5.680]	[5.864]**	[6.395]**

Note: Robust standard errors in parentheses. * Statistically significant at the 10% level, ** at the 5% level. The results of other explanatory variables are not displayed in order to save space.

At the same time, the sum of the six governance indices is also significantly correlated with the grant performance, while the CCM evaluation dummy is not significant. The estimated coefficient of the governance index is 2.1 for OLS estimates. This result indicates that a one-unit improvement in the sum of the six governance indices is associated with an increased probability of an A-rating of 2.1 per cent. It is remarkable that there is a positive correlation between the governance of the recipient country and the grant performance, whereas a negative correlation with the number of GHPs was found in Section 2. To identify which dimension of the governance indices are strongly associated with the grant performance, the six OLS estimations examining the effect of each governance index were carried out separately. The results are displayed in Table 4.12. The same explanatory variables as those presented in Table 4.11 are used for estimation. When the governance indices are estimated separately, the significance differs among the indices. (1) Voice and Accountability, (2) Political Stability/No Violence, and (4) Regulatory Quality show a positive sign but are not significantly different from zero, while (3) Government Effectiveness, (5) Rule of Law and (6) Control of Corruption are significantly positive even after the other factors are controlled. The results for the indices that were significant suggest that one increase in the indices raises the probability of a grant being A-rated from 12 per cent to 14 per cent.

4.2.4   Discussion

This empirical examination of grant rating raises implications for the design of schemes for external funds so that they function efficiently to accelerate access to required health services. The results of the estimations show that when MOF is the principal recipient the probability of a grant being A-rated is 25 per cent lower than when MOH is the principal recipient. Radelet and Siddiqi (2007) report a similar result, where grants with governmental principal recipients receive lower grant ratings. However, the study in this section found that the grant performance differs greatly even among governmental principal recipients such as the MOH and the MOF. This result may imply that the MOF has problems of bureaucracy and lacks the technical knowledge in the health sector. Although it is desirable that the MOH takes responsibility as the principal recipient to improve grant performance, this may be unfeasible due to the MOH's lack of capacity or power relationships among government ministries. At the same time, in cases where the MOF is responsible as the principal recipient, it is important to strengthen the MOH's capacity building and monitoring.

It was predicted that grant rating differs depending on LFA, but the estimation result does not support a significant difference in grant rating depending on the private accounting firm that acted as LFA even after other factors are controlled. However, a certain amount of difference in the standards of evaluation is likely to exist between UNOPS and PwC. One may expect that the difference is due to the difference in management capacity or experience in health programmes. In fact, the TERG, an independent advisory body of the Global Fund board which conducted an evaluation of LFA, also found gaps in verification and documentation, lack of a consistent management approach, and weakness in health programmatic skills, and recommended consistent auditing standards (Euro Health Group 2007).

The GDP per capita of a recipient country and the grant rating seem to be almost unrelated. The Global Fund emphasizes that the performance-based funding system does not significantly penalize poorer countries or those with weaker health systems (GFATM 2007: 52). As for the health system of a recipient country, the result of this study strongly suggests that grant programmes are likely to be successful in a country where the health system is well maintained, if it is measured by the infant mortality rate. It is important to expand the capacity of health sectors in recipient countries generally and widely so as to improve the performance of grant programmes.

Grant ratings are also affected by governance performance in recipient countries, although the abovementioned earlier study using restricted grant data could not find any relation between them. Further, the estimation succeeded in identifying the specific dimensions of governance where the positive effect on grant performance is significant. It has been found that the effectiveness of government, rule of law and control of corruption are positively related to grant performance. Consideration should be given to capacity building for these dimensions as well as for health sectors in the recipient countries.

4.3 Concluding remarks

This chapter has contributed to the deepening of the understanding of the state of deployment of global funds in developing countries. Specifically, an attempt was first made to analyse GHPs from various angles. Since there are various approaches to such partnerships, mapping out the reason why the partnership was developed will help us to understand its actual condition. Although the apparent tendency of GHPs to increase rapidly in number is a very interesting research subject, there is little research clearly focusing on this point.

As general facts concerning GHPs, the neglected diseases such as Chagas, human African trypanosomiasis (sleeping sickness), leishmaniasis and meningitis were covered by one or more partnership(s), while a large number of GHPs concentrated on the three major diseases of HIV/AIDS, tuberculosis and malaria. Further, it can also be clearly shown what kinds of organizations have played a major role in the health sector in terms of the focus of the participating partnerships and their fund donation. The contribution of the Gates Foundation is significantly high from the viewpoint of fund scale and coverage of diseases, and various other organizations have cooperatively participated in GHPs, especially in the case of large-scale partnerships such as GAVI or the Global Fund. It should be noted that substantial numbers of GHPs exist solely due to contributions from the Gates Foundation.

In the empirical analysis in Section 2, the country-specific factors determining the entry of GHPs were explored. The CMH report pointed out that donors should ensure the fund offer is subject to stringent conditions and should withhold large-scale aid to countries that engage in inefficient fund management. However, it was found that the GHPs playing a major role in external funding implemented funding in countries with a low performance of governance, and there is a strong, positive correlation between the presence of GHPs and the burden of diseases. The entry of GHPs is concentrated in countries where the burden of diseases is high, even if some of those countries have weak governance. Although one may suppose that this result is understandable because external funds are bound to go where the demand is high, the results also indicate the importance of investigating the effects of recipient countries' governance on fund efficiency as an unsolved issue requiring further examination.

In response to this issue, Section 3 conducted another empirical analysis examining what kinds of factors raise the performance of health programmes funded by external funds. Since the question of whether funds were used efficiently to improve access to health services cannot be observed from the outside, the analysis used information on grant ratings undertaken by the secretariat of the Global Fund as a proxy for an index that shows the amount of funds used efficiently to improve access to health services. The result was that, contrary to the findings in Section 2, the performance of grant programmes is strongly affected by the capacity of the health sector and governance performance in the recipient country. Through further analysis on individual governance indicators, three dimensions of governance were identified as being important for raising grant performance: effectiveness of government, rule of law and control of corruption. This finding is consistent with the recommendation in the CMH report. External funds can be observed in countries with low performance of governance, and in order to boost the efficiency of fund usage, improvement of governance is a crucial factor. Capacity-building for performance of good governance in recipient countries is recommended, along with increasing the external funding for health sectors.

The empirical analyses on external funding presented in this chapter raise policy implications for external funds that seek to efficiently improve access to required health services. Although the chapter uncovered some interesting issues, several points related to the data availability must be borne in mind. For example, estimations made in Section 2 are based on the number of GHPs instead of a funding scale and cross-sectional data, and so the results do not necessarily reflect the exact effects of GHPs' presence and the causality between the GHPs' presence and the explanatory factors. Further analyses using richer data with time sequences are essential in order to overcome this shortcoming.

Notes

1. 'Global Health Partnerships (GHPs)' is adopted as the basic general term based on the following three definitions by the health centre of the British Government's Department for International Development (DFID). The first key criterion is related to 'Partnerships'. A partnership is defined as a collaborative relationship among multiple organizations, in which risks and benefits are shared in pursuit of a shared goal. The second criterion is related to 'Health'. The purpose of partnership establishment is to solve health problems of significance for developing countries. The final criterion, 'Global', indicates that partnerships must comprise a framework to cross borders (Caines et al. 2004). This chapter follows the approach of the DFID.
2. The data on GHPs has been collected from the website of IPPPH: www.ippph.org/index.cfm?page=/ippph/partnerships (accessed September 2006).

3. There is no clear definition for 'neglected diseases'. A renowned non-governmental organization, Médecins Sans Frontières (MSF), cites malaria, human African trypanosomiasis (sleeping sickness), leishmaniasis and meningitis as neglected diseases. The WHO and the pharmaceutical industry identified the following parasitic diseases as being truly neglected: African trypanosomiasis, leishmaniasis and Chagas disease (WHO 2001b).

4. Caines (2004) found the same result, namely that 12 out of 15 of the selected neglected diseases are addressed by at least one GHP.

5. The amount of money shows the cumulative fund scale subscribed until 2003, respectively, and the commitment of fund donation is not included.

6. The Poisson regression model formulates the expected number of GHPs as an exponential function of the country-specific factors as follows: $E[p_i|X_i] = \lambda_i = \exp(X_i\beta)$ where i indexes the country, and denotes the vector of country characteristics, indicating the governance, country size, the level of health systems and burden of diseases. The parameters are estimated using the maximum likelihood estimation method. Since there is concern that the equalization feature of the conditional mean and variance in the Poisson model is rarely satisfied by the actual data, the negative binomial model which relaxes this condition is also estimated. For further details on the Poisson regression model and the negative binomial model, see Hausman, Hall and Griliches (1984) and Cameron and Trivedi (1986), respectively.

7. For further details of the indicators, see Kaufmann et al. (2004, 2005, 2006). The indicators for 1996–2005 are downloadable from the website; www.worldbank.org/wbi/governance/data (accessed February 2007).

8. For further details of DALY, see Murray and Acharya (1997) and World Bank (1993). The estimates for 2002 by cause for WHO member states are downloadable from the website: www.who.int/healthinfo/bod/en/ index.html (accessed February 2007).

9. Even if the sum total of six indexes is not used, for example, even if only one index such as the index of government effectiveness is used, the result does not change.

10. Since the estimated coefficients are interpreted as $\beta = \frac{d\lambda_i}{dX_i}\frac{1}{\lambda_i}$, the marginal effect or elasticities can be calculated.

11. This section refers to GFATM (2003, 2007).

12. A small number of key indicators, such as the rate of area/people covered by Antiretroviral (ARV) treatment for HIV/AIDS, distribution of insecticide-treated nets (ITNs) or treatment under Directly Observed Treatment, Short-course (DOTS) for tuberculosis, is used to measure the progress of the programmes.

13. The data on the grant rate after Phase I is available on the Global Fund website, www.theglobalfund.org.

14. Papke (1998) also uses the OLS method for the same reasons, namely that the interpretation of the results is easy for a linear model and understanding the ordered choice models are suitable for the case.

15. See footnote 8.

16. See footnote 7.

17. The public health expenditures in terms of GDP may be affected by other country variables. Although the sensitivity analysis was conducted whether

or not the coefficient of public medical expenditure changes by omitting other country variables such as GDP per capita, DALY and the number of GHPs, it did not vary in significance.

References

Cameron, Colin A. and Pravin K. Trivedi (1986) 'Econometric Models Based on Count Data: Comparisons and Applications of Some Estimators and Tests.' *Journal of Applied Econometrics*, Vol. 1, No. 1: 29–53.

Caines, Karen, Kent Buse, Cindy Carlson, Rose-Marie de Loor, Nel Druce, Cheri Grace, Mark Pearson, Jennifer Sancho and Rajeev Sadanandan (2004) 'Assessing the Impact of Global Health Partnerships', London: DFID Health Resource Centre. Available at: www.dfidhealthrc.org/index.html

Caines, Karen (2004) 'Global Health Partnerships and Neglected Diseases.' GHP Study Paper 4, London: DFID Health Resource Centre. Available at: www.dfidhealthrc.org/index.html

Carlson, Cindy (2004) 'Mapping Global Health Partnerships.' GHP Study Paper 1, London: DFID Health Resource Centre. Available at: www.dfidhealthrc.org/index.html

Commission on Macroeconomics and Health (2001) *Investing in Health for Economic Development*, Geneva: World Health Organization.

Euro Health Group (2007) *Evaluation of the Local Fund Agent System*, final report submitted to the Global Fund to Fight AIDS, Tuberculosis, and Malaria (the Global Fund/GFATM). Available at: www.theglobalfund.org/en/

Global Fund to Fight AIDS, Tuberculosis, and Malaria (the Global Fund/GFATM) (2003) Guidelines for Performance-Based Funding. Available at: www.theglobalfund.org/en/

Global Fund to Fight AIDS, Tuberculosis, and Malaria (the Global Fund/GFATM). (2007). *Partners in Impact – Results Report 2007*, progress report of the Global Fund to Fight AIDS, Tuberculosis, and Malaria (the Global Fund/GFATM). Available at: www.theglobalfund.org/en/

Hausman, J., B. H. Hall and Z. Griliches (1984) 'Econometric Models for Count Data with an Application to the Patents-R&D Relationship', *Econometrica*, Vol. 52, No. 4: 909–38.

Kaufmann, Daniel, Aart Kraay and Massimo Mastruzzi (2004) 'Governance Matters III: Governance Indicators for 1996, 1998, 2000, and 2002', *World Bank Economic Review*, 18: 253–87.

Kaufmann, Daniel, Aart Kraay and Massimo Mastruzzi (2005) 'Governance Matters IV: Governance Indicators for 1996–2004.' World Bank Policy Research Working Paper No 3630, Washington: World Bank.

Kaufmann, Daniel, Aart Kraay, and Massimo Mastruzzi (2006) 'Governance Matters V: Aggregate and Individual Governance Indicators for 1996–2005.' Washington: World Bank. Available at: www.worldbank.org/wbi/governance/

Murray, Christopher J. L. and Arnab K. Acharya (1997) 'Understanding DALYs', *Journal of Health Economics*, Vol. 16, No. 6 (December): 703–30.

Papke, Leslie, E. (1998) 'How are Participants Investing their Accounts in Participant-Directed Individual Account Pension Plans?, *American Economic Review*, Vol. 88, No. 2: 212–16.

Radelet, Steven and Bilal Siddiqi (2007) 'Global Fund Grant Programmes: An Analysis of Evaluation Scores', *The Lancet*, 369, issue 9575: 1807–13.

Richter, Judith (2004) 'Public–Private Partnerships for Health: A Trend with No Alternatives?', *Development*, Vol. 47, No. 2: 43–8.

WHO (World Health Organization, Commission on Macroeconomics and Health) (2001a) *Macroeconomics and Health: Investing in Health for Economic Development*, Geneva: World Health Organization.

WHO (World Health Organization, International Federation of Pharmaceutical Manufacturers and Associations) (2001b) 'Working Paper on Priority Infectious Diseases Requiring Additional R&D', at www.who.int/intellectualproperty/documents/en/

World Bank (1993) *World Development Report 1993: Investing in Health*, New York: Oxford University Press.

5
Determinants of HIV/AIDS Drug Prices for Developing Countries: Analysis of Global Fund Procurement Data*

Kensuke Kubo and Hiroko Yamane

Introduction

Pharmaceutical products form an important component of healthcare in developing and developed countries. Innovative pharmaceuticals enable new treatments and prevention of diseases. While pharmaceuticals represent only one among many health inputs, new drugs may provide an alternative to non-drug inputs such as invasive operations (Schweitzer 2007). Reflecting their importance, expenditures on pharmaceuticals take up a substantial percentage of total spending on healthcare. In 2000, this ratio was 19.2 per cent in low-income countries taken as a whole. This is even higher than the corresponding figure of 13.8 per cent for high-income countries (WHO 2004: 42). In the same year, per capita expenditure on pharmaceuticals was estimated to be only US$4.40 per year in low-income countries while it was US$396 per year in high-income countries (WHO 2004: 45).[1] Thus, there appears to be a huge disparity in the role of pharmaceuticals between rich and poor countries.

The low level of drug spending in developing countries reflects a severe lack of access. The World Health Organization (WHO) estimates that between 1.3 and 2.2 billion people (from 22 per cent to 37 per cent of the world's population) lacked access to essential medicines in 1999 (WHO 2004: 62). A series of surveys sponsored by the WHO and Health Action International shows that essential medicines are available in only 34.9 per cent of public-sector health facilities in developing countries (United Nations 2008). The proportion of private-sector health facilities having a stock of essential medicines is somewhat higher (63.2 per cent). The lack of access to medicines has serious implications for healthcare

137

in developing countries; regions with less access have significantly lower levels of disability-adjusted life expectancy (WHO 2004).

A major impediment to accessing pharmaceuticals in developing countries is the lack of a healthcare system and infrastructure in which drugs can be distributed and used properly. There is a general shortage of trained doctors and other health professionals who can properly prescribe appropriate medications (Commission on Macroeconomics and Health 2001: 86). Further, the absence of universal health insurance coverage in most developing countries means that a large part of drug consumption must be met 'out-of-pocket' by individuals, many of whom live in poverty. Even if the government rather than the individual paid for pharmaceuticals, many developing countries would still be incapable of financing the full pharmaceutical needs of their citizens (Commission on Macroeconomics and Health 2001: 86).

The issue of access is further complicated for patented drugs. A patent gives the patent holder the exclusive right to manufacture and sell the drug for a certain period. There are many circumstances in which patents and other intellectual property rights can affect access to pharmaceuticals. First, if patents exist for the medicines needed in developing countries, and the patent holder does not supply to these countries, the medicines will be inaccessible to patients. Second, the patent system allows new pharmaceuticals to be sold at prices that are higher than competitive levels. High prices for patented drugs are often justified by the patent-holder's need to recover the cost of research and development (R&D), including the clinical studies to ensure the safety and efficacy of the medicines. Such prices are affordable for patients in developed countries who are covered by health insurance but may not be so for a large number of people in developing countries. For the vast majority of essential medicines as defined by the WHO, however, these issues do not arise because very few such medicines remain under patent.[2] Nevertheless, some diseases require the use of new and patented drugs for basic treatment.

Lack of access to essential drugs has been particularly severe for acquired immunodeficiency syndrome (AIDS) patients infected by the human immunodeficiency virus (HIV). As recently as 2003, only 7 per cent of those needing treatment for AIDS in low and middle-income countries were actually receiving treatment (WHO 2006a: 19). The scourge of AIDS has been devastating, particularly in sub-Saharan Africa. It is estimated that between 1.5 and 2 million people died from the disease in sub-Saharan Africa in 2007, and more than 20 million people continue to live with the virus (UNAIDS 2007).

AIDS treatment requires the use of newer drugs. Among the products listed in the 2007 version of the Essential Medicines List of the WHO, such AIDS drugs as abacavir, lamivudine, nevirapine and nelfinavir, as well as the combination malaria drug artemether-lumefantrine, have been widely patented in developing countries.[3] In fact, most patented medicines currently included in the Essential Medicines List are AIDS-treatment drugs. This has led to concern that access to AIDS drugs in developing countries has been denied due to patents.

There have been more barriers to overcome than just patents. The underdeveloped state of healthcare systems in many developing countries, combined with the lack of financial resources, has made it difficult for patients to access even older, unpatented drugs. International organizations, governments of developed countries, and the research-based pharmaceutical industry have been slow to adopt measures responding to the urgent pharmaceutical needs arising from the HIV/AIDS pandemic. The rising sense of urgency has led to the creation of the Global Fund to Fight AIDS, Tuberculosis, and Malaria (hereafter referred to as the 'Global Fund') in 2001 to provide financial resources for countries with a need to scale up treatment and prevention programmes for these three diseases. As of mid-2007, the Global Fund board had approved more than US$7.7 billion (including monies for the purchase of pharmaceuticals) for programmes in 136 countries.[4] Due in part to these initiatives, the proportion of AIDS patients receiving drug therapy in low- and middle-income countries rose to 20 per cent by the end of 2005 (WHO 2006a: 19).

In the context of HIV/AIDS in developing countries, the pricing behaviour of pharmaceutical firms has attracted the attention of the international community, particularly because brand-name firms (also called originator firms) set a high price for AIDS medicines in the first years of their marketing in some developing countries. Manufacturers of generic versions of the same drugs could choose to offer lower prices than their originator counterparts and have introduced a certain degree of competitive pressure.[5] It was therefore argued that patents, which prevent the entry of generic medicines, were responsible for the high prices of AIDS medicines. On the other hand, 'differential pricing' by originator pharmaceutical firms, where prices are set higher in high-income countries and lower in low-income countries, can contribute to the expanded use of new pharmaceuticals in developing countries while preserving returns to R&D in the most lucrative markets.

In view of the importance of the pricing behaviour of pharmaceutical companies, the present chapter includes an examination of this issue in the context of AIDS-treatment drugs procured by developing countries under funding from the Global Fund. Global Fund procurement made up around 30 per cent of all AIDS drugs consumed in developing countries in 2005. Pricing is an important issue not only when the drugs are purchased with the internal resources of countries but also when procured with external funds. This is because financial resources are limited even in the case of large global health partnerships such as the Global Fund, and the per-unit price of the drug directly governs the amount of drugs procured and the number of patients treated.

The choice of settings is justified for the following three reasons: first, HIV/AIDS is one of the most serious health concerns in the developing world today, and treatment coverage is still far from adequate. Second, AIDS-treatment drugs are supplied to developing countries both by originator and generic pharmaceutical firms. Therefore, it is possible to observe and compare the pricing behaviour of both types of firms. Third, a large proportion (at least 50 per cent) of AIDS-treatment drug transactions in developing countries are carried out under funding from international schemes such as the Global Fund and the United States President's Emergency Plan for AIDS Relief (PEPFAR); data on these transactions are publicly available on the internet. It is therefore possible to conduct empirical analysis using a fairly representative data set.

Estimating the determinants of prices offered by originator and generic pharmaceutical firms is the main interest of the subsequent analysis. The objectives are to observe how the pricing behaviour of firms varies according to the characteristics of the recipient country (such as income level and prevalence of HIV) and to determine whether or not originator and generic firms behave differently. The analysis presented in this chapter is thus a significant improvement on previous studies, such as those of Ganslandt et al. (2005) and Vasan et al. (2006). These studies include analysis of the difference between the average prices charged by originator firms and those charged by generic firms. However, they do not include examination of how this price difference varies across countries and regions. This chapter also includes examination of the relationship between firm characteristics, such as nationality and product quality, and prices. Finally, the effect that patents have on prices offered by originator and generic firms is assessed. This provides a firm basis for discussion relating to the management and regulation of procurement programmes such as those financed by the Global Fund.

The remainder of the chapter is structured as follows: Section 1 includes explanation of the price-formation process in procurement tenders for AIDS drugs. A description of the data used in empirical analysis, which consists of drug prices, patent information and recipient-country characteristics, is provided in Section 2. Section 3 includes a description of the estimation method, and results of this estimation are presented in Section 4. Additional analyses with regard to the role of patents are discussed in Section 5, and this is followed by a concluding section.

5.1 Price formation of AIDS drugs through procurement tenders

5.1.1 Procurement of AIDS medicines

Antiretrovirals (ARVs) for AIDS treatment are used in highly active antiretroviral therapy (HAART). Since its introduction in the mid-1990s, HAART has succeeded in reducing the mortality rate due to AIDS by 60 to 80 per cent in the US and other developed countries (Bartlett 2004). HAART consists of prescribing a combination of three or four antiretroviral drugs chosen based on the stage of the patient's infection by HIV. By combining several ARVs that target different points in the lifecycle of the HIV virus, HAART is capable of suppressing the viral load far more effectively than a single-drug regimen. However, when the virus develops drug resistance, it is necessary to move to a second line of therapy that involves the use of a class of drugs not used in the first-line regimen. For example, if the first-line regimen has included two nucleoside analog reverse transcriptase inhibitors (such as lamivudine in combination with stavudine or zidovudine) plus a non-nucleoside reverse transcriptase inhibitor (such as nevirapine or efavirenz), then the second-line regimen should include a protease inhibitor (such as ritonavir-boosted lopinavir).

At the end of 2005, around 1.3 million patients were receiving ARV treatment in low- and middle-income countries. Of these, around 384,000 patients (30 per cent) were obtaining medication from programmes funded by the Global Fund. Furthermore, 471,000 patients (36 per cent) were being treated under programmes financed by the United States government's PEPFAR program. A total of 641,000 patients (49 per cent) received treatment as a result of the Global Fund and PEPFAR (WHO 2006a).[6] This means that at least half of all ARV treatments were purchased through donor-funded procurement programmes, because donors also pay for other similar but smaller schemes.

As a general rule, the transaction prices and identity of supplying firms in procurement contracts under the Global Fund are determined through sealed-bid tenders following transparent and formally written procedures (Global Fund to Fight AIDS, Tuberculosis and Malaria 2006). At the start of the tender process, the recipient country specifies the type and quantity of the drug as well as certain criteria to be met by the bidders, such as prequalification of product quality by the WHO.[7] Manufacturing firms and trading companies then respond to the tender by submitting their bids. In principle, the supplying contract is awarded to the lowest bidder among qualified suppliers. In some countries, where government policies to nurture domestic pharmaceutical industries are in place, it is possible that the local manufacturers are designated as suppliers based on considerations other than cost.[8] In such cases, the supplying firm may not necessarily be the lowest bidder.

5.1.2   Bidder behaviour

In general, bidders in sealed-bid tenders aim to maximize their expected profits. That is, each bidder i chooses its bid b_i to maximize the following quantity:

$$\Pr \left(b_i < \min_{j \neq i} b_j \right) \times (b_i - c_i)$$

where the first term represents the probability of winning the tender, and the second term is the difference between i's bid and the cost to i of supplying the product. The cost of supplying the product depends on various factors such as the pre-specified quantity of the transaction, the accessibility of the delivery location, the quality of the product, the technology employed by the manufacturer, and the geographical location of the manufacturer. The probability of bidder i winning the tender depends not only on i's own bid but also on the number of other bidders as well as their cost structures. As a general rule, the larger the number of rival bidders, the lower the probability that bidder i wins with a given bid level. The main point is that under the assumption of profit maximization, a bid depends only on cost factors and the number of rival bidders.

It is important to note that the profit-maximizing bid does not depend on demand factors such as the income level of the recipient country. This is because the transaction quantity is fixed before bidding takes place. The observation that demand factors do not influence profit-maximizing bids has important implications for the discussion on differential pricing. Pharmaceutical price differentials between rich and poor countries are thought to arise because the price sensitivity of consumers in poor countries is generally higher (Danzon 2007: 176). However, for drugs acquired through procurement tenders, price sensitivity may not affect prices at all.

5.1.3   Peculiarities of ARV transactions

In the case of tenders for ARVs supplied to developing countries, the objective of some firms may not necessarily be profit maximization. For example, Médecins Sans Frontières (2007) describes how several originator pharmaceutical firms have pre-announced steep price discounts to the poorest countries. Some manufacturers have indicated that prices subject to these discounts are 'no-profit prices', implying that the difference between bids and costs is close to zero (F. Hoffmann-La Roche 2006). Such behaviour may not be consistent with short-term profit maximization. Rather, the behaviour may reflect the concern of firms for the humanitarian needs of developing countries. If received positively by policy-makers and the general public, such behaviour may contribute to the long-term profitability of the firms.[9]

When humanitarian and/or public-relations concerns are present, the bidding behaviour of firms may indeed be affected by demand factors such as the income level and HIV prevalence rate of the recipient country. As an example, the purchasing power of patients (as captured by per capita income levels) may not affect short-term profit-maximizing prices under procurement tenders. However, by pricing lower in countries with lower per capita income, pharmaceutical firms can demonstrate to policy-makers, the general public and their shareholders that they are contributing to the welfare of the poorest countries. One objective of the analysis in this chapter is to discover whether or not there is a tendency towards such differential pricing based on country characteristics and, if so, to see what types of firms are more likely to pursue such policies.

5.2   Data description

5.2.1   Data on prices and firm characteristics

Data on ARV prices was obtained from the Purchase Price Report of the Global Fund Price Reporting Mechanism.[10] The report contains transaction-level prices and quantities of various ARVs and other medicines procured for developing countries with funding from the Global Fund. These procurements form a large part of the transactions recorded by the WHO through its Global Price Reporting Mechanism. The WHO data also contain transactions that were not paid for by the Global Fund. However, a cursory look at the Global Price Reporting Mechanism data reveals that many transactions are recorded in duplicate. Therefore, analysis concentrates on Global Fund transactions to ensure data quality.

The Purchase Price Report records the details of each transaction, including recipient country, supplying firm, product specifications, transaction value, transaction quantity and transaction terms. The database downloaded in December 2007 contains a total of 9743 transactions that took place between March 2003 and December 2007. Of these, 5585 concern ARVs. The products in these transactions include an array of active ingredients (including combinations thereof), dosage forms and strengths. Focus is placed on oral solid formulations, which represent the most commonly used form. The analysis is further limited to a set of 26 formulations that are discussed in a study by the WHO (WHO 2006b). This creates a data set of 3601 observations. Finally, the sample is limited to transactions that include complete information on International Commerce Terms (Incoterms) describing terms of the transaction (such as who pays for the insurance, freight and customs duties).[11] Only those transactions that have a non-zero price are kept in the sample.[12] The final data set contains 1668 transactions. For each of these transactions, data on product characteristics (active ingredient(s), strength of each active ingredient), name of recipient country, name of supplying firm, price per smallest unit (tablet or capsule), year of transaction, volume of transaction, and the Incoterms describing the transaction were obtained.

It is important to keep in mind that the prices contained in the data are those paid by governments and international organizations upon procurement of the drugs, not those prices at which patients purchase the drugs at the retail level. On one hand, most health facilities in developing countries provide ARVs to patients for free or at a steep discount.[13] Conversely, expenses incurred during distribution generate a potential margin above the procurement price.[14] Therefore, the prices faced by patients may be higher or lower than the procurement price depending on factors such as adequacy of the health infrastructure and efficiency of distribution networks.

Table 5.1 lists the drug formulations that appear in the data set. Eighteen of the 26 listed drugs are single-ingredient formulations; the remaining eight are fixed-dose combinations (FDCs). Seventeen drugs are categorized by the World Health Organization (2006b) as being used in a first-line regimen, and the remaining nine drugs are used primarily as part of a second-line regimen. For the purpose of identifying drugs that are novel (thus relatively expensive), an original classification was created that is similar but not identical to the WHO's first and second-line classification. Under this classification, any drug formulation containing any one of the following active ingredients was classified into Group 2: abacavir, indinavir, lopinavir, ritonavir, saquinavir

...g .... appearing in the data set

International Nonproprietary Name (INN) of Active Ingredient(s)	Strength	First or second line	Group*	Class	Number of transactions in data set
abacavir (ABC)	300 mg	2nd	2	NRTI	42
abacavir/lamivudine (3TC)/ zidovudine (ZDV or AZT)	300 mg/150 mg/300 mg	1st	2	NRTI	5
didanosine (ddI)	100 mg	2nd	1	NRTI	53
didanosine	200 mg	2nd	1	NRTI	12
didanosine	400 mg	2nd	1	NRTI	32
efavirenz (EFV or EFZ)	50 mg	1st	1	NNRTI	39
efavirenz	200 mg	1st	1	NNRTI	99
efavirenz	600 mg	1st	1	NNRTI	130
indinavir (IDV)	400 mg	2nd	2	PI	42
lamivudine	150 mg	1st	1	NRTI	169
lamivudine/stavudine (d4T)	150 mg/30 mg	1st	1	NRTI	39
lamivudine/stavudine	150 mg/40 mg	1st	1	NRTI	24
lamivudine/zidovudine	150 mg/300 mg	1st	1	NRTI	119
lamivudine/nevirapine (NVP)/zidovudine	150 mg/200 mg/300 mg	1st	1	NRTI + NNRTI	17
lamivudine/nevirapine/stavudine	150 mg/200 mg/30 mg	1st	1	NRTI + NNRTI	116
lamivudine/nevirapine/stavudine	150 mg/200 mg/40 mg	1st	1	NRTI + NNRTI	76
lopinavir/ritonavir (LPV/r)	133 mg/33 mg	2nd	2	PI	62
nelfinavir (NFV)	250 mg	1st	1	PI	44
nevirapine	200 mg	1st	1	NNRTI	141
ritonavir (RTV)	100 mg	2nd	2	PI	37
saquinavir (SQV)	200 mg	2nd	2	PI	15
stavudine	30 mg	1st	1	NRTI	94
stavudine	40 mg	1st	1	NRTI	121
tenofovir (TDF)	300 mg	2nd	2	NtRTI	18
zidovudine	100 mg	1st	1	NRTI	50
zidovudine	300 mg	1st	1	NRTI	72

* Groups 1 and 2 closely mirror the first- and second-line classifications, respectively, with the following exceptions: (1) the triple combination abacavir/lamivudine/zidovudine is classified as Group 2 even though it is recommended as a first-line treatment by the WHO; (2) didanosine is classified as Group 1 even though it is recommended as a second-line drug.

Table 5.2:   Pharmaceutical companies appearing in the data set

Company name	Classification	Headquarters location	Number of transactions appearing in data set
Abbott	Originator	USA	88
Ajanta	Generic	India	1
Aspen	Generic	South Africa	123
Aurobindo	Generic	India	78
Bayer	Originator	Germany	1
Boehringer Ingelheim	Originator	Germany	11
Bristol-Myers Squibb	Originator	USA	165
Zydus Cadila	Generic	India	4
Cipla	Generic	India	562
Emcure	Generic	India	2
Gilead Sciences	Originator	USA	16
Government Pharmaceutical Organization	Generic	Thailand	21
GlaxoSmithKline	Originator	UK	133
Hetero	Generic	India	100
McLeods	Generic	India	7
Merck	Originator	USA	149
Ranbaxy	Generic	India	130
Refasa	Generic	Peru	1
F. Hoffmann-La Roche	Originator	Switzerland	47
Strides Arcolab	Generic	India	29

and tenofovir. These drugs are novel relative to the remaining drugs which are termed Group 1.

Table 5.2 lists those pharmaceutical manufacturers that appear in the data set. A balanced mix of originator and generic firms can be observed. Originator firms generally have more transactions appearing in the data, but one Indian generic company (Cipla) overwhelms all other firms with 33.7 per cent of all transactions. Most firms listed in Table 5.2 have had their products either pre-qualified by the WHO or approved by a stringent regulatory authority such as the US Food and Drug Administration (FDA). Since pre-qualification or approval is obtained on a product-by-product and product-site basis, some products of a given firm may be pre-qualified (approved) while others may not be. From the WHO website, a list of products that have been either pre-qualified by the WHO or approved by a stringent regulatory authority was obtained and merged with the price data set.[15] This enables construction of a variable

Table 5.3:   Distribution of transactions by region and firm type

	Asia	Sub-Saharan Africa	Latin America	CIS/ Eastern Europe	All Regions
Group 1 Drugs					
Originator	77	209	58	98	442
	24.9%	28.1%	28.0%	52.7%	30.5%
Generic	232	536	149	88	1005
	75.1%	71.9%	72.0%	47.3%	69.5%
Total	309	745	207	186	1447
	100.0%	100.0%	100.0%	100.0%	100.0%
Group 2 Drugs					
Originator	32	73	35	29	169
	71.1%	88.0%	56.5%	93.5%	76.5%
Generic	13	10	27	2	52
	28.9%	12.0%	43.5%	6.5%	23.5%
Total	45	83	62	31	221
	100.0%	100.0%	100.0%	100.0%	100.0%

indicating whether or not a given transaction in the Purchase Price Report data set involved drugs meeting quality requirements.

Table 5.3 presents the distribution of transactions across regions and firm types. In the case of Group 1 drugs, 30.5 per cent of the transactions involved are supplied by an originator company. In the case of Group 2 drugs, an originator company was the supplier in 76.5 per cent of transactions. There are some regional variations as well. Countries belonging to the Commonwealth of Independent States (a group of former Soviet republics) and Eastern Europe have a higher tendency to be supplied by originator firms for both Group 1 and Group 2 drugs. In the case of Group 2 drugs, sub-Saharan African countries have a higher share of transactions with originator drugs compared to Asia and Latin America. Sub-Saharan Africa has the highest number of transactions in the data set. These include 51.5 per cent of the total for Group 1 drugs and 37.6 per cent for Group 2.

5.2.2   Patent data

One of the factors that may affect prices is the existence of patents. Information on patenting activity pertaining to ARV products by originator firms is available from Médecins Sans Frontières (2003). This report contains information on the existence of patents and their expiration dates in a subset of the developing countries that appear in the price data set. Table 5.A1 (Appendix 1) indicates the countries that are covered by the Médecins Sans Frontières (hereafter MSF) report and thus what information on patents is available.

In some cases, MSF could not ascertain whether a particular patent was actually filed in certain countries. In these situations, it is assumed that a valid patent did not exist in the country in question. There are 923 transactions in the data set for which patent data are available.

5.2.3   Country characteristics

The country receiving the drugs is identified for each transaction. In total, there are 56 recipient countries, and 19 of these belong to the least-developed-countries group as defined by the United Nations (see Table 5.A1, column 1).[16] A different group of 19 countries belongs to the low human development group as defined by the United Nations Development Programme in its Human Development Report (United Nations Development Programme 2005). A larger group of 26 countries is defined by the World Bank as including low-income economies.[17] Country characteristics such as population, gross domestic product (GDP) per capita, and HIV-infection rates were collected from the World Bank's World Development Indicators Online. Table 5.A1 contains the values of these variables.

5.3   Estimation method

5.3.1   Reduced-form model of tenders

Our main empirical analysis consists of observing how firms' pricing behaviour varies according to the types of markets they serve or the types of products that are used. This is assessed through the estimation of 'bid equations' for firms that are active in the Global Fund procurement tenders for ARVs. In these equations, bids are expressed as a function of recipient-country characteristics such as income levels and HIV prevalence, product characteristics and transaction characteristics.

Recently, several structural econometric models for analysing prices from sealed-bid, first-price auctions have been developed (see, for example, Guerre et al. 2000; Donald and Paarsch 1993). These methods estimate firms' unobserved cost in supplying the product. Firms' bids are then described as a function of their costs as well as of the competitive environment they face, such as the number of rival bidders. In our empirical analysis, we do not employ the structural econometric approach. This is because the structural approach is based on the assumption that all firms submit their bids with the objective of maximizing profits. Profit maximization may not necessarily be the objective in the case of pharmaceutical firms participating in tenders to supply ARVs to poor countries.

Our approach can be interpreted as a reduced-form model of the tender process. We estimate the overall effect that market characteristics have on the winning bids. This includes not only the impact of market characteristics on bids through costs, but also the indirect impact through the effect that market characteristics have on the competitive environment. We do not directly estimate how country, product and transaction characteristics (collectively called 'market characteristics') affect the cost of supplying drugs. Nor do we estimate how costs, in conjunction with the competitive environment, influence firms' bids.

5.3.2 Bid equations for originators and generics

Taking each transaction in the data set as a unit of observation, we estimate separate bid equations for originator firms and generic firms as distinct groups. Each transaction can be defined by the following set of bid equations:

$$b_{io}^* = \beta_o' X_i + \varepsilon_{io}$$
$$b_{ig}^* = \beta_g' X_i + \varepsilon_{ig} \tag{5.1}$$

where b_{io}^* denotes the bid by an originator firm, and b_{ig}^* is the bid by a generic firm. X_i is a vector of market characteristics, while β_o and β_g are vectors of coefficients. ε_{io} and ε_{ig} are independent and identically distributed random error terms.

By estimating the respective equations for originators and generics, it is possible to see if pricing behaviour varies across different types of firms. The purpose is to test whether originator firms are more likely to practice differential pricing than generic firms.

The prices recorded in the Purchase Price Report represent the winning bids for each transaction; the losing bids – bids that are higher than the winning bid – are not recorded. Our data is therefore censored, in that the outcome variable – the firm's bid – is observed if and only if the firm is the winning bidder. One way to deal with this type of data is to ignore the censoring problem and to estimate the bid equations with the available data, using standard methods such as ordinary least squares (OLS). However, the OLS results are likely to be biased, unless the winner of each tender is determined exogenously. Clearly, winners are not determined exogenously, but are decided through a process where various bids are compared. Fortunately, there are methods to obtain unbiased estimates under these circumstances. The method we apply is called the 'switching regression model with endogenous switching' (Maddala and Nelson 1975; Lee 1978).

Appendix 2 explains the derivation of the switching regression model. For practical purposes, we apply the model by first estimating a binary-choice regression model describing how the identity of the winning firm (originator or generic) is determined across transactions. We call this the first-stage regression. We use the probit specification of binary choice, and let the identity of winners be determined by the following process:

$$\Pr\,(\text{Winner in tender } i \text{ is originator firm}) = \Phi(\delta'Z_i) \qquad (5.2)$$

where $\Phi(\cdot)$ is the standard normal distribution function, Z_i is a vector of explanatory variables for tender i, and δ is a vector of coefficients.

Next, we use the probit regression results to construct a set of 'generated regressors' that are described in Appendix 2. These generated regressors are then combined with the market characteristics X as explanatory variables to estimate the bid equations in (1), which we call the second-stage regression.

5.3.3   Dependent variable

We employ two measures of price as the dependent variable in the bid equations. The first one, called *PRICE PER DDD*, is the price per tablet/capsule, in US dollars, multiplied by the defined daily dose. Although this is an accurate representation of the price of a drug, it has the disadvantage of not always being comparable across products. In particular, the price of a fixed-dose combination (FDC) that contains three active ingredients cannot be meaningfully compared to the price of a single-ingredient formulation. The second price measure, called *RATIO TO US PRICE*, is meant to be comparable across different products. It is the ratio of the reported price per tablet/capsule to the price of an equivalent product – supplied by the originator firm – in the US market. For FDCs that are not marketed in the US, the US prices are computed by adding up the prices of each component drug.

5.3.4   Explanatory variables

The market characteristics contained in X are as follows: Country characteristics including *PER CAPITA GDP* (annual per capita GDP in 2004 in US$100), *LOG POPULATION* (logarithm of population in 2004),

HIV RATE (HIV infection rate among people of ages 15 to 49), *LOW HUMAN DEVELOPMENT* (according to UNDP's definition), *ODA SHARE* (official development assistance as a percentage of GDP), and regional dummy variables (*SUBSAHARAN AFRICA, LATIN AMERICA, CIS/EASTERN EUROPE*); product characteristics including *GROUP 2* (dummy variable indicating Group 2 drugs) and *FDC* (dummy variable indicating fixed-dose combination); and transaction characteristics including *QUANTITY* (volume of each transaction in terms of defined daily dose), year dummy variables, and dummy variables for various Incoterms.

We also include some firm characteristics in the price equations. *PREQUALIFY* is a dummy variable equal to one if the winning bidder's product has either been pre-qualified by the WHO or approved by a stringent regulatory authority such as the US FDA. *HOME* is a dummy variable indicating whether the winning bidder is located in the purchasing country.

The *Z* variables include all of the market characteristics contained in *X*, as well as an additional variable called *PHARMA INDUSTRY*. This dummy variable is equal to one if the purchasing country has a significant generic pharmaceutical industry that manufactures ARVs.[18] The existence of a generic pharmaceutical industry is expected to influence the choice between originator and generic products. However, it may not affect the actual bids, beyond the effects captured by the *HOME* variable. For this reason, the *PHARMA INDUSTRY* variable is included in *Z* but not in *X*.[19] The definitions of all the variables used in the econometric analysis are found in Table 5.4.

5.4   Estimation results

5.4.1   First-stage probit regression

We first discuss the results of the probit regression model (equation (2)), presented in Table 5.5. The first column presents the coefficient estimates as well as their standard errors. In the second column, we present the marginal effect of each variable on the probability that the winning firm is the originator firm.[20]

Starting with country characteristics, we find that countries with high per capita GDP are more likely to have transactions with originator firms. Countries with large populations are also likely to be served by originator firms. Taken together, this implies that larger markets are more likely to be supplied by originator firms. This may be because originator firms are less localized than generic firms. Given that there are fixed costs to entering a new country, such as the cost of drug registration, all firms are

Table 5.4: Variables used in empirical analysis

Variable name	Unit	Description
Country characteristics		
PER CAPITA GDP	100 US dollars	Annual per capita GDP in 2004
LOG POPULATION		Log of total population in 2004
HIV RATE	proportion	Percentage of the population, ages 15–49, who were HIV-positive in 2005
LOW HUMAN DEVELOPMENT	zero-one indicator	Indicates that the country belonged to the 'low human development' group, as defined by the UNDP's Human Development Report 2005
ODA SHARE	proportion	Proportion of total official development assistance to GDP in 2004
ASIA, SUBSAHARAN AFRICA, LATIN AMERICA, CIS/EASTERN EUROPE	zero-one indicators	Region dummy variables (ASIA was dropped from the estimation)
PHARMA INDUSTRY	zero-one indicator	Indicates that the country has a significant generic pharmaceutical industry that manufacturers ARVs
Product characteristics		
GROUP2	zero-one indicator	Indicates that the product belongs to a group of newer, more expensive ARVs
FDC	zero-one indicator	Indicates that the product is a fixed-dose combination
Firm characteristics		
PREQUALIFY	zero-one indicator	Indicates that the firm has obtained prequalification for the product in question under the WHO Prequalification Project, or obtained approval from a stringent regulatory authority
HOME	zero-one indicator	Indicates that the firm is located in the recipient country
Transaction characteristics		
QUANTITY	Defined daily dosages	Volume of transaction
YEAR 2003, YEAR 2004, YEAR 2005, YEAR 2006, YEAR 2007	zero-one indicators	Year dummy variables (YEAR 2003 was dropped from the estimation)
CIF, CIP, CPT, FOB	zero-one indicators	Incoterm dummy variables (FOB was dropped from the estimation. Coefficients estimates are not reported in Tables 5 and 6, but are available upon request.)*

* See United States Government Accountability Office (2005) for the definitions of various Incoterms. For our purposes, DDU is included in CIF, DDP is included in CIP, and FCA is included in FOB. Observations with other Incoterms as well as those without Incoterm designations were dropped.

Table 5.5: Probit model of firm type determination

	Dependent variable: *ORIGINATOR = 1* *GENERIC = 0*	Marginal effects
Country characteristics[1]		
PER CAPITA GDP	0.0318***	0.0054
	0.0050	
LOG POPULATION	0.2889***	0.0490
	0.0406	
HIV RATE	0.0058	0.0010
	0.0057	
LOW HUMAN DEVELOPMENT	0.4370**	0.0549
	0.1852	
ODA SHARE	0.2069	0.0351
	0.7712	
SUBSAHARAN AFRICA	−0.2064	−0.0399
	0.1981	
LATIN AMERICA	−0.0400	−0.0070
	0.1521	
CIS/EASTERN EUROPE	0.2833*	0.0397
	0.1474	
PHARMA INDUSTRY	−1.3567***	−0.4240
	0.1820	
Product characteristics		
GROUP 2	1.5034***	0.0930
	0.1111	
FDC	−0.8271***	−0.2199
	0.0920	
Transaction characteristics[2]		
QUANTITY	−0.3680**	−0.0624
	0.1643	
YEAR 2004	−1.1951***	−0.3596
	0.3046	
YEAR 2005	−1.3325***	−0.4144
	0.3022	
YEAR 2006	−1.8330***	−0.6048
	0.3050	
YEAR 2007	−1.7705***	−0.5827
	0.3068	
CONSTANT	−4.0104***	
	0.7650	
Number of observations:	1668	

Notes: Figures in lower rows are standard errors. The marginal effects were calculated using the mean values for the continuous explanatory variables, while the binary variables were set to zero.

***, **, and * represent statistical significance at the 1%, 5%, and 10% levels, respectively.

1. The regional dummy variable representing Asia has been dropped.
2. The year 2003 dummy variable has been dropped.

likely to prefer larger markets to smaller markets. This is because in larger markets, the fixed entry costs can be spread over a larger volume, leading to lower average costs. On the other hand, some generic companies are located within recipient countries and face relatively low entry costs for those markets. Originator firms are generally located in developed countries and lack such proximity advantages. As a result, originator firms may be more sensitive to market size than generic firms.

Meanwhile, countries classified as having Low Human Development have a higher propensity towards being supplied by originator companies. According to the corresponding marginal effect estimate, a Low Human Development designation is likely to increase the probability of being served by an originator firm by 5.49 percentage points. This suggests that originators give priority to such countries.

The *PHARMA INDUSTRY* variable has a negative and statistically significant coefficient, implying that countries with pharmaceutical manufacturing capabilities are less likely to have originator firms as their suppliers. In fact, the probability of being supplied by an originator firm is lower by 42.4 percentage points in countries with pharmaceutical manufacturing capability. This could be due to several factors. The first possibility is that originator firms are less inclined to enter tenders in countries that are capable of manufacturing their own ARVs. The second possibility is that the procurement tender process is biased in favour of domestic generic firms in those countries. Third, it is possible that the *PHARMA INDUSTRY* variable is correlated with some unobservable country characteristics, such as insufficient enforcement of intellectual property rights, and those characteristics have a negative impact on originator firms' propensity to enter.

Turning to the product characteristics, it is found that Group 2 drugs are more likely to be supplied by originator firms (probability is higher by 9.3 percentage points). This is consistent with what we saw in Table 5.3, and can be explained by the novelty of the Group 2 drugs. On the other hand, fixed-dose combinations are more often supplied by generic companies.

The last set of variables pertains to transaction characteristics. We find that larger transactions are more likely to be awarded to generic firms. The significantly negative coefficients on the year dummy variables imply that the share of generic firms is increasing over time.

5.4.2   Second-stage OLS regression

Table 5.6 presents the ordinary least squares (OLS) estimates of the bid equations where the explanatory variables consist of X as well as the generated regressors. While two different definitions for the price variable were employed, the results are broadly similar across the definitions.

The most striking aspect of Table 5.6 is that the coefficients of the originator equation (columns 1 and 3) have a clearly different pattern compared to the coefficients of the generic equation (columns 2 and 4).

The effect of country characteristics

We find that originator firms' bids are sensitive to the purchasing country's per capita GDP level, while those of generic firms are not. Namely, originator firms tend to offer lower prices in countries with lower per capita income. This is evidence of differential pricing by originator firms based on income levels.

At first glance, it is puzzling that originators offer lower prices in lower-income countries, because the first-stage regression results showed that originator firms are *less likely* to be the winning bidder in countries with lower incomes. A likely explanation is that originator firms are selective about which tenders to participate in; they only enter a subset of the tenders in low-income countries, but when they do enter, they tend to bid low prices. The results of the first-stage regression (Table 5.5) suggest that the markets that are avoided by originator firms may be those low-income countries that have significant local pharmaceutical manufacturing capabilities.

Originator firms also tend to bid higher in countries with higher populations, while generic firms are not shown to have such a tendency. This is in spite of our previous finding that originator firms are more likely to be the winning bidder in larger countries. Once again, this can be explained by allowing originator firms to be selective about which tenders to enter. In other words, originators do not enter all the tenders in countries with small populations, but where they do enter, their bids tend to be low.

Both originator and generic firms are sensitive to the HIV infection rates in the recipient countries: both groups are found to offer lower prices in countries with high infection rates. This provides additional evidence of differential pricing, pursued by both originator and generic companies.

The *LOW HUMAN DEVELOPMENT* variable has a significantly positive coefficient in the originator equations. This is a somewhat puzzling finding. It may be because supplying to countries with low human development costs more, but we do not have sufficient evidence to support this claim.

Table 5.6: Determinants of ARV prices

Two-stage Switching Regression Model

Dependent variable:	PRICE PER DDD		RATIO TO US PRICE	
	(1) Originator firms	**(2)** Generic firms	**(3)** Originator firms	**(4)** Generic firms
Country characteristics[1]				
PER CAPITA GDP	0.0681***	0.0037	0.0050***	−0.0002
	0.0155	0.0106	0.0013	0.0005
LOG POPULATION	0.4961***	0.0684	0.0227*	0.0020
	0.1418	0.0764	0.0119	0.0039
HIV RATE	−0.0386*	−0.0435***	−0.0032*	−0.0024***
	0.0199	0.0112	0.0017	0.0006
LOW HUMAN DEVELOPMENT	2.1716***	0.1690	0.1556***	−0.0005
	0.6705	0.3879	0.0565	0.0198
ODA SHARE	1.3630	5.8260***	0.1291	0.2944***
	2.6827	1.2940	0.2259	0.0662
SUBSAHARAN AFRICA	−1.2119*	0.4305	−0.1006*	0.0335*
	0.6620	0.3963	0.0558	0.0202
LATIN AMERICA	0.9915**	0.3267	0.0739*	0.0277*
	0.4633	0.3205	0.0381	0.0164
CIS/EASTERN EUROPE	3.3376***	0.5516*	0.1998***	0.0290*
	0.4992	0.3243	0.0411	0.0166
Product characteristics				
GROUP 2	2.3800***	1.0336	0.0772	0.0547
	0.5891	0.6554	0.0487	0.0337
FDC	0.4770	0.2777	−0.0495	−0.0115
	0.4516	0.2459	0.0376	0.0125
Firm characteristics				
PREQUALIFY	−0.2296	−0.2608	−0.0026	−0.0120
	0.2218	0.1679	0.0195	0.0086
HOME	2.4541	0.1381	0.7352***	0.0366*
	2.2159	0.3689	0.2043	0.0189
Transaction characteristics[2,3]				
QUANTITY	−2.3389***	−0.1663	−0.1601***	−0.0082
	0.4976	0.1292	0.0406	0.0066
YEAR 2004	−0.7077	−0.6165	−0.0023	−0.0139
	0.8072	1.2808	0.0646	0.0607
YEAR 2005	−0.9587	0.1169	−0.0065	0.0220
	0.8247	1.2782	0.0662	0.0605
YEAR 2006	−1.6945*	−0.8166	−0.0363	−0.0242
	0.9552	1.3260	0.0774	0.0633

(Continued)

Table 5.6:   Continued

Two-stage Switching Regression Model

Dependent variable:	PRICE PER DDD		RATIO TO US PRICE	
	(1) Originator firms	(2) Generic firms	(3) Originator firms	(4) Generic firms
YEAR 2007	−2.0616**	−0.8315	−0.0634	−0.0288
	0.9118	1.3285	0.0736	0.0634
CONSTANT	−9.7605***	−0.6193	−0.4285*	−0.0185
	2.8294	1.8178	0.2389	0.0897
σ_{ou}, σ_{gu}	1.9188***	−0.4343	0.0676	−0.0083
	0.6878	0.6090	0.0579	0.0311
Number of observations:	611	1057	611	1057

Notes: Figures in lower rows are standard errors.
***, **, and * represent statistical significance at the 1%, 5%, and 10% levels, respectively.
1. The regional dummy variable representing Asia has been dropped.
2. The year 2003 dummy variable has been dropped.
3. Dummy variables representing different Incoterms were used in estimation, but their coefficients are not reported here.

The *ODA SHARE* variable is positive and significant in the bid equation for generic firms. This may be because countries receiving large amounts of development aid have a higher willingness to pay for pharmaceuticals, and generic firms are pricing accordingly. The coefficients on the regional dummy variables suggest that originator firms tend to offer lower prices in sub-Saharan Africa, relative to Asia. On the other hand, both originator and generic firms tend to have higher prices in Latin America and CIS/Eastern Europe.

The effect of product characteristics

We find that originator firms tend to charge higher prices for Group 2 drugs compared to Group 1 drugs. On the other hand, such a tendency could not be found in the case of generic firms. The coefficient on the dummy variable representing fixed-dose combinations was not found to be significantly different from zero.

The effect of firm characteristics

The coefficient on the *PREQUALIFY* variable is not significantly different from zero, and the point estimates are all negative. One of the main arguments against imposing adequate quality regulation for pharmaceuticals in developing countries has been the high cost of compliance, which could lead to shortages and possibly higher prices (Broun 2005). Our results show that compliance costs have not resulted in higher drug prices. On the other hand, we do not have sufficient information to assess the effect of quality regulation on the availability of drugs.

The *HOME* variable has a positive and significant coefficient when the *RATIO TO US PRICE* variable is used as the dependent variable. One possible reason is that the cost of drugs supplied by companies residing in the same country is inclusive of transport and other costs. Although we have employed dummy variables to account for price differences across different Incoterms, it is possible that the dummy variables have not fully captured such differences. Another possible reason is that procurement tenders are biased in favor of domestically manufactured drugs.

The effect of transaction characteristics

Turning to the transaction characteristics, the significantly negative coefficient for the *QUANTITY* variable in columns 1 and 3 suggests that originator firms practice quantity discounts. It should be recalled, however, that larger transactions are more likely to be won by a generic company. Thus, it is likely that originator firms sometimes choose not to enter tenders involving large volumes, even though they may have been ready to provide quantity discounts.

The year dummy variables for 2006 and 2007 are negative and significant in the case of originator firms, suggesting that they have lowered prices more aggressively in recent years.

Covariance between error terms

The σ_{ou} parameter measures the covariance between the error term in the second-stage price equation for originator firms on the one hand, and the error term in the first-stage binary choice model on the other (see Appendix 2). We estimate σ_{ou} to be significantly positive. This implies the following: tenders where originator firms are likely to submit higher bids (those with a high value of ε_{io}) are more likely to have originator firms as the winning bidder (u_i also has a high value).

This is a somewhat counterintuitive finding, because the winning bidders are generally those with the lowest bids. In order to explain the positive covariance between the error terms, we must once again allow for the possibility that originator firms are selective about which tenders to enter. In other words, originators seem to be deciding *not* to enter some tenders where they would have submitted lower bids.

5.4.3 Expected bids

The estimated coefficients in Table 5.6 clearly indicate that the bidding policies of originator and generic firms are different. In particular, we find that originator firms have a higher tendency to price differentially according to countries' income levels. On the other hand, the coefficients by themselves do not tell us about the comparative affordability of originator and generic products.

In order to address this question, we use our coefficient estimates to compute the expected bids for both originator and generic firms in sub-Saharan African countries. We chose to focus on sub-Saharan Africa because approximately half the transactions in our data set are located in that region. Rather than calculating the overall average bid, we calculate the bids that are expected in different groups of countries. In particular, we are interested in knowing how expected bids vary between countries with high income levels and low income levels, as well as between those with high HIV infection rates and low infection rates.

Table 5.7 presents our estimates. The expected bids are expressed as a ratio of the originator's price for the same drug in the US. To produce the expected bids, we chose representative values for the explanatory variables, as explained in the footnote to the table, and interacted them with the estimated coefficients. Standard errors were also computed using a standard formula.[21] Note that these bids are conceptually different from the observed prices in the Purchase Price Report database. The observed prices consist only of winning bids, while the prices presented in Table 5.7 are the values that originator and generic pharmaceutical companies are expected to bid, *regardless of whether or not they win the tender.*

Several interesting patterns emerge from the results. In countries with low per capita GDP (defined as lower than US$500 per year), the point estimates for expected bids by originator firms are lower than the corresponding point estimates for generic firms. In other words, originator firms tend to bid lower than generic firms in low-income countries. This is true for both Group 1 drugs and Group 2 drugs. On the other hand, in countries with higher per capita GDP (defined as US$500 per year or higher), the point estimates for expected bids by originator firms are higher than the corresponding point estimates for generic firms. This means that originator firms tend to bid higher than generic firms in developing countries with higher income levels.

Taken together, these findings imply that the pricing behaviour of originator firms exhibits a far clearer pattern of differential pricing, in

Table 5.7:   Predicted bids for ARV supply in Sub-Saharan African countries

| | Predicted ratio to US price | | | | | |
| | Group 1 drugs | | | Group 2 drugs | | |
	Originator	Generic	Difference	Originator	Generic	Difference
Low Per Capita GDP, Low HIV Rate Countries	0.0614 0.0811	0.1287 0.0232	−0.0673	0.1503 0.0481	0.1841 0.0520	−0.0338
Low Per Capita GDP, High HIV Rate Countries	0.0363 0.0730	0.1065 0.0219	−0.0702	0.1251 0.0402	0.1618 0.0517	−0.0367
High Per Capita GDP, Low HIV Rate Countries	0.1720 0.0691	0.1223 0.0265	0.0497	0.2608 0.0435	0.1777 0.0557	0.0831
High Per Capita GDP, High HIV Rate Countries	0.1437 0.0508	0.0748 0.0268	0.0689	0.2326 0.0340	0.1302 0.0568	0.1024

Notes: Figures in lower rows are standard errors.

'Low Per Capita GDP' is defined as less than US$500 per year, while 'High Per Capita GDP' is US$500 per year or higher. Similarly, 'Low HIV Rate' is defined as infection rates below 5% of the population, while 'High HIV Rate' is 5% or higher.

To represent Low Per Capita GDP-Low HIV Rate countries in Sub-Saharan Africa, we use the mean per capita GDP for this group, US$262, and the mean HIV rate, 2.34%. The mean values used for the other groups of countries are as follows: Low Per Capita GDP-High HIV Rate: (US$365, 11.67%); High Per Capita GDP-Low HIV Rate: (US$2538, 3.13%); High Per Capita GDP-High HIV Rate: (US$3245, 22.64%).

For the other explanatory variables, we used either the mean (for continuous variables) or representative values (for discrete variables) for Sub-Saharan African countries: LOG POPULATION = −2.486; LOW HUMAN DEVELOPMENT = 1; ODA SHARE = 0.066; FDC = 0; PREQUALIFY = 1; HOME = 0; QUANTITY = 0.004; YEAR = 2005; INCOTERM = CIF.

comparison to the behaviour of generic firms. In fact, while originator firms have a clear tendency to bid lower in countries with lower income levels, the same cannot be said for generic firms.

It is somewhat surprising that generic firms do not offer lower prices in countries with lower per capita GDP. As a possible explanation, tenders held by higher-income countries may involve more bidders. The economic theory of auctions shows that when firms maximize profits, their bids decrease the higher the number of rival bidders (Krishna 2002). We can therefore argue that the bidding strategies of generic firms – who may be more likely than their originator counterparts to be behaving in a profit-maximizing manner – are more responsive (negatively) to the number of rival bidders, resulting in relatively low bids by generic firms in higher-income countries. As mentioned in the previous section, however, our methodology is not capable of discerning how bids are affected by the competitive environment, including the number of rival bidders.

5.5 The role of patents

In order to investigate how patents relate to the pricing of drugs, we combined the Purchase Price Report data with data on ARV patents. Each transaction in the Purchase Price Report is identified by the name of the drug, the name of the recipient country, and the date on which the product was ordered. Meanwhile, the patent data tells us whether or not a given ARV was protected by a patent in a given country, on a given date. By merging the two data sets, we can tell whether or not a given transaction was conducted in the presence of a valid patent.

Table 5.8 presents the distribution of transactions according to patent status. For Group 1 drugs, we find that only 27.9 per cent of the transactions that occurred under a valid patent were actually supplied by the originator company, while the remaining 72.1 per cent were supplied by a generic firm. Remarkably, the corresponding ratios for transactions that occurred outside of patent protection are quite similar: 28.3 per cent supplied by originator firms, and 71.7 per cent supplied by generic firms. This implies that the existence of patents has no bearing on whether a Group 1 ARV is supplied by an originator firm or a generic firm. In the case of Group 2 drugs, originator firms supplied all of the transactions that occurred under patent protection, while they supplied 72.1 per cent of the transactions that took place outside of patent protection. Thus, in the case of Group 2 drugs, the existence of patents seems to have an effect on the identity of supplying firms.

In Tables 5.9 and 5.10, we examine whether the prices of drugs supplied under patent protection differ significantly from the prices that were realized outside of patent protection. In the case of Group 1 drugs, prices realized under patents are significantly *lower* than prices realized outside of patent protection, whether the drug was supplied by an originator firm or by a generic firm. In the case of Group 2 drugs, the same result holds in the case of drugs supplied by originator firms. In the case of generic firms, we are not able to assess the difference, because generic firms never supplied Group 2 drugs in countries where they were patented.

It is rather surprising that the existence of patents is associated with lower prices, rather than higher prices. One possible explanation is that patents are filed by originator firms in countries where they are likely to offer lower prices. Before assessing the effect of patents on prices, it is necessary to examine and model the patenting decisions of originator

Table 5.8:   Distribution of transactions by patent status and firm type

	Group 1 drugs			Group 2 drugs		
	Patented	Not patented	Total	Patented	Not patented	Total
Originator	102	127	229	22	62	84
	27.9%	28.3%	28.1%	100.0%	72.1%	77.8%
Generic	264	322	586	0	24	24
	72.1%	71.7%	71.9%	0.0%	27.9%	22.2%
Total	366	449	815	22	86	108
	100.0%	100.0%	100.0%	100.0%	100.0%	100.0%

Table 5.9:   Mean price per DDD by patent status and firm type

	Group 1 drugs		p-value for difference between means	Group 2 drugs		p-value for difference between means
	Patented	Not patented		Patented	Not patented	
Originator	1.1491	1.5002	0.0627	2.0364	3.9248	0.0532
	0.0949	0.1499		0.2291	0.5655	
Generic	0.3162	0.5568	0.0000	–	1.2717	–
	0.0268	0.0467		–	0.2590	

Note: Figures in lower rows are standard errors.

Table 5.10:   Mean ratio to US price by patent status and firm type

	Group 1 drugs		p-value for difference between means	Group 2 drugs		p-value for difference between means
	Patented	Not patented		Patented	Not patented	
Originator	0.0920	0.1344	0.0128	0.0961	0.2138	0.0087
	0.0093	0.0132		0.0103	0.0257	
Generic	0.0210	0.0459	0.0000	–	0.0974	–
	0.0015	0.0037		–	0.0104	

Note: Figures in lower rows are standard errors.

firms. This is, however, not possible with the limited amount of patent data that is available to us.

5.6   Conclusion

Access to pharmaceuticals in developing countries has been hindered by various factors such as the underdevelopment of healthcare systems and the inability of governments and individuals to pay for a sufficient quantity of even off-patent essential drugs. In the case of newer drugs that are under patent protection (such as ARVs used to treat AIDS), the question of pricing further complicates the picture. For example, if countries in sub-Saharan Africa were to purchase ARVs to treat all of their AIDS patients and pay prices prevalent in the United States, the total cost would surpass the combined GDP of these countries (Ganslandt et al. 2005).

Rising concern within the international community and the resulting advent of funding schemes such as the Global Fund have reduced financial and logistical constraints to some extent. An important issue is the pricing of pharmaceuticals because prices determine the number of patients that can be treated with a given amount of funding. The increasing need for second-line treatment in various countries has contributed to further concern regarding prices.

This chapter addressed the following questions relating to the pricing behaviour of originator and generic pharmaceutical firms in the context of procurement tenders for ARVs in developing countries: Do firms practice differential pricing? Are there differences in behaviour between originator and generic firms? How are product quality and firm nationality related to prices? Do patents have a significant impact on pharmaceutical prices?

There appears to be a clear tendency for originator pharmaceutical firms to offer lower prices in countries with low per capita GDP, but such behaviour is not found among generic firms. Without controlling for market characteristics, previous studies have only noted that the average price of drugs supplied by originators is higher than that of drugs supplied by generic firms (Vasan et al. 2006; Chien 2007). In fact, the results of this chapter indicate that there are significant differences in pricing behaviour between the two types of firms. As a result of these behavioural differences, originator firms tend to supply at prices that are lower than those of generics in lower-income countries. Countries with high HIV-infection rates also tend to be offered price discounts by both originator and generic firms.

The process by which the identity of the winning bidder is determined (whether the winner is an originator or a generic firm) was also estimated. Results show that the winning bidder is more likely to be an originator firm in countries with higher per capita GDP and higher population. At first glance, these results are surprising because originator firms tend to bid high in such countries, and this makes them less likely to win. However, the puzzle can be explained by the possibility that originator firms are selective about which tenders to enter. Originator firms may have a tendency to refrain from entering certain low-income countries such as those having local pharmaceutical manufacturing capabilities even though they are likely to bid low in those countries.

Regression results also give insight into the relationship between prices and firm characteristics. Most notably, higher quality (measured by WHO pre-qualification or approval by a stringent regulatory authority) does not appear to increase the price of the drug. This is contrary to the traditional argument that stringent quality regulation will lead to higher prices for drugs in developing countries. The results also suggest that locally manufactured drugs do not tend to be cheaper. It is possible that local firms are awarded contracts even if they are not the highest bidder (see footnote 8). Thus, while policies allowing the use of suboptimal-quality drugs and policies that promote the use of locally manufactured drugs may lead to reduced drug safety, they are not effective at lowering drug costs.

Analysis of the role of patents yields two interesting findings: first, patents do not seem to have a significant effect in determining the winning bidder for older ARVs. Second, patents are associated with lower (rather than higher) ARV prices. The first result may well be due to the fact that in certain developing countries, originator firms have not insisted on being the sole supplier based on their patent rights (Chien 2007). In order to explain the second result, future studies must examine in detail the patenting behaviour of originator firms. It may be the case that firms are more likely to file patent applications in certain countries while those same countries tend to attract lower prices, and this leads to the negative relationship observed between patents and prices.

The above findings have implications for ARV procurement and financing by the Global Fund and by national governments. First, given that the objective of internationally funded procurement is to provide high-quality medicines in a cost-effective manner, procurement of suboptimal-quality drugs should not be allowed, particularly because the quality factor does not add to the cost of AIDS drugs. Second, given that originator firms tend to offer lower procurement prices in poorer countries, governments should not assume that AIDS drugs supplied by originator pharmaceutical firms are always more expensive than their generic counterparts. Third, given the risk that poorer and smaller countries may have to face extremely high prices for newer ARVs that are subject to patent protection, the Global Fund should strengthen its price-monitoring efforts and provide some mechanism for intervention to adjust procurement prices, taking into account not only recipient characteristics, but also the cost of R&D.

Appendix 1

Table 5.A1: Countries appearing in the data set

Country name	Least developed countries group	Low human development group	Low-income economies group	GDP per capita in 2004 (US$)	Total population in 2004 (million)	HIV prevalence in 2005 (%)	Patent information available from MSF	No. of transactions in data set
Sub-Saharan Africa								
Benin	yes	yes	yes	495	8.2	1.79	yes	7
Burkina Faso	yes	yes	yes	377	12.8	2.01	yes	20
Burundi	yes	yes	yes	91	7.3	3.26	no	8
Cameroon	no	yes	no	988	16.0	5.43	yes	40
Central African Republic	yes	yes	yes	329	4.0	10.73	yes	1
Côte d'Ivoire	no	yes	yes	866	17.9	7.06	no	37
Djibouti	yes	yes	no	847	0.8	3.11	yes	37
Equatorial Guinea	yes	no	no	6,562	0.5	3.20	yes	17
The Gambia	yes	yes	yes	271	1.5	2.44	no	11
Ghana	no	no	yes	409	21.7	2.27	no	4
Guinea-Bissau	yes	yes	yes	175	1.5	3.79	no	18
Kenya	no	yes	yes	481	33.5	6.09	yes	25
Madagascar	yes	yes	yes	241	18.1	0.51	no	16
Malawi	yes	yes	yes	151	12.6	14.09	yes	7
Mali	yes	yes	yes	373	13.1	1.73	yes	8
Namibia	no	no	no	2,842	2.0	19.56	no	2
Niger	yes	yes	yes	226	13.5	1.10	yes	12
Nigeria	no	yes	yes	559	129.0	3.86	no	2
Rwanda	yes	yes	yes	206	8.9	3.07	no	33

(Continued)

Table 5.A1: Continued

Country name	Least developed countries group	Low human development group	Low-income economies group	GDP per capita in 2004 (US$)	Total population in 2004 (million)	HIV prevalence in 2005 (%)	Patent information available from MSF	No. of transactions in data set
Senegal	yes	yes	yes	669	11.4	0.91	yes	1
Sierra Leone	yes	yes	yes	201	5.3	1.56	no	1
South Africa	no	no	no	4,725	45.5	18.78	yes	264
Swaziland	no	yes	no	2,250	1.1	33.38	no	213
Tanzania	yes	yes	yes	301	37.6	6.46	no	13
Togo	yes	no	yes	344	6.0	3.24	yes	2
Uganda	yes	no	yes	245	27.8	6.66	yes	4
Zimbabwe	no	no	yes	364	12.9	20.12	yes	25
CIS/Eastern Europe								
Armenia	no	no	no	1,183	3.0	0.15	no	7
Azerbaijan	no	no	no	1,045	8.3	0.11	no	2
Belarus	no	no	no	2,351	9.8	0.34	no	5
Bulgaria	no	no	no	3,131	7.8	0.10	no	7
Georgia	no	no	no	1,135	4.5	0.22	no	16
Kyrgyz Republic	no	no	yes	434	5.1	0.14	no	7
Rep. of Macedonia	no	no	no	2,645	2.0	0.10	no	2
Moldova	no	no	no	614	4.2	1.05	no	15
Russian Federation	no	no	no	4,097	144.0	1.09	no	59
Tajikistan	no	no	yes	322	6.4	0.14	no	12
Ukraine	no	no	no	1,366	47.5	1.40	yes	77
Uzbekistan	no	no	yes	458	26.2	0.21	no	8

Asia							
Cambodia	yes	no	354	13.8	1.64	yes	263
China	no	no	1,485	1,300.0	0.08	yes	5
Islamic Rep. of Iran	no	no	2,433	67.0	0.15	no	6
Mongolia	no	yes	640	2.5	0.10	no	6
Nepal	yes	yes	253	26.6	0.53	no	41
Thailand	no	no	2,543	63.7	1.40	yes	25
Vietnam	no	yes	550	82.2	0.51	no	8
Latin America							
Belize	no	no	3,680	0.3	2.49	no	5
Colombia	no	no	2,156	44.9	0.61	no	5
Dominican Republic	no	no	2,110	8.8	1.11	no	6
El Salvador	no	no	2,336	6.8	0.92	no	42
Guatemala	no	no	2,228	12.3	0.90	yes	4
Haiti	yes	yes	456	8.4	3.81	no	1
Honduras	no	no	1,046	7.0	1.54	no	71
Nicaragua	no	no	837	5.4	0.24	no	7
Peru	no	no	2,489	27.6	0.57	yes	88
Suriname	no	no	2,576	0.4	1.94	no	40

Sources: United Nations Development Programme (2005), Médecins Sans Frontières (2003), and references listed in footnotes 16 and 17.

Appendix 2   Derivation of the switching regression model

Either an originator firm's bid (b_{io}^*) or a generic firm's bid (b_{ig}^*) is observed in each transaction – but never both – depending on which one is the winning bid. Therefore, we need to describe the process through which the winning bidder is determined. As a general rule, the winner is an originator firm only if the originator firm submits a lower bid. However, some firms may be selective about which tenders to enter, and this may distort the lowest-bid rule. For example, a firm may decide not to enter a particular tender, even though it would have submitted the lowest bid had it entered. In addition, some countries may have a preference for originator products, while others may prefer local generic products. These preferences can also distort the lowest-bid rule.

Taking these considerations into account, the winner is an originator firm if and only if the following condition holds:

$$b_{io}^* - b_{ig}^* < \lambda' W_i + \eta_i$$
$$\Leftrightarrow \quad \beta_o' X_i - \beta_g' X_i - \lambda' W_i < \varepsilon_{ig} - \varepsilon_{io} + \eta_i$$
$$\Leftrightarrow \quad (\beta_o - \beta_g)' X_i - \lambda' W_i < \varepsilon_{ig} - \varepsilon_{io} + \eta_i$$

The expression $\lambda' W_i + \eta_i$ captures firms' entry behavior into tenders, as well as the purchasing country's preference for originator products. This expression may be either positive or negative. The probability that the winner is an originator firm can then be expressed as follows:

$$\Pr\left[(\beta_o - \beta_g)' X_i - \lambda' W_i < \varepsilon_{ig} - \varepsilon_{io} + \eta_i\right] = \Pr\left(u_i < \delta' Z_i\right) = \Phi(\delta' Z_i) \quad \text{(A2.1)}$$

where $u_i \equiv \varepsilon_{io} - \varepsilon_{ig} - \eta_i$, Z_i consists of the elements in X_i and W_i, and δ is a vector of coefficients. It has been assumed that u_i has a standard normal distribution.

Equation (A2.1) is useful for two reasons. First, it can be used to describe how the winning firm type – originator or generic – is determined in the sample. Second, the estimated parameters can be employed for obtaining unbiased estimates of the bid equations in (1). This is because the 'conditional expectation of bids' has the following forms (Lee 1978):

$$E(b_{io} | u_i < \delta' Z_i) = \beta_o' X_i - \sigma_{ou} \frac{\phi(\delta' Z_i)}{\Phi(\delta' Z_i)}$$

$$E\left(b_{ig} | u_i \geq \delta' Z_i\right) = \beta_g' X_i + \sigma_{gu} \frac{\phi(\delta' Z_i)}{1 - \Phi(\delta' Z_i)} \quad \text{(A2.2)}$$

where $\phi(\cdot)$ is the probability density for the standard normal distribution, $\sigma_{ou} \equiv Cov(\varepsilon_{io}, u_i)$, and $\sigma_{gu} \equiv Cov(\varepsilon_{ig}, u_i)$. The first equation in (A2.2) describes the expected bid by an originator firm, conditional on the winner being an originator firm. The second equation is the expected bid by a generic firm, conditional on the winner being a generic firm.

In the empirical implementation, we first estimate the parameter vector δ in (A2.1) using the probit regression model. Next, for each transaction in the data set, we calculate $\frac{\phi(\delta'Z_i)}{\Phi(\delta'Z_i)}$ and $\frac{\phi(\delta'Z_i)}{1-\Phi(\delta'Z_i)}$ using the parameter estimates $\hat{\delta}$. Third, OLS regressions for the equations in (A2.2) are run separately to estimate the β and σ parameters; transactions involving winning bids by an originator firm are used to estimate the first equation, while those involving winning bids by a generic firm are used to estimate the second equation. The variables in X as well as the calculated ratios are used as explanatory variables. Finally, the standard errors for the parameter estimates are calculated through the formula presented in Maddala (1983: 225–7).

Notes

*   This chapter refines the analytical method used in the earlier study on ARV prices by the same authors (http://www.ide.go.jp/English/Publish/Download/Jrp/pdf/jrp_142_05.pdf), so that bidding behaviour of drug companies could be taken into account. The present analysis also takes more care in assessing the relationship between patents and drug prices.

1. According to a more recent survey, annual per capita spending on pharmaceuticals ranges from US\$0.04 to US\$16.30 in developing countries and from US\$26.67 to US\$505.46 in developed countries (United Nations 2008).

2. The WHO Essential Medicines List was established in 1977 by World Health Assembly Resolution 28.66 to serve as a model for national essential medicines lists. The WHO list is renewed approximately every two years: see www.who.int/medicines/publications/essentialmedicines/en/

3. WHO 15th Essential Medicines List, March 2007: see www.who.int/medicines/publications/08_ENGLISH_indexFINAL_EML15.pdf

4. Chapter 4 of this book provides a detailed analysis of the funding activities of the Global Fund.

5. Generic drugs are defined here as 'copies of patented drugs'. A webpage of the World Trade Organization provides different usages of the term based on the intellectual property status of the product: see www.wto.org/English/tratop_e/trips_e/factsheet_pharm03_e.htm

6. The combined number of patients treated through the Global Fund and PEPFAR is smaller than the sum of 384,000 and 471,000 because 214,000 patients were treated under programmes jointly funded by the Global Fund and PEPFAR.

7. Pre-qualification signifies that the drug has been assessed for quality, safety and efficacy, and is thus found to be acceptable by the WHO (Dekker et al. 2006).
8. This is based on interviews with Global Fund officers and participants in tenders, November 2007.
9. Ellison and Wolfram (2006) discuss another example where pharmaceutical prices may have been set out of motives other than short-term profit maximization. They find that during the early 1990s originator pharmaceutical firms coordinated their efforts to hold down price increases, possibly in an attempt to influence policy discussions on healthcare reform.
10. The data can be accessed at the Global Fund Price Reporting Mechanism website: www.theglobalfund.org/en/funds raised/price_reporting/
11. Previous studies using Global Fund price data, such as those by Vasan et al. (2006) and Chien (2007), have ignored the significant price differentials that exist between different transaction types as defined by Incoterms. According to the United States Government Accountability Office (2005), these price differentials range from 3 per cent to 15 per cent.
12. There are several transactions reporting a price near zero, but a close look reveals that many of these are the result of unrealistically large volumes. Since prices are calculated as total value divided by total volume, a large figure for volume leads to a low figure for price. Consequently, observations having near-zero price were dropped.
13. It appears somewhat unreasonable that some governments of developing countries are charging their citizens for drugs whose costs are paid by donors. However, patient out-of-pocket payments may be necessary in these countries because their governments cannot finance the health infrastructure required for drug provision (Philips 2007).
14. The United Nations (2008) found that in developing countries, the retail-level price of a basket of essential drugs was more than 2.5 times the average government procurement price.
15. A current list of pre-qualified products was obtained from the following webpage: http://mednet3.who.int/prequal/lists/hiv_suppliers.pdf
16. See the UN's List of Least Developed Countries, at: www.un.org/special-rep/ohrlls/ldc/list.htm
17. See the World Bank's Country Classification Table at : http://siteresources. worldbank.org/DATASTATISTICS/Resources/CLASS.XLS
18. To construct the *PHARMA INDUSTRY* variable, we tabulated all the transactions in the data set according to the country of manufacture. If a country is the manufacturing site of a generic product in two or more transactions, then the *PHARMA INDUSTRY* variable is given a value of 1. Otherwise, it takes the value of 0. *PHARMA INDUSRY* equals 1 for the following countries: Guatemala, India, Peru, South Africa and Thailand.
19. As a technical matter, the exclusion of the *PHARMA INDUSTRY* variable from the bid equations helps to identify the estimated model (Willis and Rosen 1979).
20. The magnitude of marginal effects depends on the values assigned to the explanatory variables. Therefore, in order to evaluate the marginal effects, the continuous variables were assigned their mean values, while the binary variables were given a value of zero.

21. The predicted value for a country with characteristics X_0 is $b_0 = \beta' X_0$, and its variance is $Var(b_0) = X_0' Var(\beta) X_0$. The standard error is the square root of the estimate of $Var(b_0)$.

References

Bartlett, John (2004) 'Antiretroviral Therapy', in *A Guide to Primary Care of People with HIV/AIDS*, United States Department of Health and Human Services.

Broun, Denis (2005) *Global Fund Policy on Quality Assurance for Pharmaceutical Products: Procurement of Single and Limited Source Pharmaceuticals*, Geneva: World Health Organization.

Chien, Colleen (2007) 'HIV/AIDS Drugs for Sub-Saharan Africa: How do Brand and Generic Supply Compare?', *PLoS ONE*, issue 3: e278.

Commission on Macroeconomics and Health (2001) *Macroeconomics and Health: Investing in Health for Economic Development*, Geneva: World Health Organization.

Danzon, Patricia (2007) 'At What Price?', *Nature*, 449: 176–9.

Dekker, Theo, Adriaan van Zyl, Olivier Gross, Ivana Tasevska, Matthias Stahl, Marie Rabouhans and Lembit Rägo (2006) 'Ongoing Monitoring of Antiretroviral Products as Part of WHO's Prequalification Project', *Journal of Generic Medicines*, Vol. 3: 96–105.

Donald, Stephen and Harry Paarsch (1993) 'Piecewise Pseudo-Maximum Likelihood Estimation in Empirical Models of Auctions', *International Economic Review*, Vol. 34, No. 1: 121–48.

Ellison, Sara Fisher and Catherine Wolfram (2006) 'Coordinating on Lower Prices: Pharmaceutical Pricing under Political Pressure', *RAND Journal of Economics*, Vol. 37: 324–40.

F. Hoffmann-La Roche (2006) *Removing Barriers, Increasing Access: Roche's Commitment to Increase Access to HIV Medicines in Resource-limited Countries*, at: www.roche.com/ pages/downloads/sustain/pdf/removing_barriers_e.pdf

Ganslandt, Matthias, Keith Maskus and Eina Wong (2005) 'Developing and Distributing Essential Medicines to Poor Countries: The DEFEND Proposal', in Carsten Fink and Keith Maskus (eds) *Intellectual Property and Development: Lessons from Recent Economic Research*, New York: World Bank and Oxford University Press.

Global Fund to Fight AIDS, Tuberculosis, and Malaria (2006) *Guide to the Global Fund's Policies on Procurement and Supply Management*, at: www.theglobalfund. org/en/about/procurement/

Guerre, Emmanuel, Isabelle Perrigne and Quang Vuong (2000) 'Optimal Nonparametric Estimation of First Price Auctions', *Econometrica*, Vol. 68: 525–574.

Krishna, Vijay (2002) *Auction Theory*, New York: Academic Press.

Lee, Lung-Fei (1978) 'Unionism and Wage Rates: A Simultaneous Equation Model with Qualitative and Limited Dependent Variables', *International Economic Review*, Vol. 19: 415–33.

Maddala, G. S. (1983) *Limited-Dependent and Qualitative Variables in Econometrics*, Cambridge: Cambridge University Press.

cins Sans Frontières (2003) *Drug Patents under the Spotlight: Sharing Practical Knowledge about Pharmaceutical Patents*, at: www.who.int/3by5/en/patents_2003.pdf

Médecins Sans Frontières (2007) *Untangling the Web of Price Reductions: A Pricing Guide for the Purchase of ARVs for Developing Countries*, 10th ed., at: www.accessmed-msf.org/main/hivaids/untangling-the-web/

Philips, M. (2007) 'Making AIDS Patients Pay for their Care: Why Does Evidence Not Change Anything in International Donor Policies?', in Médecins Sans Frontières, *Humanitarian Stakes: MSF Switzerland's Review on Humanitarian Stakes and Practices*.

Schweitzer, Stuart O. (2007) *Pharmaceutical Economics and Policy*, 2nd ed., Oxford: Oxford University Press.

United Nations (2008) *Delivering on the Global Partnership for Achieving the Millennium Development Goals: MDG Gap Task Force Report 2008*, New York: United Nations.

United Nations Development Programme (2005) *Human Development Report 2005 – International Cooperation at a Crossroads: Aid, Trade and Security in an Unequal World*, New York: UNDP.

United States Government Accountability Office (2005) 'Global HIV/AIDS Epidemic: Selection of Antiretroviral Medications Provided under US Emergency Plan is Limited', Report to Congressional Requesters.

UNAIDS (2007) *2007 AIDS Epidemic Update*, Geneva: Joint United Nations Programme on HIV/AIDS.

Vasan, Ashwin, David Hoos, Joia Mukherjee, Paul Farmer, Allan Rosenfield and Joseph Perriëns (2006) 'The Pricing and Procurement of Antiretroviral Drugs: An Observational Study of Data from the Global Fund', *Bulletin of the World Health Organization*, Vol. 84, No. 5: 393–8.

WHO (World Health Organization) (2004) *The World Medicines Situation 2004*, Geneva: World Health Organization.

WHO (2006a) *Progress on Global Access to HIV Antiretroviral Therapy: A Report on '3 by 5' and Beyond*, Geneva: World Health Organization.

WHO (2006b) 'Prices Paid for Antiretroviral Drugs by Low and Middle Income Countries from January 2004 to June 2006, Breakdown in Semester.' Summary report from the Global Price Reporting Mechanism on Antiretroviral Drugs, at: www.who.int/hiv/amds/grpm_aug06.pdf

Willis, Robert and Sherwin Rosen (1979) 'Education and Self-Selection', *Journal of Political Economy*, Vol. 87, No. 5 (October), Part 2, S7–S36.

6
How to Manage Out-Migration of Medical Personnel from Developing Countries: The Case of Filipino and South African Nurses and Doctors Leaving for Saudi Arabia, the UK and the US

Tatsufumi Yamagata

Introduction

A shortage of medical personnel has become a critical problem for developing countries and hinders them from providing medical services to the poor. Two aspects of the issue are of vital importance, one related to the demand and the other to the supply of medical personnel.

The demand for medical personnel has risen in developing countries because of the persistently widespread occurrence of serious infectious diseases such as HIV/AIDS, tuberculosis, and malaria and also because of the intensification of efforts by the international community to combat such diseases. The growing concern of the international community is symbolized by the Millennium Development Goals (MDGs) which were agreed upon at the United Nations Millennium Summit in 2000 and by the establishment of the Global Fund to Fight AIDS, Tuberculosis, and Malaria (the Global Fund) established in 2002. MDGs include an improvement in the health of the poor. In association with efforts for this, substantial funds have been raised and the necessary medicines have been made available for HIV/AIDS, tuberculosis and malaria. Therefore, the shortage in medical personnel willing to serve in developing countries has become more pronounced.[1]

The demand for medical personnel in developing countries is further expanded by the aging of the population, and aging of the population is even more marked in developed countries. Because of the fall in fertility and the decline in mortality, the percentage of elderly people is steadily increasing worldwide, and the aged population boosts the demand for medical services all over the world.

In most of developed countries, the local supply of medical personnel is insufficient to meet the growing demand. As a result, driven by the huge wage gap between developing and developed countries, the increasing demand in developed countries is, at least partially, met by migration of doctors and nurses from developing countries. This movement of human resources aggravates the shortage of medical personnel in developing countries, where an insufficiency in medical services may be fatal due to the emerging infectious diseases.

Hence, how to increase the supply of medical personnel is a serious and acute issue in the developing countries. A long-term solution is to expand the capacity of medical educational institutions and to increase the local supply of medical personnel. In the meantime, the outflow of such personnel abroad is a most urgent issue and has to be addressed at once. Otherwise, the stock of medical personnel will be quickly and dramatically eroded in developing countries, and the investment in human capital funded by governments in low-income countries will end up wasted.

What complicates the profit-and-loss arithmetic of emigration of medical personnel from developing countries is the high reward for their services in developed countries and the great amount of the remittances sent back to their countries of origin, which may substantially enhance the living standards of the recipients. This benefit is highly appreciated in some developing countries such as the Philippines.

Taking into account the two contrasting consequences of outflow of medical personnel, prohibition of the outflow of medical personnel is not among the best countermeasures because prohibition would halt access to the high earnings which can be attained by medical personnel who have emigrated from developing countries. The best measure will be harmonious with the motivations and incentives which doctors and nurses in developing countries have in their minds.

This chapter describes what is occurring in typical source and destination countries and how policies taken in both groups of countries affect the current worldwide distribution of medical personnel. An important observation presented in this chapter is that influential destination countries attempt to steadily expand the supply of medical personnel to their labour markets, which imposes the role of adjustment valve on the source countries.

The remainder of this chapter is organized as follows. Section 1 gives a general overview of the shortage problem in medical services in developing countries, which is caused by the emigration of medical personnel. Section 2 describes the current situation and policies taken to deal with this issue in two representative source countries: the Philippines and South Africa. On the other hand, Saudi Arabia, the United Kingdom and the United States are among the greatest absorbers of doctors and nurses from these two source countries. The situations and policies of these three destination countries are summarized in Section 3. Finally, two feasible measures to mitigate the tension caused by the massive outflow of medical personnel are discussed in Section 4. Concluding remarks are presented at the end.

6.1   Unequal distribution of medical personnel around the world

It is widely known that people in low-income countries suffer from poor-quality health, a state of affairs that is characterized, amongst other things, by low life expectancy. These health problems are deep-seated and have long presented a challenge to people in low-income countries and in the international community. However, the situation may well be aggravated by outflows of medical personnel from low-income countries to high income countries (Ahmad 2005; Bach 2003; Kapur and McHale 2005: 25–9; Mejia 1978; Physicians for Human Rights 2004; WHO 2004).

Table 6.1 indicates the resources for medical services available through-out the world by region. It is clear that resources in terms of human and physical capital are more abundant in the Commonwealth of Independent States (CIS), Europe and North America.[2] In these regions, more than two physicians are available for every thousand people, and more than 90 per cent of births are supervised by skilled health staff. In addition, more than three hospital beds are available for every thousand people.

By contrast, sub-Saharan Africa ranks as the worst region in terms of all three indicators. In rounded figures, only one physician is available for every 15,000 people, while only one hospital bed is available for every 1000 people. Only half of all births are attended by skilled health staff. East and South Asia is the second worst region, followed by Oceania, the Middle East and North Africa. However, the inferiority of available resources in sub-Saharan Africa is striking.

The shortage of human capital for medical services in developing regions such as sub-Saharan Africa and East and South Asia can be

Table 6.1:   Indicators of resources for medical services by region

	Physicians per 1000 people	Hospital beds per 1000 people	Births attended by skilled health staff (%)
East and South Asia	0.895 (23)	2.710 (15)	57.4 (22)
Commonwealth of Independent States	3.366 (11)	7.164 (11)	93.6 (9)
Europe	3.010 (35)	5.792 (34)	99.2 (17)
Middle East and North Africa	1.479 (20)	2.379 (19)	80.1 (11)
Sub-Saharan Africa	0.204 (46)	0.907 (3)	52.0 (43)
Canada and USA	2.200 (2)	3.500 (2)	98.0 (1)
Latin America and Caribbean	1.550 (20)	2.410 (31)	85.3 (27)
Oceania	1.123 (7)	4.014 (7)	82.2 (5)

Note: The figures are regional averages of variables in the latest year when the value was available in the range of years between 2000 and 2004. The numbers in parentheses indicate the sample size of countries for each average.
Source: World Bank (2006b).

attributed partly to the outflow of medical personnel to developed countries. The World Health Organization (WHO 2006: 100) demonstrates that a high proportion of medical doctors trained in sub-Saharan Africa work in developed countries. This source states 23 per cent as the ratio of doctors trained in ten sub-Saharan African countries[3] and working in eight OECD countries in Europe and North America[4] to doctors working in the ten sub-Saharan African countries. If this figure is applicable throughout sub-Saharan Africa, then almost a fifth of the doctors trained in sub-Saharan Africa are working in the OECD countries. The WHO (2006: 100) has also compiled data on nurses and midwives trained in 19 sub-Saharan African countries[5] and working in seven OECD countries.[6] The equivalent ratio for nurses and midwives is 5 per cent. Though this proportion is lower than that for medical doctors, there are some countries where the ratio is higher. The proportion of Zimbabwean nurses and midwives working in seven OECD countries is 34 per cent of the same number of nurses and midwives working in Zimbabwe. The equivalent ratios are 18 per cent for Lesotho and Mauritius and 13 per cent for Ghana. Thus, it is apparent that, for some sub-Saharan African countries, the outflow of medical personnel is substantial and that, potentially, it may have a highly harmful effect on health services in the countries from which the massive outflows of medical personnel are occurring.

In theory, emigration of the educated may work to the benefit of the educated labour force remaining in the country of origin and may actually cause it to increase. The opportunity to emigrate increases the returns on education and leads more people to invest in education with the expectation of emigration. However, only part of the educated population will succeed in emigrating. This being the case, the amount of human capital in the whole economy increases if the loss in human capital due to emigration is smaller than the gain in human capital due to the rise in expected returns on education. This effect is called 'brain gain', by contrast with brain drain (Beine, Docquier and Rapoport 2001; Mountford 1997; World Bank 2006a: 68). However, there is not enough evidence to suggest that, in reality, the brain-gain effect outweighs the brain-drain effect, and it is still generally believed that the outflow of medical personnel from developing countries is detrimental to the availability of medical personnel in the source countries (WHO 2006). Some observations on the case of the Philippines, which are offered in the following section, suggest that the effects of brain drain outweigh those of brain gain.

6.2   What is happening in the sending countries?: the cases of the Philippines and South Africa

The following two sections present case studies highlighting five countries that are deeply involved in the international migration of medical personnel: the Philippines, South Africa, Saudi Arabia, the United Kingdom and the United States. The former two are known as source countries, while the latter three are destination countries for medical personnel. The circumstances, mechanisms, environments and policies affecting the migration of medical personnel are described in turn below.

6.2.1   The Philippines

The Philippines has been a leading source country of labour in Southeast Asia for decades (Catholic Institute for International Relations 1987: 13–19; Chalamwong 2005; Sagalla 1988). It is one of the best organized developing countries in terms of the management of private recruiting agencies and the provision of care for its citizens working abroad through diplomatic missions in foreign countries. It follows that it is also a leading country in the dispatch of medical personnel overseas,[7] as data of the selected host countries makes evident later. In contrast to women from neighboring Muslim societies, Filipina women experience few cultural restrictions on working overseas and large numbers of female nurses and midwives leave the Philippines to work abroad.

Trends in outflow

The scale of out-migration for work from the Philippines is great. In 2005, the outflow of Filipino workers amounted to as many as one million persons. Moreover, a rising trend is apparent in the number of both land-based and sea-based migrants. The government of the Philippines operates an agency, the Philippine Overseas Employment Administration (POEA), whose task is to secure overseas employment for Filipinos. POEA advertises job openings abroad, supervises recruitment agencies, and checks the contracts between overseas employers and Filipino workers before the workers leave the country (Achacoso 1987). More than other countries in Southeast Asia, the Philippines emphasizes the role of overseas employment in its economic development. It follows that the government of the Philippines, in general, has taken better care of its workers than most other labour-exporting countries (Abella and Abrera-Mangahas 1997: 32; ILO 1988; UNESCAP 1987: 156–202).

The amount of remittances from overseas Filipino workers is enormous, too. In 2006, the amount was US$12.8 billion. In recent years, remittances have grown more rapidly than exports, such that the remittance-to-export ratio increased steadily from 15.9 per cent in 2000 to 26.9 per cent in 2006. More than half of the remittances originated from the United States.[8]

Among occupations of migrant workers from the Philippines, most of medical personnel are counted as skilled workers, and the massive outflow of medical personnel has drawn attention because of the attendant risk of substantial deterioration in medical services in the Philippines. On the other hand, the potential for employment of Filipino medical personnel is promising especially in countries where the population pyramid is skewed as a result of contraction in the number of youth and where the income level causes physically demanding jobs such as nursing and care-giving to be viewed as unattractive occupations. For their part, Filipino workers have shown aptitude for occupations that involve interaction with people, including occupations such as housemaids and entertainers in addition to nurses, midwives and caregivers. Thus, the increasing demand for medical personnel in high-income countries is opening up favourable prospects for new employment opportunities for Filipino workers.

Figure 6.1 shows the scale of temporary migration of Filipino nurses, by destination country, for 1992–2005. The order of emigration is from

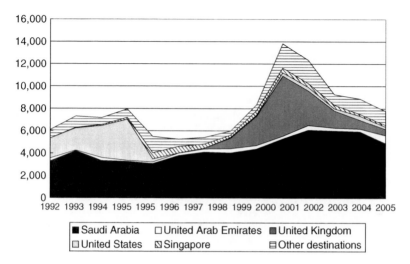

Figure 6.1:   Outflow of migrating Filipino nurses (unit: persons)

Note: The number of nurses immigrating to the United States shown above does not include those leaving for the United States through the 'employment-based immigration scheme'.

Source: Philippine Overseas Employment Administration (2007).

some thousands to less than 15,000. A conspicuous feature of the trend is the great fluctuation according to changes in demand from the United States and the United Kingdom. The number of Filipino nurses who temporarily emigrated dropped by more than 2000 when the US suddenly closed the doors to them in 1996. Meanwhile, the demand for Filipino nurses in the United Kingdom has grown since 1999. The outflow to the United Kingdom was a little over 6000 persons in 2001, and the United Kingdom became the most important destination for Filipino nurses at that time. Since then, the number of emigrants to the UK visibly and continuously decreased until 2005. By contrast, Saudi Arabia has been a steady absorber of Filipino nurses for some time and continuously receives 4000 to 6000 nurses per annum, displaying a moderately rising trend. Thus, Saudi Arabia provides a steady and reliable demand for Filipino nurses working abroad, while demand in other destination countries tends to be more capricious.

There is a reservation on the trend in emigration to the United States. Figure 6.1 covers only temporary migrants who do not gain citizenship and who are monitored by the POEA. Most Filipino nurses currently leave for the United States under the 'employment-based immigration

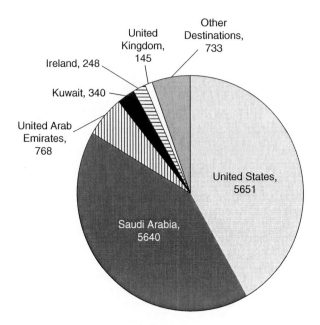

Figure 6.2:   Outflow of migrating Filipino nurses in 2006 (unit: persons)
Note: The figures for the United States include those with visas through the 'employment-based immigration scheme'.
Source: Internal document of the Philippine Overseas Employment Administration.

scheme', and they are counted as permanent migration with citizenship and not included in the number shown in Figure 6.1.

Only for the year 2006 is data on those who went to the United States under the employment-based immigration scheme available. Figure 6.2 shows the integrated number of emigrating Filipino nurses. The United States turns out to be the greatest host country, barely surpassing Saudi Arabia in terms of integrated figure.[9]

The large and continuous outflow of nurses from the Philippines to other countries is motivated by the huge wage gap. According to interviews at the College of Nursing, University of the Philippines, a typical Filipino nurse working in the United States in 2007 earns US$40 per hour and works for 12 hours per day, three days a week. Multiplied by 52 weeks, the estimated annual earnings amount to US$75,000 per annum.[10] At the same time, the average monthly wage rate of professional nurses in the Philippines in June 2004 was 8669 pesos,[11] which was almost equivalent to US$1856 per annum in 2004. Hence, nurses'

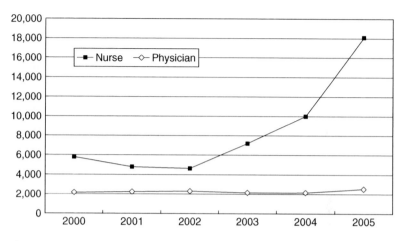

Figure 6.3: Number of newly registered physicians and nurses in the Philippines (unit: persons)
Source: Department of Labour and Employment (2007), Table 12.8.

earnings in the United States are about 30 times greater than their counterparts' earnings in the Philippines.[12]

Supply of medical personnel

This opportunity greatly stimulates the supply of nurses in the Philippines. Figure 6.3 demonstrates the rapid growth of newly registered nurses in the country for 2003–5. The new registration as nurses tripled in 2005 compared to the period of 2000–2, while the number of newly registered physicians remained stable (Figure 6.3).

This dramatic increase in newly registered nurses might be interpreted as evidence supporting the brain-gain hypothesis which was raised in the previous section. In fact, the number of newly registered nurses exceeds that of the outflow of nurses in 2005 (compare Figures 6.1 and 6.3).[13] These observations seemingly testify to the positive effect of employment opportunities abroad on the supply of medical workers in local labour markets. However, the reality is not so simple. An interesting fact is that there are many cases of medical doctors and clinical technologists as well as information and technology professionals quitting their jobs and attempting to become nurses, even if it requires two years of nursing school.[14] As a result, the number of applicants for medical school in the Philippines has also plummeted.[15] The huge wage gap between nurses in the United States and skilled workers in the Philippines is sufficient for the skilled workers to throw away their accumulated human capital in the form of high skills and to embark upon a new career. The average annual earnings of medical doctors in private hospitals in June 2004 were as low as 204,828 pesos,[16] which is equivalent to US$3,655. So, although the number of registered nurses has dramatically increased, it is not the case that the brain-gain effect outweighs the brain-drain effect.

The current situation of medical services in the Philippines, with its massive outflows of medical personnel, is often referred to as 'crisis'. In September 2005, the head of the World Health Organization Country Office in the Philippines, Jean Marc Olive, loudly warned of the crisis.[17] Landingin (2005) reported that 115 towns out of more than 1500 in the whole country did not have a doctor. Rodolfo and Dacanay indicated that both the number of private hospitals and their beds decreased markedly from 1964 to 2003 (2006: 93). The few optimistic views[18] are essentially outweighed by these pessimistic observations. The Philippines suffers the loss of human capital investments, which are made substantially by the government, when Filipino nurses leave for abroad, and the human capital investments made in the Philippines will benefit the destination countries. Moreover, when it comes to persons trained as doctors going abroad as nurses instead, the investments made for them to become doctors are completely lost. Thus, these externality[19] and inefficiency problems have to be addressed somehow.

6.2.2 South Africa

Trends in outflow

South Africa is one of the greatest source countries for medical personnel in sub-Saharan Africa (WHO 2006: 100). The data on emigration from, and immigration to, South Africa is collected by the Department of Home Affairs. Figure 6.4 shows that immigration and emigration are negatively associated and fluctuate strongly. Since the 1990s, there has been an upward trend in emigration and a downward trend in immigration.

Figure 6.5 shows that the number of emigrating medical doctors and nurses increased from 1997 to 2003.[20] The magnitude of emigration of nurses displayed in Figure 6.5 is far smaller than that of the Philippines as displayed in Figures 6.1 and 6.2. As shown later, the figures incorporating total outflows of nurses from South Africa are far smaller than the figures of the flow of nurses coming from South Africa to the United Kingdom which are collected by the latter country (see Figure 6.10). This discrepancy seems to testify to the underestimation of emigration data collected by South Africa in general, as is claimed by Brown, Kaplan and Meyer (2002).

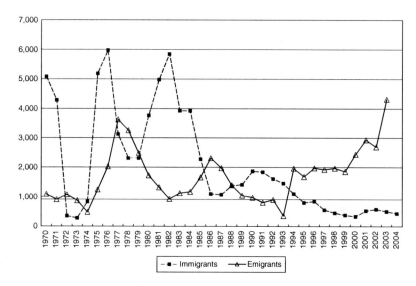

Figure 6.4: Trends in immigration and emigration in South Africa (unit: persons)

Source: Simelane (1999); Statistics South Africa (SSA), *Documented Migration*, Pretoria: SSA, various issues; SSA, *Bulletin of Statistics*, Vol. 39, No. 4, December 2005

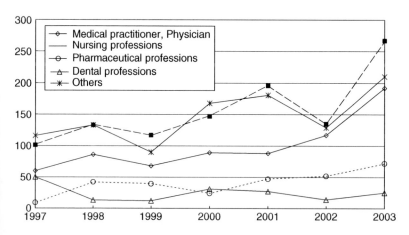

Figure 6.5: Outflow of medical personnel from South Africa (unit: persons)

Source: Statistics South Africa (SSA), *Documented Migration*, Pretoria: SSA, various issues.

Outflow offset by inflow from lower-income countries

South Africa is known as a highly diverse society. The country is one of the most advanced countries in science and technology in the African continent, while poverty remains a serious problem throughout the country, as does the spread of HIV/AIDS. South African workers trained in the use of high technology participate in international labour markets where their skills can be most effectively utilized and highly rewarded (*The Economist* 2005; Kahn et al. 2004). This situation applies to medical personnel, too. As a result, high percentages of medical doctors, nurses and midwives trained in South Africa go abroad to work and earn a larger income. As a result, skilled medical personnel are in short supply throughout the country, and this is an issue that has become particularly serious in rural areas (Padarath, Ntuli and Berthiaume 2004; Paton 2006). The shortage of skilled workers has been recognized by the government of South Africa as a critical problem which is likely to impede the country's further development. In 2006, the government launched the Joint Initiative for Priority Skills Acquisition (JIPSA) and has requested all stakeholders to participate in this initiative. However, the first priority is placed on the employment of engineers and artisans for infrastructure development, and the plan is to include 'high-level planning and management skills in public health and education' in the second phase of JIPSA (Mantashe 2006).

A feature which distinguishes South Africa from other source countries that supply medical personnel is that the country is richer than its neighbouring countries, and so the shortage in medical personnel is partly filled by an inflow of recruits to South Africa from low-income countries in the same region (*The Economist* 2005). Aware that this compensating inflow may aggravate the shortage of medical personnel in its neighbouring countries, the South African government has followed a policy of orderly recruitment. South Africa is a signatory of the Commonwealth Code of Practice for the International Recruitment of Health Workers (Padarath, Ntuli and Berthiaume 2004: 302; WHO 2006: 104–5). Moreover, the country has published a Policy on Recruitment and Employment of Foreign Health Professionals in the Republic of South Africa (National Department of Health 2006). In short, disorderly recruitment of foreign health workers is strongly discouraged by the government, though whether this policy penetrates to South Africa's rural areas is not altogether clear. The government maintains bilateral agreements with Cuba, Iran and Tunisia for the orderly recruitment of health workers.[21] The agreement with Cuba has been maintained since 1996 (Mine 1996: 220; OECD 2004). In addition, in 2003 a bilateral

agreement was concluded with the United Kingdom on both the outflow and inflow of medical personnel. A favourable evaluation of this
agreement was made in April 2006.[22] The experiences of South Africa
imply that bilateral agreements and codes of conduct between countries may mitigate market-driven flows of medical personnel, if a strong
commitment is made by the relevant parties.

6.3   What is happening in the receiving countries?: the cases of Saudi Arabia, the United Kingdom and the United States

International labour markets are most likely to be buyers' markets
because of the competition among the many competing labour-sending
countries and the ample labour force in large host countries. Changes
in the economic and political situations in the host countries critically
affect employment of foreign workers, even those with special skills such
as medical services. Therefore, it is important to review the economic,
political and social environments of the main recipient countries in order
to investigate the prospects for international migration by medical personnel. Saudi Arabia, the United Kingdom and the United States are
chosen for case studies because of their great influence.

6.3.1   Saudi Arabia

Saudi Arabia has been a destination for migrant workers ever since oil
was discovered there in the 1930s. The country became the top recipient in the Middle East of Asian workers in the 1980s and continues to
be a favourite destination (UNESCAP 1987:18, Table 3). As a spacious,
resource-rich, but labour-poor country, Saudi Arabia has continuously
attracted a large number of contract workers, except for the period of
the Gulf War in 1991. Because of the small size of the Saudi population
and a low labour participation ratio, particularly for women, Saudi Arabia has generated a steady demand for the labour of foreign workers.[23]
Medical services are one of several sectors that demonstrate Saudi Arabia's
dependence on foreign labour power.

Structure of health institutions

The data on medical personnel in Saudi Arabia is examined in detail
below, but it is first necessary to take into account the structure of health
institutions in Saudi Arabia. The main elements of this structure are
displayed in Figure 6.6.

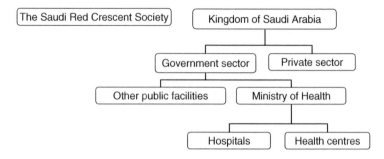

Figure 6.6:   Structure of health-related institutions in Saudi Arabia

Health services in the Kingdom of Saudi Arabia are supplied by both the government and the private sector. In addition, the Saudi Red Crescent Society provides medical services for pilgrims going to Mecca. The scale of the private sector is fairly small. In the field of medicine in Saudi Arabia, the private sector plays only a small part, and the main institution responsible for the provision of health services for Saudis is the government, in the form of the Ministry of Health. The Ministry supervises hospitals and health centres.

There were gently rising trends in the total number of medical personnel working for the kingdom throughout the 1990s.[24] The trends reflect a steady but moderate growth in demand for medical personnel. By contrast, the growth in foreign physicians, nurses and other health personnel has been less rapid. As a result, there was an increase in the Saudi share of the medical personnel working in the kingdom in the 1990s, as shown in Figure 6.7. This is a result of policies that have placed a high priority on employment of Saudis over non-Saudis, known as 'Saudization'.

Saudization partially comes into effect

Viewed in historical terms, the share of Saudis in the number of medical personnel employed in Saudi Arabia has followed a long-term pattern (Figure 6.7 for medical staff working for the Ministry of Health[25]). In terms of the Saudi ratio of physicians, there has been a shallow U-shaped trend that bottomed out in 1979–80.[26] In 1970–1, only 12.8 per cent of the physicians working for the Ministry of Health were Saudi. The percentage thereafter declined further, probably reflecting the accumulation of abundant financial resources following hikes in the oil price.

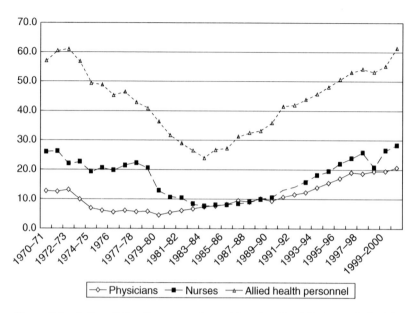

Figure 6.7: Ratio of Saudi personnel working for the Ministry of Health (unit: per cent)

Source: Kingdom of Saudi Arabia, Ministry of Economy and Planning, Central Department of Statistics, *Statistical Yearbook*, various years.

Since then, the Saudization ratio has increased steadily, and by 2000–1, it amounted to 20.7 per cent. Even so, approximately four out of five doctors working for the Kingdom of Saudi Arabia were foreigners in 2000–1. The Saudization ratios for nurses and for allied health personnel show initial medium-term decreases and subsequent medium-term increases, though the two ratios are distinct from each other.

Another kind of structural change is apparent in the long-term trend in the Saudization ratio of nurses. The number of female nurses increased in the 1970s and a majority of them came from abroad. According to the *Statistical Yearbook* published by the Central Department of Statistics, in the early 1960s there were as many males as females working as nurses for the Ministry of Health.[27] In the late 1960s, the number of male nurses was double that of female nurses. Then, a structural change in the composition of nurses occurred in the 1970s. In 1970–1, there were only 60 Saudi female nurses and the number of non-Saudi female nurses, 720, was smaller than that of non-Saudi male nurses, which was 946.

Throughout the 1970s, the number of male nurses, irrespective of origin, remained stable at around 1000 persons, while the number of Saudi female nurses increased slightly. By contrast, the number of non-Saudi female nurses increased dramatically. The number of non-Saudi female nurses grew by more than 800 per cent between 1970–1 and 1980–1. In other words, the development of medical services in Saudi Arabia during the 1970s involving the recruitment of female nurses resulted in the feminization of the profession.

As mentioned above, the Saudization policies work to a certain extent. The policies date back to 1970 (Ramady 2005: 355). However, so far as medical personnel were concerned, they had little effect until the mid-1980s. The estimated ratio of expatriate workers to total employment increased from 14.1 per cent in 1963 to 53.3 per cent in 1980 (Sirageldin, Sherbiny and Serageldin 1984: 66, Table 4.2). The period when the policies were geared up was during the third development plan for 1980–5. While the second development plan for 1975–80 featured quantitative expansion of the economy, such as building physical infrastructure and human resources, the third development plan focused more on qualitative issues, such as better utilization of infrastructure and human resources (UNESCAP 1987: 146–50). Along the line, the priority on utilization of Saudi labour power was made explicit. The fourth development plan took a step forward toward Saudization. It set a numeric target, calling for a reduction in the number of foreign workers by 600,000 by 1990, while the number of Saudi workers would be augmented by 375,000. At the same time, the education of Saudis was prioritized. Moreover, the government of Saudi Arabia did not authorize the hiring of foreign workers if Saudi workers were available to undertake the job sufficiently well.

Even though considerable progress was made toward Saudization in the late 1990s, the Saudi share of medical personnel is still low. The ratio was 21.3 per cent for physicians working in the whole kingdom in 2000–1, while the ratios for nurses and allied health personnel were 19.3 per cent and 45.9 per cent respectively.

To sum up, the oil-price hike in 1973 enabled Saudi Arabia to hire more workers from abroad than hitherto. Medical doctors and female nurses were introduced on a substantial scale, and foreigners came to assume a virtually dominant position among the medical personnel of the country in the 1980s. Since then, Saudization has gradually come into effect, and the share of Saudi medical personnel has increased, though a great majority of the physicians and nurses are still non-Saudi. In any event,

Saudi Arabia had its own reasons for adjusting the inflow of medical personnel and requested source countries to accommodate to them accordingly.

6.3.2 The United Kingdom

The United Kingdom finds it difficult to secure a sufficient number of medical personnel irrespective of job category. The problem is structural in the sense that it stems from the British population pyramid, which is skewed towards older people. The rise of the nuclear family is another trend that is generating a greater demand for hospital medical services. These factors have facilitated the international recruitment of medical personnel by the state-run National Health Service. A substantial wage gap between the United Kingdom and low-income countries has caused a massive flow of medical personnel from developing countries to Britain (Bach 2003: 21–4, Yamada 2004).

Mandela's criticism and codes of practice

In 1997, Nelson Mandela criticized the United Kingdom for recruiting nurses from South Africa and argued that British policy was threatening to cause a shortage of nursing staff which would put at risk the health of South African nationals. Since then, the British government's Department of Health has taken two approaches to address the criticism. One of these approaches has been to preserve ethical standards by establishing codes of conduct for employers and agents, and the other has been to sign bilateral agreements with the governments of the source countries (Bach 2003).

In response to various criticisms including that of Mandela, in 1999 the Department of Health issued guidelines to employers in the public sector, advising them to refrain from 'actively' recruiting nurses from developing countries that are suffering from shortages of nursing staff. South Africa and the Caribbean were listed as territories from which recruitment should be avoided. In the terminology employed by the government, 'actively' also rules out the employment of unsolicited applicants (Bach 2003: 22). As long as employers did not actively solicit immigration and did not recruit nurses from unlisted countries, they were not held to blame. It should be noted that the private sector lay outside the scope of these guidelines.

In 2001, a new code of practice was issued by the Department of Health. The new code suggests that employers should not target developing countries for the recruitment of medical personnel. A difference between the guidelines issued in 1999 and 2001 is that, in the 2001 guidelines, employers in the private sector were also strongly encouraged to sign the code.

In July 2006, the United Kingdom issued a policy that resembled the code of practice of 2001, but with a different goal. The government had decided not to issue work permits to newly qualified foreign nurses unless they were employed for some specific jobs that are not easily filled by nurses trained in the European Economic Area (EEA)[28] or in the United Kingdom. The main purpose of this policy change is not to address the shortage of medical personnel in developing countries, but to help home-grown nurses find employment. In this regard, it should be noted that only 20 per cent of newly graduating nurses in the United Kingdom found jobs in the summer of 2006 (Hall 2006).

Bilateral agreements

The second approach to address criticisms of British recruitment policy is reflected in the bilateral agreements that Britain has signed with the developing countries from which medical personnel have immigrated to the United Kingdom. In this connection, Britain has concluded agreements with several countries, including Egypt, India, the Philippines, Spain and South Africa (Bach 2003: 23; WHO 2006: 104). The agreement with the Philippines was concluded between the British Department of Health and the POEA in 2002. The agreement sets out, among other things, the standard rates of various fees, such as the cost of the initial application for registration as a nurse in the United Kingdom, the entry visa application cost, the processing fee for employers to pay the POEA, and the contribution to the Workers' Welfare Fund. This means that unscrupulous charges are less likely to be imposed on immigrant Filipino workers entering the UK (Bach 2003: 23–4).

The UK's bilateral agreement with South Africa, signed in 2003, recognizes an unusual feature of the South African situation in that in the case of South Africa, not only outflow but also inflow of medical personnel is substantial. Thus, the agreement stresses the necessity of mutual exchange of information and expertise and also covers UK health professionals immigrating to South Africa, even though the scale of such emigration is far less than the flow in the opposite direction. The agreement also covers the training and study needed for a health professional of one country to undertake work in the other country. Behind this scheme lies the notion that, after the exchange period, the professional returns to her/his home country, and her/his post is kept open for her/him to reoccupy without difficulty (WHO 2006: 104). As mentioned

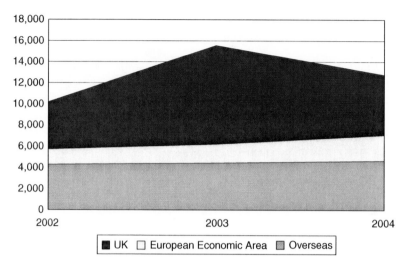

Figure 6.8: Newly registered doctors in the United Kingdom (unit: persons)
Source: General Medical Council (2005).

in the subsection on South Africa, the effectiveness of this agreement was evaluated by the two countries in April 2006, and both countries' evaluations were favourable regarding continued implementation of the agreement.

Trends in inflow

As a result of changes in British policy, the number of foreign medical personnel fluctuates more than that of native medical personnel, and the composition of medical personnel by source country has changed substantially. Figure 6.8 indicates that the number of registered doctors who were educated overseas varies for 2002–4, while those educated in the United Kingdom and the EEA increase smoothly and moderately. This trend is reproduced for registered nurses and midwives. Figure 6.9 demonstrates that the number of overseas workers is somewhat more volatile than that of the UK and the EEA. Those from overseas act like an adjustment valve for those trained in the UK and the EEA.

The backdrop of the volatility is the change in the composition of the source countries. Regarding nurses, data on the number of them by country of origin is available. Figure 6.10 displays the fluctuations in the number of nurses by major source countries. It is apparent that since South Africa was included in the list of source areas from which

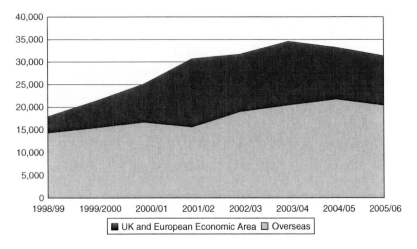

Figure 6.9:   Newly registered nurses and midwives in the United Kingdom (unit: persons)
Source: The Nursing and Midwifery Council (NMC), *Statistical Analysis of the Register*, various issues, London: NMC.

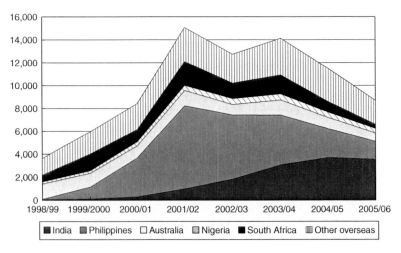

Figure 6.10:   Newly registered overseas nurses and midwives in the United Kingdom by source country (unit: persons)
Source: As for Figure 6.9.

active recruitment of medical personnel should be avoided, inflow from the Philippines and India has grown as a result. After the conclusion of the bilateral agreement between the UK and the Philippines in 2002, the number of nurses coming from the Philippines seems to have been strictly controlled and has decreased up to the time of this writing. In the meantime, inflow from India was on the rise by 2004–5.

6.3.3 The United States

The United States is a large country which always exerts a large impact on the global market of medical personnel. Moreover, the atmosphere of the country is open and liberal toward migrants since the country was founded by immigrants from Europe and, later, the rest of the world. There are societies of various ethnic origins which accommodate new-comers of the same origin. Therefore, the United States is a favourite destination for all immigrants except when the political situation in the United States is at odds with immigration.

In fact, the country was a major destination for Filipino nurses up to the first half of the 1990s, as shown in Figure 6.1. Note that the Philippines is one of the most important countries in terms of outflow of medical personnel. However, the momentum of recruitment of Filipino nurses somehow weakened in the second half of the 1990s (Figure 6.1). This drop in the supply of nurses was a general tendency seen among nurses working in the United States overall. Figure 6.11 displays the trend in the number of newly qualified nurses by place of education. The figure shows that the number of US-educated nurses who passed the examination on their first try declined in the second half of the 1990s.

This drop in the supply of nurses was taken seriously by the Department of Health and Human Services in 2000 (Brush, Sochalski and Berger 2004: 78–9). Brush, Sochalski and Berger stated that the department immediately started attempting to address the shortage in medical personnel. A new set of policies was adopted to increase the recruitment of foreign nurses, and this set of policies was powerful in the following three respects: 1) its expansion of organized international nurse recruitment; 2) its involvement of private and for-profit agencies to hire foreign nurses; and 3) its increase of the number of source countries.

These policy changes resulted in an increase in the number of 'internationally educated'[29] nurses, as shown in Figure 6.12. The figure in 2005 almost tripled from that in 2000. The number of US-educated nurses in 2005 also returned to the level of 1995, as demonstrated in Figure 6.11. The third policy, which was the diversification of source countries, was

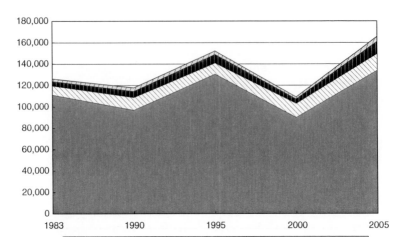

Figure 6.11:   Newly qualified nurses in the United States by place of education

fulfilled too. It is apparent in Figure 6.12 that, in addition to nurses educated in the Philippines, those from India, the Republic of Korea and
'Others' increased between 2000 and 2005.

An initiative that symbolizes the strengthened recruitment efforts is
the conducting of examinations overseas for accreditation as US nurses.
The first overseas examination took place in August 2007 in Manila in
the Philippines.[30] Such convenience undoubtedly facilitates Filipinos'
applications to work as nurses in the US.

Due to the abovementioned new policies, the United States is currently
regarded as a popular destination. The employment-based immigration
scheme, which was mentioned in the subsection on the Philippines,
offers immigration visas to nurses. Moreover, the nurse's family is also
allowed to come to the United States with the nurse (Rodolfo and
Dacanay 2006: 78). Thus, the United States will continue to be a magnet
for foreign nurses.

6.4   How to manage migration of doctors and nurses from developing countries

All five countries presented here as case studies are ambivalent about
the international migration of medical personnel. Source countries such

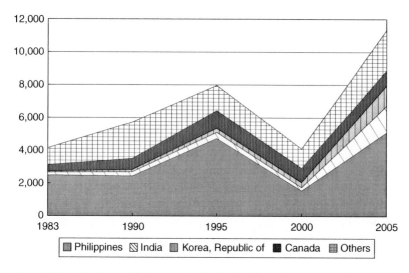

Figure 6.12: Newly qualified nurses in the United States by country of education (internationally educated and passed in the first examination)
Note: Both 'registered' and 'licensed practical/vocational' nurses are included.
Source: National Council of State Boards of Nursing (1985, 1991); Brown, Yocom and White (1997); Crawford et al. (2001); Kenward et al. (2006).

as the Philippines and South Africa welcome the substantial amount of earnings raised abroad and remitted back. At the same time, both countries worry about the damaging effects of the outflow on their own national health systems. Meanwhile, the host countries are not entirely pleased about the prospect of foreign professionals becoming dominant in domestic health sectors, which are of crucial importance to the welfare of their nationals. However, they desperately need help from abroad to sustain medical service at home.

There are two points of view on how to better handle migration of medical personnel for both source and destination countries. First, formal nation-to-nation agreement on migration of medical personnel should be established. The examples of this are the agreement between the Philippines and the United Kingdom and the code of conduct among the British Commonwealth countries, both of which were mentioned in previous sections.

There are advantages to these kinds of formal relationships. The first advantage is facilitation of monitoring of the migration processes. Close monitoring will result in better protection of workers. With closer monitoring according to an agreement, there will be less likelihood that migration contracts will be implicit, and migrants' human rights will be more likely to be protected.

The second advantage is high predictability as to the amount of flows of migration. As described above, the destination countries have changed their policies from time to time. Lenient and open policies may be quickly followed by restrictive policies, according to changing economic and political circumstances in the destination countries. In most cases, the bargaining power of the source countries is so weak that they find themselves obliged to adjust to changes in demand for medical personnel generated in destination countries. As a result, even the Philippines, which is one of the most important suppliers of medical personnel in the world, faces large and unpredictable variations in demand over time. Bilateral or multi-country agreements make the future of labour flows more foreseeable and reduce the probability that destination countries will suddenly shut the door to migrant workers.

The second viewpoint on how to better handle migration of medical personnel involves promotion of medical tourism. Medical tourism is a reverse flow of migration of consumers for medical services to the countries which would otherwise send medical personnel abroad. Modern transportation allows consumers to travel at a low cost as well as take advantage of low labour costs. If consumers travel to a developing country to receive medical services, instead of workers moving from developing countries to the country of origin of the consumers, then the pressure for emigration of medical personnel from the developing country to the developed country will be attenuated. Although medical tourism to developing countries is unlikely to substitute completely for the outflow of medical personnel, it will help in keeping medical personnel at home in developing countries to a certain extent. As a matter of fact, some developing countries, such as Cuba, Malaysia, Singapore and Thailand, have already started encouraging medical tourism to their countries (Rodolfo and Dakanay 2006: 90–1).

The main purpose of medical tourism is to provide high-quality medical service to foreigners for cheaper costs. The resources for medical services will be mobilized for foreign tourists rather than local people. Therefore, it seems there is no point for local people to facilitate medical tourism. One of the benefits of medical tourism is the transfer of advanced skills and technology maintained or gained in host countries through personnel and facilities employed for foreign patients. This spillover effect is lost if the medical professionals emigrate. A caveat is the same loss in technology transfer is applicable if the hospitals are isolated from the local communities, becoming nothing but enclaves of foreigners and medical personnel working exclusively for them.

Secondly, some hospitals which have already established medical tourism have begun providing medical services to local communities by fulfilling their 'corporate social responsibility'.[31] As long as the hospitals are located in developing countries and medical personnel remain in the country, both intentional and spontaneous spillover effects, either through technology transfer or direct provision of medical services to local communities, may be present. Such an 'externality' generated by highly skilled medical staff and advanced medical technology is completely lost once the medical personnel leave the home country for developed countries.

In the age of globalization, both medical personnel and patients are mobile. Given this, the situation where the patients are mobile and the medical personnel are stationary is more beneficial to developing countries than the situation where the medical personnel are mobile and the patients are stationary. In this sense, medical tourism is a valuable experiment for a developing country suffering from loss of medical personnel. This policy may help the country forestall potential emigration and attract investments in medical services to the country.

6.5   Concluding remarks

How to secure medical personnel is a critical problem in both developed and developing countries. Some developing countries, in particular middle-income countries which have a certain amount of skilled medical personnel, are losing medical professionals due to emigration to higher income countries.

Various efforts by trial and error have been attempted by both source and destination countries to address this issue. Saudi Arabia, the United Kingdom and the United States are main recipient countries, and they have both an intention to attract foreign doctors and nurses and a hesitation about raising dependence on them. Source countries, such as the Philippines and South Africa, are obliged to respond to such capricious changes in policies in the destination countries passively, playing the role of an adjustment valve.

Two feasible measures to address the difficulties faced by the source countries were reviewed: one is formal agreements between the source and destination countries, while the other is promotion of the medical tourism industry in the source countries. The former helps monitor the migration processes effectively and makes the flow of migration more predictable. This policy is widely applied and looks to be working effectively. The latter is an experimental idea which may mitigate the loss of medical personnel from the source countries and would generate a positive spillover effect for the local economy, an effect that is created by the highly skilled medical personnel remaining at home and by the foreign capital attracted by the medical tourism industry. These measures, hopefully, will make the outflow of medical personnel from developing countries more orderly and will enhance their incentives to stay in the source countries.

Notes

1. It is well known that the supply of medical personnel is critically insufficient to take care of people living with HIV/AIDS, now that antiretroviral medicines have become more widely available in developing countries thanks to the Global Fund and other initiatives (WHO 2006: 144; Dräger, Gedik and Dal Poz 2006).
2. Note that Mexico is included under 'Latin America and Caribbean'.
3. The countries are Angola, Cameroon, Ethiopia, Ghana, Mozambique, Nigeria, South Africa, Uganda, United Republic of Tanzania, and Zimbabwe.
4. They are Australia, Canada, Finland, France, Germany, Portugal, the United Kingdom and the United States.
5. The countries are Angola, Botswana, Cameroon, Ethiopia, Ghana, Guinea-Bissau, Kenya, Lesotho, Malawi, Mauritius, Mozambique, Namibia, Nigeria, South Africa, Swaziland, Uganda, United Republic of Tanzania, Zambia and Zimbabwe.
6. The countries are Canada, Denmark, Finland, Ireland, Portugal, the United Kingdom and the United States.
7. Emigration of medical personnel dates back to 1965 when the US Immigration Act abolished the national origin quota system. Filipino doctors, nurses, dental technicians and dietitians took advantage of this to immigrate to the United States (Catholic Institute for International Relations 1987: 17). For readers who can read Japanese, see Yamada (2004, 2006) on contemporary emigration of Filipino medical personnel.
8. The data on remittance is cited from Bangko Sentral ng Pilipinas, *Selected Philippine Economic Indicators*, September 2007. The export data is found on the website of the Philippine National Statistics Office: www.census.gov.ph/data/sectordata/tsft.htm.
9. According to internal information, out of 5651 Filipino nurses migrating to the United States in 2006, 5449 nurses, or 96.4 per cent, were covered by the employment-based immigration scheme.
10. The estimate is calculated assuming US$40/hour, 12 hours/day, 3 days/week, 52 weeks/year, which equals US$74,880. Brush, Sochalski and Berger (2004) state that foreign nurses earned US$43,850 per annum in 2002. Rodolfo and Dacanay indicated the earnings of nurses in the United States were around US$48,000 (Rodolfo and Dacanay (2006: 78)).
11. This figure is cited from Table 8.6 of the Department of Labour and Employment (2007).

12. According to the same source, some Filipino nurses are employed by two hospitals so that they work for six days a week and earn twice as much as the typical nurse. Those who desperately want to earn money work on the remaining day so that they work seven days a week.

13. Again, notice that the outflows exhibited in Figure 6.1 do not include workers going to the United States under the employment-based immigration scheme.

14. For the trend wherein medical doctors go to the United States as nurses, see Landingin (2005) and Rodolfo and Dacanay (2006: 78–82), among others.

15. The number of National Medical Admission Test examinees dropped from 6245 in 2000 to 2912 in 2005 (Rodolfo and Dacanay 2006: 78–9).

16. The source is the same as that given in Footnote 11.

17. See *Balita*, an online journal based in the Philippines (http://ofw.balita.ph/ html/article.php/20050921004055668) and *Mainichi Shimbun*, published in Japan, on 21 and 22 September 2005.

18. See a news article by the DOLE on November 12, 2003 (www.dole.gov.ph/ news/print.asp?id=N000001030), among others.

19. The benefit, which is not paid by the beneficiaries through market transactions, is called an 'externality' in economics.

20. Data was not collected between 2003 and 2006 because of an institutional change, which was revoked in 2006. See Statistics South Africa (2004, 2006).

21. This information was provided by Ms T. R. Mdlalose (Director, Human Resource Stakeholder Relations and Management, Department of Health) and Mrs Gcinile Buthelezi (Director, Human Resource Policy Research and Planning, Department of Health) on 12 December 2006 at the Department of Health, Republic of South Africa.

22. The source is the same as the previous footnote.

23. A counteracting factor is the high fertility rate. The fertility rate defined as the number of infants per woman is 6.2 in Saudi Arabia, while the same figure is 4.1 on average for all Arab countries and 3.1 on average for all developing countries for 1995–2000 (Ramady 2005: 354).

24. For details on the time series of foreign medical personnel in Saudi Arabia, see Section 4 of Yamagata (2007).

25. Only data of non-Saudi personnel working for the Ministry of Health are available for the 1970s.

26. All statistics for Saudi Arabia in this chapter are based on the Hegira calendar. The Hegira calendar starts on the day that the Prophet Mohammed migrated from Mecca to Medina. The Hegira year has 354 days divided into 12 lunar months (Kingdom of Saudi Arabia 2004: 15).

27. The data on the number of nurses by sex and origin is available only for 1970/71 to 1980/81 in the *Statistical Yearbook*. Precisely speaking, 'female nurses' include midwives and their assistants, too.

28. The European Economic Area includes Austria, Belgium, Cyprus, Czech Republic, Denmark, Estonia, Finland, France, Germany, Greece, Hungary, Iceland, Irish Republic, Italy, Latvia, Liechtenstein, Lithuania, Luxembourg, Malta, the Netherlands, Norway, Poland, Portugal, Slovakia, Slovenia, Spain, Sweden, and Switzerland. Travel among the EU member countries is substantially liberalized.

29. The term 'internationally educated' implies that the nurse has been educated outside the United States immediately before taking the examination.

30. This was announced at www.ncsbn.org/1282.htm. See Matsuno (2007), as well.
31. See the website of the Bumrungrad Hospital, which is one of the pioneers in this industry in Thailand, as an example (www.bumrungrad.com/overseas-medical-care/About-Us/Factsheet.aspx). This site indicates that the hospital is dedicated to helping the underprivileged in Thailand, offering access to free healthcare services.

References

Abella, M. I. and M. A. Abrera-Mangahas (1997) *Sending Workers Abroad: A Manual for Low- and Middle-Income Countries*, Geneva: International Labour Office.
Achacoso, T. D. (1987) *Market Development and Organizational Change in the Field of Overseas Employment Administration: The Philippine Experience*, Manila: Philippine Overseas Employment Administration.
Ahmad, O. B. (2005) 'Managing Medical Migration from Poor Countries', *British Medical Journal*. CCCXXXI (July 2, 2005): 43–5.
Amante, M. S. V. (2007) *Labour Dimension of the Japan-Philippine Economic Partnership Agreement (JPEPA)*, Visiting Research Fellow Monograph Series No. 429 (Chiba, Japan: Institute of Developing Economies, Japan External Trade Organization), at: www.ide.go.jp/English/Inter/Vrf/pdf/vrf_429.pdf
Bach, S. (2003) *International Migration of Health Workers: Labour and Social Issues*, Working Paper, Sectoral Activities Programme, Geneva: International Labour Office.
Beine, M., F. Docquier and H. Rapoport (2001) 'Brain Drain and Economic Growth: Theory and Evidence', *Journal of Development Economics*, LXIV: 275–89.
Brown, M., D. Kaplan and J.-B. Meyer (2001) 'The Brain Drain: An Outline of Skilled Emigration from South Africa', in D. A. McDonald and J. Crush (eds) *Destinations Unknown: Perspectives on the Brain Drain in Southern Africa*: Pretoria: Africa Institute of South Africa: 99–112.
Brown, V. D., C. J. Yocom and E. L. White (1997) *1995-1996 Licensure and Examination Statistics*, Chicago: National Council of State Boards of Nursing.
Brush, B. L., J. Sochalski and A. M. Berger (2004) 'Imported Care: Recruiting Foreign Nurses to US Health Care Facilities', *Health Affairs*, XXIII: 78–87.
Catholic Institute for International Relations (1987) *The Labour Trade: Filipino Migrant Workers around the World*, Manila: Friends of Filipino Migrant Workers, Inc. [KAIBIGAN] and National Secretariat for Social Action [NASSA].
Chalamwong, Y., 'The Migration of Highly Skilled Asian Workers to OECD Member Countries and Its Effects on Economic Development in East Asia', in K. Fukasaku, M. Kawai, M. G. Plummer and A. Trzeciak-Duval (eds) *Policy Coherence towards East Asia: Development Challenges for OECD Countries*, Paris: Organization for Economic Cooperation and Development [OECD], 487–523.
Crawford, L., C. Marks, S. H. Gawel, E. White and L. Obichere (2001) *2000 Licensure and Examination Statistics*, Chicago: National Council of State Boards of Nursing.
Department of Labour and Employment (DOLE), The Philippines (2007) *2006 Yearbook of Labour Statistics*, Manila: DOLE.

Dräger, S., G. Gedik, and M. R. Dal Poz (2006) 'Health Workforce Issues and the Global Fund to Fight AIDS, Tuberculosis, and Malaria: An Analytical Review', *Human Resources for Health*, IV, at: http://www.human-resources-health.com/content/4/1/23.

Economist, The (2005) 'African Migration: Home, Sweet Home – For Some', 13 August, 37-8.

General Medical Council (GMC) (2005) *Annual Review 2004/05*, London: GMC.

Hall, S. (2006) 'Foreign Nurses Barred in Attempt to Help Homegrown Candidates', *The Guardian*, 4 July.

International Labor Organization (ILO) (1988) *Agenda for Policy: Asian Migration Project*, Bangkok: ILO.

Kahn, M., W. Blankley, R. Maharajh, T. E. Pogue, V. Reddy, G. Cele and M. du Toit (2004) *Flight of the Flamingos: A Study on the Mobility of R&D Workers*, Cape Town: Human Sciences Research Council Publishers.

Kapur, D. and J. McHale (2005) *Give Us Your Best and Brightest: The Global Hunt for Talent and Its Impact on the Developing World*, Washington DC: Center for Global Development.

Kenward, K., T. R. O'Neill, M. Eich and E. White (2006) *2005 Nurse Licensee Volume and NCLEX Examination Statistics, NCBN Research Brief* XXV, Chicago: National Council of State Boards of Nursing.

Kingdom of Saudi Arabia, Ministry of Economy and Planning, Central Department of Statistics (2004), *Statistical Yearbook, 2003*, Kingdom of Saudi Arabia.

Landingin, R. (2005) 'Philippines Faces Healthcare Crisis as Doctors Leave for Better Paid Jobs Abroad', *Financial Times*, 26 September.

Mantashe, G. (2006) 'Comment: Universities Drawn into Skills Development Scheme', *Mail and Guardian*, South Africa, 10–16 November.

Matsuno, A. (2007) 'Nurse Migration: The Asian Perspective', mimeograph, Bangkok: International Labor Organization.

Mejia, A. (1978) 'Migration of Physicians and Nurses: A Worldwide Picture', *International Journal of Epidemiology*, VII (1978): 207–15.

Mine, Y. (1996) *Minami Afurika: Niji no Kunie no Ayumi* [South Africa: Towards the Rainbow Nation], Tokyo: Iwanami-Shoten.

Mountford, A. (1997) 'Can a Brain Drain be Good for Growth in the Source Economy?', *Journal of Development Economics* LIII: 287–303.

National Council of State Boards of Nursing (1985) *1983 and 1984 Licensure and Examination Statistics*, Chicago: National Council of State Boards of Nursing.

National Council of State Boards of Nursing (1991) *1990 Licensure and Examination Statistics*, Chicago: National Council of State Boards of Nursing.

National Department of Health, Republic of South Africa (2006) 'Policy: Recruitment and Employment of Foreign Health Professionals in the Republic of South Africa', mimeograph, Pretoria: National Department of Health.

Organisation for Economic Co-operation and Development (OECD) (2004), 'The International Mobility of Health Professionals: An Evaluation and Analysis Based on the Case of South Africa', *Trends in International Migration, Annual Report, 2003 Edition*, Paris: OECD, Part III.

Padarath, A., A. Ntuli and L. Berthiaume (2004) 'Human Resources', in P. Ijumba, C. Day and A. Ntuli (eds) *South African Health Review 2003/04*, Durban: Health Systems Trust: 299–315.

Paton, C. (2006) 'Terminally Ill: Public Hospitals are Missing a Third of the Doctors They Need', *Financial Mail*, South Africa, 14 April, 16–19.

Philippine Overseas Employment Administration (POEA) (2007) *OFW Global Presence: A Compendium of Overseas Employment Statistics 2006*, Manila: POEA.

Physicians for Human Rights (2004) *An Action Plan to Prevent Brain Drain: Building Equitable Health Systems in Africa*, Boston: Physicians for Human Rights.

Ramady, M. A. (2005) *The Saudi Arabian Economy: Policies, Achievements and Challenges*, New York: Springer.

Rodolfo, M. C. L. S. and J. C. Dacanay, 'Challenges in Health Services Trade: The Philippine Case', in G. O. Pasadilla (ed.) *The Global Challenge in Services Trade: A Look at Philippine Competitiveness*, Manila: Philippine Institute for Development Studies, 55–97.

Sagalla, L. B. (1988) 'Study on Overseas Contract Workers (Part 1)', *CB Review* (the Central Bank of the Philippines), XL (1988): 20–6.

Simelane, S. E. (1999) 'Trends in International Migration: Migration among Professionals, Semi-professionals and Miners in South Africa, 1970-1997', paper presented at the Annual Conference of the Demographic Association of Southern Africa (DEMSA), 5–7 July, at Saldanha Bay, Western Cape.

Sirageldin, I. A., N. A. Sherbiny and M. I. Serageldin (1984) *Saudis in Transition: The Challenges of a Changing Labor Market*, New York: Oxford University Press.

Statistics South Africa (2004) *Statistical Release: Tourism and Migration*, Pretoria: Statistics South Africa, April.

Statistics South Africa (2006) *Statistical Release: Tourism and Migration*, Pretoria: Statistics South Africa, August.

United Nations Economic and Social Commission for Asia and the Pacific (UNESCAP) (1987) *International Labour Migration and Remittances between the Developing EACAP Countries and the Middle East: Trends, Issues and Policies*, Development Papers No. 6, Bangkok: UNESCAP.

WHO (World Health Organization) (2004) *Addressing Africa's Health Workforce Crisis: An Avenue for Action*, Abuja, Nigeria: WHO.

WHO (World Health Organization) (2006) *The World Health Report 2006: Working Together for Health*, Geneva: WHO.

World Bank (2006a) *Global Economic Prospects: Economic Implications of Remittances and Migration*, Washington: World Bank.

World Bank (2006b) *2006 World Development Indicators*, CD-Rom, Washington: World Bank.

Yamada, R. (2004) '*Gurobarizeshon to Kango-roudouryoku-ido* (Globalization and International Migration of Nurses)', *Nagoya-Tanki-Daigaku-Kenkyukiyo* (Nagoya, Japan), XLII: 159–76.

Yamada, R. (2006) '*Filipin Kango-roudouryoku no Gurobaruna Ido to Sono Kadai* (Global Movement of Filipino Nurses and Challenges to It)', *Business Labor Trend* (Japan), CCCLXXIII (April): 16–21.

Yamagata, T. (2007) 'Securing Medical Personnel: Cases of Two Source Countries and Two Destination Countries.' Discussion Paper No. 105 (Chiba, Japan: Institute of Developing Economies), at www.ide.go.jp/English/Publish/Dp/Abstract/105.html.

7
Publicly Provided Primary Healthcare Services in Rural India: Achievements, Problems and Possible Solutions

Seiro Ito and Hisaki Kono

Introduction

The recent decades of poverty research have convincingly shown the value of a well-functioning health system in the development process. One of the ways in which poverty manifests itself is in the vicious cycle of ill-health and low income. Many studies have documented how temporary shocks to people's health can have long-lasting effects on their welfare when healthcare is not available at affordable costs. Acknowledging this, more emphasis is now being placed on health outcomes as a primary policy goal across the developing world. The Millennium Development Goals notwithstanding, the Government of India (GOI) has always been a keen advocate of achieving good health among the general public.

However, despite health being set as the overarching goal in general welfare and despite the government's efforts to expand the network of public sector hospitals, the health outcome indicators of India have been slow to respond. As numerous government reports rightly point out, ready access to quality healthcare at an affordable cost remains an illusion for most of the poor. There are many anecdotes that relate the difficulty of accessing quality care, but it is relatively rare to see analysis of the common mechanism behind them. The government reports also are to blame for their scant focus on analysing the mechanism behind inadequate healthcare provision for the poor.

The purpose of this chapter is threefold: to show the government's achievements so far in terms of infrastructure, to show the government's impact on one of the policy goals as described below, and to discuss the possible ways to improve the functioning of the existing hospital network. We show the extent of the effects of the government's effort on hospital network expansion and estimate its impact on one of the health-policy goals, which is the sex ratio of children below six. The results suggest the mere construction of buildings has not been effective in achieving the policy goal, and we point to the incentive problem as the primary issue that the government should tackle. After surveying the existing literature, we list possible interventions that would instill a mechanism to ensure the provision of quality healthcare in the rural Indian context.

7.1 Primary healthcare policies

7.1.1 Health outcome overview

It is widely acknowledged that maternal and child health can be good indicators of the state of the national primary healthcare system. This is justifiable on the grounds that a dismal record in these essential areas of health should be interpreted as a sign of a dismal primary healthcare system. Figure 7.1 shows the national average of infant mortality rates (IMR). As often discussed, early neonatal mortality is high and lowering it has a significant impact on bringing down the IMR. It can also be seen that stillbirths, which are not accounted in computing IMR, are high.

It has been indicated in the literature that the stillbirths are correlated with maternal health status before and after pregnancy, and the early neonatal mortality is correlated with low birth weights. Therefore the policies for promoting maternal health are expected to play a larger role.

The risk of perinatal diseases can be significantly reduced by prior arrangements through periodic prenatal checkups, the provision of which is the state governments' responsibility.

As the data on institutional births (Figure 7.2) and maternal mortality ratio (MMR, Figure 7.3) show, despite the progress being made, fewer than 50 per cent of all births were institutional births in 2002 even in the high-performing states, and MMR is well above the MDG of 105 per 100,000 births. The state governments still have far to go in achieving these health-related goals.

Figure 7.4 shows the disease burden estimated by the WHO in terms of DALY (disability adjusted life years) and deaths. The data shows that the most serious malaise is infectious and parasitic diseases, followed by neuropsychiatric, perinatal, cardiovascular and respiratory diseases. The GOI shows strong interest in particular infectious diseases such as tuberculosis, malaria, Japanese encephalitis, kala azar, dengue fever, chikungunya, polio, leprosy, and HIV/AIDS, but not in other infectious

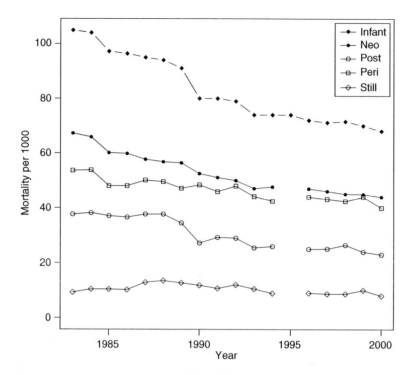

Figure 7.1:   Infant mortality rates (1983–2000)

Notes: 1. Infant mortality is defined as the deaths among 0–1 year olds per 1000. Neonatal mortality is mortality up to 28 days after birth per 1000; perinatal mortality is defined as mortality over the 22nd week of pregnancy until 7 days after birth per 1000; postnatal mortality is after birth until 42 days per 1000; stillbirth is mortality after the 20th week's gestation until birth per 1000.
2. For 1995, only infant mortality information is available.
Source: Compiled by the author using Indiastat (www.indiastat.com). Accessed on 22 June 2007.

diseases and parasitic diseases which manifest symptoms such as diarrhoea or respiratory infection and which can be prevented by providing hygienic conditions through public investment.

Deaths data show that the major killer is cardiovascular diseases, followed by infectious and parasitic diseases, respiratory diseases, perinatal diseases, and malignant neoplasms. We see that the general public suffers in their daily lives from infectious diseases and other acute symptoms, but causes of deaths are mostly cardiovascular, hence the chronic symptoms. This suggests the need for more emphasis on promotional medicine.

206

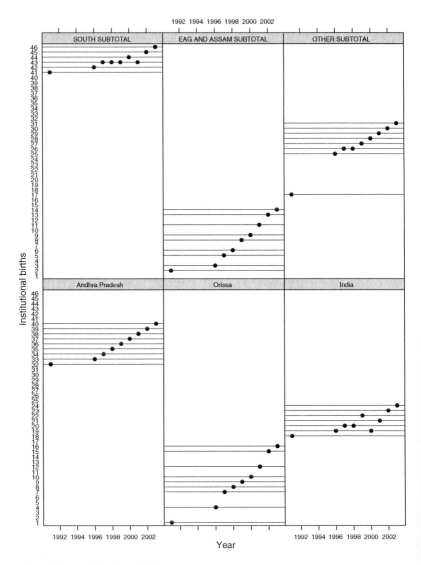

Figure 7.2: Institutional births

Notes: 1. EAG states are Uttar Pradesh, Madhya Pradesh, Orissa, Bihar, Jharkhand, Chattis-garh, Rajasthan and Uttaranchal.
2. South states are Andhra Pradesh, Karnataka, Kerala and Tamil Nadu, and the union terri-tories of Lakshadweep and Pondicherry.
Source: Compiled by the author using Registrar General (2006).

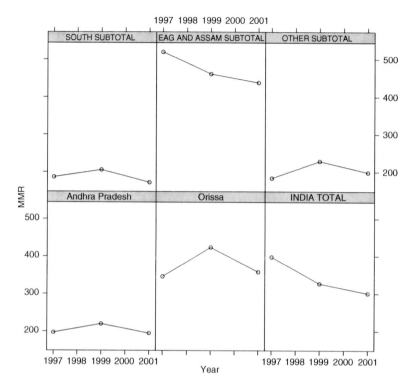

Figure 7.3: Maternal mortality ratio

Notes: 1. Maternal mortality ratio is maternal deaths per 100,000 births. 2. EAG states are Uttar Pradesh, Madhya Pradesh, Orissa, Bihar, Jharkhand, Chattisgarh, Rajasthan and Uttaranchal. 3. South states are Andhra Pradesh, Karnataka, Kerala and Tamil Nadu, and the union territories of Lakshadweep and Pondicherry.
Source: Compiled by the author using Registrar General (2006).

7.1.2   Health policies

The backbone of healthcare policies in India was established by the National Health Policy of 1982, pursuant to the Health for All (HFA) goal announced in the Alma Ata Declaration. The primary goals of NHP-1982 are: 1) to set up a well-dispersed network of comprehensive primary healthcare services; 2) to provide intermediation through health volunteers having appropriate knowledge, simple skills and requisite technologies; 3) to establish a well-worked-out referral system; and 4) to create an integrated network of evenly spread specialty and super-specialty services. Under this policy, although there were significant

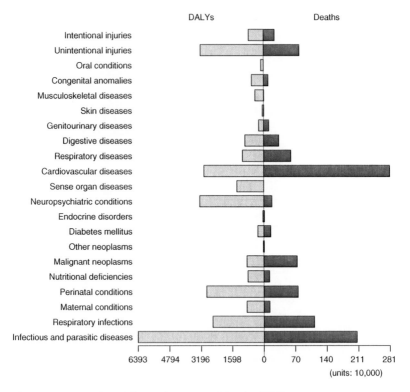

Figure 7.4:   DALY-based disease burden and deaths (2002)

Notes: 1. DALY: disability adjusted life years. Total life years lost due to deaths and illnesses. Life years lost due to death are computed from cohort average life years. Life years lost due to illnesses are computed using the standard duration by illness.

2. Deaths are the actual number of deaths.

Source: Compiled by the author using www.who.int/entity/healthinfo/statistics/bodgbddeathdalyestimates.xls.

improvements in controlling some of the major infectious diseases, there still was wide variation in health outcomes among states and between social groups, especially in the morbidity and mortality rates. In light of this, the National Health Policy was revised in 2002. NHP-2002 acknowledges that NHP-1982 produced a 'limited success' (NHP-2002: 3). The document states the reason for the limited success as being that 'the financial resources and public health administrative capacity was far short of that necessary to achieve such an ambitious and holistic goal' (NHP-2002: 4–5).

The goal of NHP-2002 (22, Table 3.1) is to achieve acceptable standard of good health amongst the general population. This is pursued by making the healthcare system more decentralized, by establishing the new infrastructure in the deficient areas to ease access, and by upgrading the infrastructure in the existing institutions.[1] While NHP-2002 lays out the goals, it is silent on how they should be achieved. More importantly, it lacks analysis of the current situation. It falls short in showing why the health outcomes are not improving as much as being hoped for. Without understanding a mechanism behind the failure, it is impossible to come up with an improved set of policies. It is no surprise that NHP-2002 was succeeded by a new initiative within a few years after it was launched.

In 2005, the government of India started a new initiative, the National Rural Health Mission (NRHM). The descriptive style of NRHM mission statement (MHFW 2005a) is qualitatively different from NHP-2002 in that it presents analysis on why certain goals are failing. It also shows how to fix such bugs in the policy. In this sense it is more complete and intellectually more sincere than NHP-2002. Of course, this does not guarantee that the mechanism it presents is true or that the bug fixes will actually work, but it stands in sharp contrast to NHP-2002.

MHFW (2005a) states the objectives of NRHM are:

- Reduction of child and maternal mortality.
- Universal access to public services for food and nutrition, sanitation and hygiene and universal access to public healthcare services with emphasis on services addressing women's and children's health and universal immunization.
- Prevention and control of communicable and non-communicable diseases, including locally endemic diseases.
- Access to integrated comprehensive primary healthcare.
- Population stabilization, gender and demographic balance.
- Revitalization of local health traditions and mainstreaming AYUSH.
- Promotion of healthy lifestyles.

The main vehicles for change are decentralization and public-private partnership (PPP). However, in the year 2001–2, the state and central governments jointly spent 6100 times more than their local counterparts, which negates the notion of decentralization despite its often-heard rhetoric.

Decentralization requires careful preparation and decisive concession of authority to local bodies (MHFW 2006a, 2006b). In NRHM's mission statement (MHFW 2005a), however, despite its note in the bold characters that '(t)he committees that are formed at various levels must have concomitant authority, i.e., they must have the power to initiate action', it fails to show what the authority is. Despite calling for local communities to participate, it does not give any power over budgets or human resource management. The only provision to the Village Sanitation and Health Committees is untied funds in the amount of Rs. 10,000 (US$250) per year. It is questionable how much can be done by the VSHCs with this amount, especially without authority over the health- and sanitation-related arms of the state government. As policy planning is fundamentally conducted in the bottom-up style, policy planning also calls for local communities to submit information in a timely manner in the form of plans. However, it is questionable that accurate information will be submitted just by commanding it, unless a higher tier of government ensures that the submitted information will be utilized to the benefit of local bodies. To ensure such a promise, it is necessary not only to require local bodies to collect information but also to transfer to them the power to draw up policies based on the collected information. Overall, NRHM lacks an appreciation of incentives and still suffers from the traditional input-oriented mindset of planned-economy era. This holds true with the arguments of PPP. As we will see in section 7.3, existing incentives for personnel in the healthcare system are the key to understanding the functioning of (or the lack thereof) the current healthcare system.

7.2   Primary healthcare services in rural Andhra Pradesh

7.2.1   Policy implementation

In this section, we will examine the characteristics of two locality groups: one with PHC and another without. We will then assess to what extent the government's effort to expand the Subcentres, the bottom tier of the healthcare system, in rural areas contributed to one of the key policy goals, female birth and survival of under-6 females relative to their male counterparts. The data we use is drawn from the village censuses conduced by the Andhra Pradesh (AP) state government in two rounds, in 1991 and 2001.

The state of Andhra Pradesh (AP), a home to 76 million people, is organized into a three-tier administrative hierarchical structure: 23 districts, 1109 mandals, and 28,123 villages.[2] Villages may be further divided into natural hamlets that may have their own village forum called *gram sabha* (village council), and administrative villages that represent their own governing body called *gram panchayat* (elected village assembly) which covers a few hamlets. The median population for village, mandal, and district are, 1202, 48,795, 2,592,055, respectively.

We take up the AP state because it has large and fairly diverse population in terms of social classes, and has reputation for effectively providing the social services to the poor as one of the progressive southern states.

The healthcare system is organized into three-tier system consisting of primary, secondary and tertiary levels. At the bottom tier, a Subcentre is staffed with an ANM (auxiliary nurse midwife) and a multipurpose health worker (MPHW), and several Subcentres are supervised by a Primary Health Centre (PHC) which is managed by a medical officer with professional training in medical college. PHCs are further organized by secondary-level hospitals called Community Health Centres (CHCs), and CHCs are further overseen by higher-tier district hospitals. Tertiary institutions are mostly in the capital city of Hyderabad. According to national norms, Subcentres are supposedly built for every 5,000 population, PHCs for every 30,000, and CHCs for every 120,000.

There are also private clinics, both medically licensed and unlicensed. Unlicensed clinics are called rural medical practitioners (RMPs).[3] RMPs are 'quacks' and are notoriously ill-trained and have almost no qualifications to practise medicine. They charge the maximum of several hundred rupees for a shot of painkillers, aspirin or similar, without diagnosing the condition of patients. Some of them even perform C-section operations with anaesthetics. According to the villagers we have talked with in several villages, and NGO staffs, many of them unofficially work as middlemen for the licensed private hospitals in towns, sending the patients whom RMPs cannot cure for commission. While RMPs may serve as painkillers for the minor ailments, just like an incompetent druggist does, a substantial part of their service is detrimental to public health. This is the case because they refer patients only at an advanced stage of illnesses, after a few rounds of pointless out-patient visits and associated non-negligible fees and pains born by the patients. There are other medical professions even more questionable than RMPs – the traditional healers, whose arsenals for cure are herbs and prayers. But we will omit them from our scope. We will also ignore the vast repository of 'doctors' in AYUSH, or the Indian System of Medicine.[4]

Location of PHCs: some eyeball tests

In this subsection, we will visually inspect the characteristics of medical facility location. Table 7.1 shows the achievements made in terms of number of facilities between round 1 and round 2 of the AP census: 486 new PHCs were built, increasing from 1404 to 1890, which is an increase of 34.6 per cent. CHCs increased by 166 per cent from 212 to 564, Subcentres increased by staggering 566.3 per cent from 1533 to 10,215, but

Table 7.1: Increase of medical care facilities

	round 1	round 2	change	rate	norm in rd 1	norm in rd 2
Subcentres	1533	10,215	8682	5.663	31,442	5424
PHCs	1404	1890	486	0.346	34,331	29,313
CHCs	212	564	352	1.66	227,362	98,229
RMPs	4256	16,531	12,275	2.884	11,325	3351

Source: Authors' calculation based on AP survey.
round 1: Round 1 of AP survey
round 2: Round 2 of AP survey
change: Change in establishments between rounds 1 and 2
Notes: rate: Rate of change in establishments between rounds 1 and 2
norm in rd 1: Establishments per norm population in round 1
norm in rd 2: Establishments per norm population in round 2

RMPs, who have no medical qualification, also increased by 288.4 per cent from 4256 to 16,531. With this increase, the 'plane' population norm[5] for PHCs at the state level was achieved in round 2, the population covered by one PHC decreased from 34,331 to 29,312. The population norm for Subcentres had not been met in round 2, standing at 5423 despite the rapid reduction from 31,442. CHCs had population coverage of 227,362 in round 1 but it declined to 98,228 in round 2. All these were done under the population of 4.82 million in round 1 to 5.54 million in round 2 with the relatively low rate of increase at 1.26 per cent per annum.

Figure 7.5 shows the quantile-quantile plot (qqplot) of population in the locality with and without PHC in round 2. A qqplot is convenient for visual examination of the characteristics of two distributions because it directly compares the quantiles of the two. In a qqplot, a point in the figure indicates a percentile. For example, if the 5th percentile (the bottom 5 per cent point) of the distribution is chosen, a qqplot enables comparison of the values of 5th percentiles of two distributions. If, in Figure 7.5, the 5th percentile value is greater for the group of locality with PHC, meaning that, if the village corresponding to the bottom 5 per cent of the PHC group has larger population than the village corresponding to the bottom 5 per cent of the non-PHC group, then a point for the 5th percentile will be plotted above the 45-degree line. If the values are the same, then the point will be on the 45-degree line, and if the value for the group of locality without PHC is greater, it will be plotted below the 45 degree line.

Figure 7.5 shows that the population size is consistently greater in the locality with PHC for the same percentile. This means that the distribution of PHC locality is shifted to the right as compared to the distribution of the non-PHC group. As Figure 7.5 is in log-scales, the persistent gap

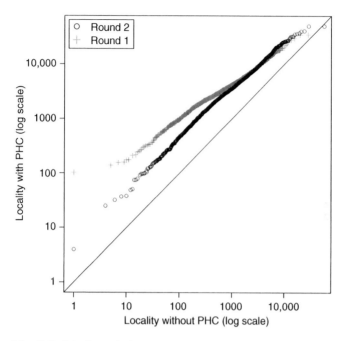

Figure 7.5: QQ-plot of population

Notes: 1. Quantile-quantile plots are shown. If the quantiles are the same between localities with and without PHC, plots will be on the 45 degree line. If the localities with PHCs have greater quantiles, the plot will be above the 45 degree line.
2. Log scales are used for both axises.
Source: Compiled by the author using AP survey.

between the quantile plots and the 45-degree line indicates the growing gap between two distributions. So the upper tail of the PHC locality group is longer than the non-PHC locality group. This makes sense because PHCs are located in larger villages and towns. Note, however, the change through time: in round 1, the plots are further up from the 45-degree line for a smaller locality (lower quantiles). This means that the state government established PHCs mainly in smaller communities between round 1 and round 2.

Figure 7.6 shows a qqplot of distance to the nearest city. The city defined here is greater in size than a mandal (area roughly equivalent to a small, city-sized municipality) headquarters and are roughly equivalent to district (area roughly equivalent to a county in the US) capitals. As the plot shows, in round 2, both groups are virtually indistinguishable in their distributions. This shows that the chance of having a PHC may not be systematically related to the distance to the nearest city. That is, combined with the finding shown in Figure 7.5, there are more PHCs located

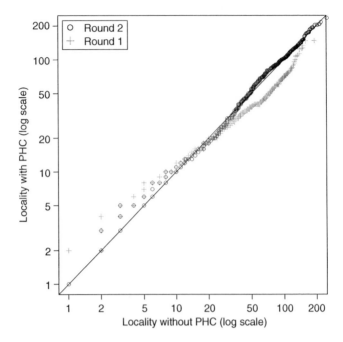

Figure 7.6:   QQ-plot of distance to towns

Notes: 1. Quantile-quantile plots are shown. If the quantiles are the same between localities with and without PHC, plots will be on the 45-degree line. If the localities with PHCs have greater quantiles, the plot will be above the 45-degree line.
2. Log scales are used for both axes.
Source: Compiled by the author using AP survey.

closer to cities simply because there are more localities closer to cities. Within the same distance grid, PHCs are located in larger communities. So, one sees that it is not the case that the state government disproportionately neglects remote localities when setting up PHCs. As the change in plots reveals, the state government has set up PHCs in remote locations of the state, between 50 to 120 km away from cities. This does, however, show that remote localities are not necessarily favoured in terms of PHC construction, as seen by the fact that the plot goes below the 45-degree line at the upper tail area. This absence of corrective actions in favour of remote localities may exist out of necessity, yet it still is problematic given that there are fewer choices for quality services in remote localities than in semi-urban localities. This implies that the government attaches importance to the size of the population covered within a given radius. We will further examine the rules for facility establishment followed by the government later.

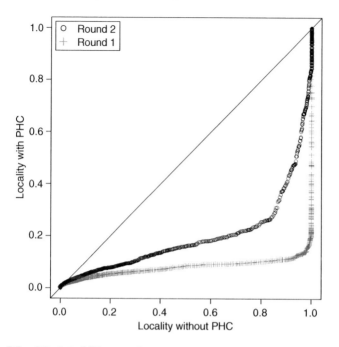

Figure 7.7: QQ-plot of ST proportion

Notes: 1. Quantile-quantile plots are shown. If the quantiles are the same between localities with and without PHC, plots will be on the 45-degree line. If the localities with PHCs have greater quantiles, the plot will be above the 45-degree line.
2. Log scales are used for both axes.
Source: Compiled by the author using AP survey.

As the more remote and smaller localities are handicapped by PHC absence, it may be of interest to know the characteristics of the residents. We will look at the proportions of Scheduled Tribes (STs) and Scheduled Castes (SCs) as the indicators of poverty and social exclusion. STs are original residents of India and are outside the caste system, and SCs, also known as untouchables, occupy the lowest tier of the caste hierarchy. Both are traditionally considered to be the poorest in India.

Figure 7.7 and Figure 7.8 show the qqplots of the proportion of ST and SC population in localities with and without a PHC. As the plots stay below the 45-degree line, the ST proportion is larger in the non-PHC group. This is a well-known fact, as the ST population tends to live in the remote hills away from urban areas. The relatively intensive plot pattern in the lower quantiles indicates that there are more localities with a lower ST proportion for both groups. ST population in round 1 has a curious shape, with an almost horizontal segment. This implies that the

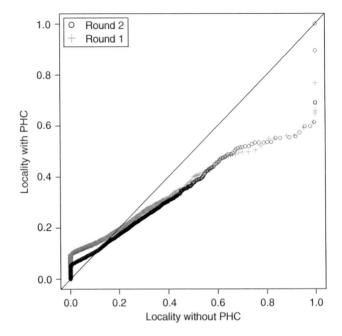

Figure 7.8:   QQ-plot of SC proportion

Notes: 1. Quantile-quantile plots are shown. If the quantiles are the same between localities with and without PHC, plots will be on the 45-degree line. If the localities with PHCs have greater quantiles, the plot will be above the 45-degree line.
2. Log scales are used for both axes.
Source: Compiled by the author using AP survey.

PHC group is heavily concentrated in the localities with a low ST proportion, while the non-PHC group is not. The steep ascent in the upper tail of distributions also confirms that the PHC group does not have many ST-dominant localities while the non-PHC group does. The last segment of the qqplot is vertical, meaning that the non-PHC group has many 100 per cent ST localities, while the PHC group has few of them. This is best understood as meaning that the ST population is being neglected, as there are a small number of communities with a high ST proportion in the PHC group. The decade of policy efforts shifted the plot toward the equitable 45-degree line; however, there still remains a considerable gap between the two groups in terms of ST proportion. Figure 7.7 shows the marginalization of ST population in terms of PHC availability. This is a topic more intensively treated in Chapter 8 by D'Souza and Abrahams.

While the ST population receives fewer benefits relative to the average residents, Figure 7.8 shows a different story for the SC population. At the lower quantiles, the PHC group has more SC population than the non-PHC group, which suggests a non-negligible proportion of SC population migrates to semi-urban areas. The plot pattern of Figure 7.8 also shows a 'J' shape, but only at the upper tail. The points in the upper quantiles are sparse, which indicates there are only a small number of SC-dominated localities. The slope of the plot is less steep and closer to the 45-degree line than in the ST case. This means that there is smaller difference between the PHC and non-PHC groups in terms of SC proportions. This difference in terms of PHC access between SCs and STs is also well documented. Banerjee and Somanathan (2007), who used the district level data of 1971 and 1991 and converted it into parliamentary constituency-based data, attribute this to the politicization of SC statuses, while STs did not form political parties of their own that were strong enough to influence budget allocation at the state level. We note little change between round 1 and round 2 for SCs in our data.

Econometric investigation of the medical facility location rule: efficiency versus equity

As seen in Figure 7.5 and Figure 7.6, the government sets up new PHCs in smaller and more remote localities. We will examine the factors that affected the government's decision. We will also examine whether the government follows the efficiency rule or the equity rule in medical facility establishment.

The state governments are supposed to satisfy the population norms set by the central government. It is, however, ambiguous as to what level the state government should satisfy the norms, at state, district, mandal or village, and also ambiguous how they choose the locality in setting up a new PHC. One can argue that, for sake of efficiency, the unserved locality with larger population should be given priority. This will help the government achieve the goal faster at the mandal level, and more population will be served by an additional PHC.[6] Another argument can be made that, on the equity ground, one should establish a new PHC away from large settlements that may already have private clinics. One can also expect that larger settlements are more likely to exist closer to the even larger settlements through the agglomeration process. By placing a new PHC away from the large settlements, population with no effective choice in seeking quality medical services, hence a more desperate one, will be served better.

One can examine which one, the efficiency rule or the equity rule, is more likely to hold in reality by using the distance and population data. The argument is as follows: suppose that we have two 'towns' or large settlements. Assuming the symmetry of population distribution over the space around each town, one can deduce that the segments between two towns, call it the inside area, have a larger population than the outside segments, or the outside area, for a given distance away from the town. That is, for a given radius around a town, there will be more people living between the towns than outside that area. If efficiency is the priority when the government sets up a new PHC in a certain radius from a town, they will choose a location in the inside area. If equity is the priority when choosing the location in a certain radius, they will choose a location in the outside area. For a given distance, the efficiency rule predicts that population is positively correlated with new PHC establishment, while the equity rule predicts a negative correlation. For a given population, the efficiency rule predicts a positive correlation between new establishment and distance, and the equity rule a negative correlation. This follows because the population of the inside area declines more slowly with distance than does the population of the outside area.

We have a panel of 26,730 villages of rural AP in round 1 and round 2. We have 1558 PHCs in round 2 and 1369 PHCs in round 1. This amounts to the change in mean PHC presence from 5.05 per cent to 5.81 per cent in a village, and any estimation using a change in such a small fraction should proceed with caution. This applies also to CHCs, which changed from 0.79 per cent to 1.90 per cent. However, this is not the case with Subcentres and RMPs, which expanded from a mean presence of 5.33 per cent to 33.60 per cent and from 12.92 per cent to 27.29 per cent, respectively. Therefore we will focus more on Subcentres and RMPs in the subsequent analysis.

Table 7.2 shows excerpts from probit estimates of various health facility establishments between round 1 and round 2 using 26,730 localities which did not have their respective health facilities in round 1. A probit model is a statistical model that is suited to analysing the probability of a chosen event taking place, in our case the existence of a medical facility of interest, and it shows how the variables (called covariates or explanatory variables) influence the probability of existence. Full results are shown in the Appendix (Table 7.A1). A positive estimate on a covariate is interpreted as indicating a relationship in which a larger value of covariate increases the probability of existence, while a negative estimate decreases it.

Columns (1) and (2) give the results for PHCs. In (1), only the village-level variables are used, and in (2) mandal-level and district-level variables are added. The results in (1) for PHCs show what we have confirmed so far: as evidenced by positive estimates for ST population,

Table 7.2: Probit estimates of health facility establishment

Variables	PHC		Subcentre		CHC	
	(1)	(2)	(3)	(4)	(5)	(6)
(Intercept)	-2.561***	-1.669***	-2.146***	-2.037***	-3.197***	-3.018***
	(0.066)	(0.330)	(0.047)	(0.151)	(0.139)	(0.340)
total population	19.087***	28.258***	121.573***	117.256***	-2.672	-3.817
	(6.366)	(6.708)	(5.022)	(5.208)	(5.413)	(5.661)
population below age 6	-43.304	-40.566	-268.036***	-244.538***	42.954*	38.950
	(28.421)	(29.701)	(22.130)	(22.913)	(23.881)	(25.008)
ST population	20.016***	5.850	41.094***	33.159***	-3.420	-2.182
	(4.621)	(5.406)	(4.030)	(4.583)	(4.949)	(5.393)
SC population	-13.218**	-5.160	28.827***	28.688***	-8.882	-7.859
	(6.425)	(7.491)	(4.893)	(5.660)	(5.514)	(6.382)
literate population	5.342	-9.963	-96.144***	-92.757***	14.071***	14.670***
	(5.918)	(6.144)	(5.275)	(5.528)	(5.202)	(5.332)
water tap	0.074	0.125**	0.124***	0.138***	0.137***	0.173***
	(0.057)	(0.061)	(0.032)	(0.033)	(0.053)	(0.054)
paved road	-0.022	0.419***	0.700***	0.701***	0.837***	0.872***
	(0.065)	(0.076)	(0.047)	(0.050)	(0.136)	(0.146)
unpaved road	-0.143**	0.249***	0.449***	0.431***	0.480***	0.530***
	(0.063)	(0.072)	(0.047)	(0.050)	(0.137)	(0.146)
distance	883.296***	205.137	153.832***	298.516***	470.522***	517.802***
	(64.478)	(130.513)	(46.430)	(95.381)	(89.877)	(194.334)
number of CHCs	0.276*	0.264*	1.042***	1.025***		
	(0.148)	(0.151)	(0.142)	(0.143)		
number of PHCs			0.689***	0.692***	0.458***	0.514***
			(0.055)	(0.056)	(0.057)	(0.058)
number of Subcentres	0.333***	0.557***			0.010	0.101
	(0.060)	(0.076)			(0.064)	(0.076)
number of RMPs	0.022	0.030	0.107***	0.102***	0.016	0.004
	(0.034)	(0.035)	(0.024)	(0.024)	(0.029)	(0.029)
mandal and state level controls	no	yes	no	yes	no	yes

Note: Regressors are round 1 values. Population, literacy, and distance are divided by 100,000.

the government gives the ST population priority when setting up PHCs, despite the fact that they live far away from the cities. In (1), while the ST population is awarded more PHCs, the SC population is shown to have fewer because its coefficient is negative. The number of Subcentres is also positively correlated. This may be due to the fact that PHCs oversee Subcentres, so the more Subcentres, the more need for supervision. Column (2) shows the importance of controlling the mandal and district level variates. As shown in Table 7.A1, adding the ST population ratio at the mandal level makes the ST and SC populations of villages insignificant, while addition of the district-level ST ratio does not change the results. This means that PHC targeting at the ST population is done at the mandal level and is not geared toward the ST population at the village level. This is appropriate, as a PHC is expected to cover roughly three-quarters of a median-sized mandal and cannot be built only for ST-dominated villages. However, given the difficulty that people in ST-dominated localities have in reaching the towns due both to poor road conditions and to cultural barriers, corrective measures in Subcentre establishments may be desirable.

Within the mandal, the estimates in Table 7.2 suggest they choose to set up a new PHC in larger villages with mains water and a paved road approach, but do not worry about the distance. A positive correlation with presence of water taps, paved roads and large population indicates the characteristics of better equipped, larger settlements.[7] Population variates are both positive and significant in (1) and (2), but the distance in (2) becomes insignificant after the mandal and district variables are added. Given the crudeness of our distance which measures the distance to cities but not to mandal headquarters, measurement errors may have attenuated our distance estimates. The results thus weakly support the efficiency rule of PHC establishment, which agrees with our earlier eyeball tests on population and distance qqplots. While the government may seek efficiency in setting up a new PHC, it also favours the ST-dominated communities at the mandal level. However, not having an effective sample size of newly established PHCs, we must not stretch the implication of the estimates on PHCs.

Subcentres follow a similar pattern, while there are some differences. First, targeting on ST and SC persists even after adding mandal and district-level covariates, and Table 7.A1 shows that district-level covariates are significant while mandal-level covariates are not. This means that the government compensates them for its inability to set up PHCs in ST and SC-dominated villages, and the targeting is done both at the district and village levels. The focus on ST and SC-dominated communities also results in the targeting of less literate societies, explaining the negative estimates on literacy. However, secondly, distance is positive and significant, supporting the efficiency rule. This means that, under the assumption that population tapers off monotonically as we move away from the settlements, the government tries to set up Subcentres closer to larger localities. This is confirmed by the negative estimates on average distance at the mandal level, implying Subcentres are established in mandals closer to cities.[8] Third, the number of RMPs is positively correlated, so Subcentres are established where there are more RMPs. This is good for public health if the presence of Subcentres drives unqualified RMPs out of the village.

CHCs follow a distinctively different rule, they are in more literate communities with more paved road approaches. Estimates in Table 7.A1 show that CHCs are set up in large, remote communities with more variable village and mandal population, and with more variable PHC norm achievements. Remoteness is logical since CHCs need to be spaced out geographically. This indicates that establishment of CHCs between the two rounds of the census had mostly taken place in remote, backward, yet large communities to provide public secondary healthcare services which were previously nonexistent.

In Table 7.3, the presence of rural medical practitioners (RMPs) is analysed. Again, the full results are shown in the Appendix (Table 7.A2). One of the problems in rural health is that RMPs thrive and people support them. It is documented in some surveys, including ours, that villagers do not feel strongly betrayed by RMPs even when they fail to provide effective treatment. Anecdotes indicate that villagers favor RMPs over PHCs or Subcentres because the attitude of the personnel is better, personnel are available onsite, the relatively effective cost disadvantage at RMPs is fairly small due to the long distance to and the stockout of free drugs at PHCs, despite the free provision of drugs there, and villagers are not knowledgeable enough about medicine to differentiate RMPs from PHC doctors.

Columns (1) to (2) in Table 7.3 give probit estimates of presence of RMPs in a village on a sample of 23,277 villages with no RMPs in round 1, and columns (3) to (4) give difference-in-differences (DID) estimates on the number of RMPs in a village on the full sample of 26,720 villages. One sees that, between probit and DID estimates, signs change with the parameters of population, literate population, and paved road. This suggests the presence of the following village fixed effects spurring RMP presence: positively correlated with population, negatively correlated with literate population, and positively correlated with paved roads.

Table 7.3: Probit and DID estimates of RMP presence

Variables	(1)	(2)	(3)	(4)
intercept	−2.102***	−2.777***		
	(0.051)	(0.161)		
total population	52.903***	63.691***	−8.183**	−11.350***
	(4.370)	(4.612)	(3.956)	(4.027)
population below age 6	−88.138***	−171.720***	−80.080***	−73.912***
	(19.265)	(20.318)	(14.239)	(14.369)
ST population	22.769***	30.904***	42.055***	39.187***
	(3.658)	(4.374)	(6.611)	(6.693)
SC population	35.176***	19.317***	12.097**	32.387***
	(4.418)	(5.179)	(6.015)	(6.384)
literate population	−52.752***	−44.116***	75.639***	74.062***
	(4.668)	(4.948)	(3.464)	(3.548)
water tap	0.020	0.036	0.101***	0.005
	(0.033)	(0.034)	(0.013)	(0.015)
paved road	0.969***	0.820***	−0.052*	−0.081***
	(0.052)	(0.059)	(0.027)	(0.028)
unpaved road	0.778***	0.576***	−0.009	0.003
	(0.052)	(0.058)	(0.026)	(0.027)
distance	−185.349***	325.599***		
	(49.475)	(108.792)		
number of PHCs	0.190***	0.234***	0.103***	0.120***
	(0.048)	(0.050)	(0.039)	(0.039)
number of Subcentres	−0.256***	0.074	0.258***	0.254***
	(0.043)	(0.052)	(0.016)	(0.016)
mandal Subcentre norm		−0.100*		−0.074***
		(0.052)		(0.016)
mandal population		−0.139		−0.516**
		(0.113)		(0.212)
STD of village population		4.987***		−0.486
		(1.355)		(1.599)
area of mandal		0.001***		
		(0.000)		
average distance of villages in mandal		−382.673***		
		(141.184)		
mandal ST population ratio		−1.174***		−0.506
		(0.108)		(0.484)
mandal SC population ratio		−0.488***		−1.083**
		(0.239)		(0.531)
district level controls	no	yes	no	yes

Notes: 1. (1) and (2) are probit estimates of RMP presence in round 2 for the sample with no RMPs in round 1. Size is 23,277.
2. (3) and (4) are difference-in-differences estimates for the full sample. Size is 26,730.
3. Population, literacy, and distance are divided by 100,000.

A positive correlation with population size and paved roads suggest RMPs are active in large settlements with better infrastructure. A negative correlation with literate population indicates that the educational backwardness of a village is associated with the presence of RMPs.

Inspection of (1) and (2) shows that new RMP establishments are in: large-area mandals with smaller SC and ST populations, and closer to cities; and within mandals, in more populous villages with more illiterate persons; and ST- and SC-dominant, remote locations, with more paved roads and having PHCs but not Subcentres. This gives us an impression that RMPs exist in mandals closer to cities but also in the remote villages of each mandal. So they seem to be seeking a niche, but are not necessarily concerned with Subcentre presence as estimates for this are positive in (2) to (4). The number of PHCs in a village is also positively correlated in all specifications. Both imply that Subcentres and PHCs are not driving out RMPs from villages. It also implies a puzzling phenomenon in which RMPs and public healthcare are seemingly complementing each other.

7.2.2   Health outcome indicators of AP

When we look at maternal health, as indicated in Figure 7.2 and Figure 7.3, AP state is a relatively high performer. However, it is not the highest among the high-performing southern state pack. Figure 7.3 shows the maternal mortality ratio to be declining non-monotonically despite its high level. Figure 7.2 shows a low level of institutional births which has not changed much from round 1. This is despite the infrastructural achievement of expanding the primary healthcare services.

One can assess the policy goals more directly in terms of child health by looking at the sex ratio below the age of six. Table 7.4 shows the estimated average treatment effects (ATE) of Subcentre construction on the under-six sex ratio at the village level, defined by total male population below the age of six divided by total female population below the age of six.

ATE is a popular statistic that captures the average effectiveness of a policy on the outcome that is of interest across the villages. Columns (1) to (3) give propensity score matching (PSM) estimates, and columns (4) to (6) give difference-in-differences (DID) estimates. The idea behind PSM is that it finds a village without a Subcentre similar in observable characteristics to a village with a Subcentre, so they can safely be compared on the outcome indicator, i.e., the sex ratios, to see the effects

Table 7.4: Propensity score matching and DID estimates of ATE

Variables	(1)	(2)	(3)	(4)	(5)	(6)
intercept	1.009***	0.975***	0.957***	0.015***	0.015***	0.022**
	(0.02)	(0.023)	(0.024)	(0.004)	(0.005)	(0.011)
Subcentre construction	−0.037	−0.007	−0.007			
	(0.031)	(0.033)	(0.036)			
ST population	−0.314	−1.261***	−1.044**	−3.945***	−5.169***	−5.345***
	(0.37)	(0.424)	(0.432)	(1.784)	(1.823)	(1.829)
SC population	0.084	−0.337	−0.707	7.134***	6.452***	6.617***
	(0.47)	(0.542)	(0.552)	(1.561)	(1.657)	(1.669)
male literate population	1.537**	1.881**	1.887**	−1.473	−1.32	−1.883
	(0.724)	(0.783)	(0.844)	(1.787)	(1.808)	(1.846)
female literate population	−2.172**	−2.207**	−2.064*	1.272	1.415	1.836
	(0.929)	(0.983)	(1.059)	(1.851)	(1.863)	(1.928)
tap water	0.002	0.004	0.005	0.013***	0.012***	0.01**
	(0.004)	(0.004)	(0.004)	(0.004)	(0.004)	(0.005)
paved road	0.034*	0.069***	0.073***	0.038*	0.045**	0.043**
	(0.02)	(0.022)	(0.022)	(0.02)	(0.02)	(0.02)
unpaved road	0.045**	0.077***	0.079***	0.033	0.041**	0.04*
	(0.02)	(0.022)	(0.022)	(0.02)	(0.02)	(0.02)
RMP	−0.001	0	0	0	0	−0.001
	(0.001)	(0.001)	(0.001)	(0.002)	(0.002)	(0.002)
mandal population		−0.039**	−0.072***		−0.124**	−0.129**
		(0.016)	(0.018)		(0.051)	(0.058)
mandal ST population		0.154***	0.117***		0.71***	0.478**
		(0.031)	(0.036)		(0.187)	(0.228)
mandal SC population		0.146**	0.309***		0.402*	0.438
		(0.066)	(0.077)		(0.233)	(0.305)
district population			0.003***			0.001
			(0.001)			(0.002)
district ST population			0.001			0.018
			(0.002)			(0.011)
district SC population			−0.014***			−0.005
			(0.003)			(0.009)

interacted with Subcentre construction

	(1)	(2)	(3)	(4)	(5)	(6)
ST population	0.158	0.911*	0.666	3.787	4.618*	4.826*
	(0.475)	(0.547)	(0.557)	(2.408)	(2.579)	(2.586)
SC population	−0.455	−0.492	−0.157	−7.257***	−6.16***	−6.322***
	(0.629)	(0.725)	(0.734)	(2.016)	(2.169)	(2.179)
male literate population	0.065	0.155	0.498	−3.281	−3.806	−3.166
	(1.035)	(1.098)	(1.151)	(2.391)	(2.433)	(2.477)
female literate population	0.176	−0.053	−0.7	3.873	4.064	3.54
	(1.305)	(1.356)	(1.427)	(2.595)	(2.622)	(2.694)
tap water	0.002	0	−0.002	−0.008	−0.007	−0.004
	(0.005)	(0.005)	(0.005)	(0.006)	(0.006)	(0.006)
paved road	0.038	0.007	0.003	−0.024	−0.033	−0.031
	(0.031)	(0.032)	(0.032)	(0.028)	(0.028)	(0.028)
unpaved road	0.015	−0.014	−0.016	−0.024	−0.034	−0.033
	(0.032)	(0.032)	(0.033)	(0.027)	(0.028)	(0.028)
RMPs	0.001	0.001	0.001	0.001	0.001	0.001
	(0.002)	(0.002)	(0.002)	(0.002)	(0.002)	(0.002)
mandal population		0.016	0.054**		0.166**	0.172**
		(0.022)	(0.025)		(0.07)	(0.079)
mandal ST population		−0.11**	−0.069		−0.648**	−0.432
		(0.043)	(0.048)		(0.283)	(0.326)
mandal SC population		−0.02	−0.224**		−0.577*	−0.58
		(0.09)	(0.104)		(0.329)	(0.413)
district population			−0.003***			−0.003
			(0.001)			(0.004)
district ST population			−0.001			−0.018
			(0.002)			(0.015)
district SC population			0.016***			0.004
			(0.004)			(0.012)

Notes: 1. Average treatment effect of Subcentre presence on the under-6 sex ratio, defined by male population below age 6 divided by female population below age 6.

2. (1) to (3) are propensity score matching estimates. Matching was done on the nearest neighbour. Size is 15,321.

3. (4) to (6) are difference-in-differences estimates after propensity score matching. Size is 15,321.

of having a Subcentre. DID also estimates the effect of having Subcentres, but inferences based on DID estimates are known to be more robust than those using PSM. This is because DID estimates are not affected by the unobservable village fixed effects that may influence the difference in outcome indicators between any two villages, whereas PSM estimates are.

The point estimates of level effect of Subcentre construction in (1) to (3) show a negative value, implying more girls were born and survived relative to boys after the construction of a PHC in a village. They are, however, all statistically insignificant. These become significant and positive in more robust DID estimates in (4) to (6). A Subcentre, by itself, increases the sex ratio; hence relatively fewer female children are born and survive than male children, with the order between .015 and .022. Looking at (4) to (6), sex ratios become higher in SC-dominated communities, but equally negative effects are observed in SC-dominated communities with Subcentre construction, virtually cancelling out each other. This means that a Subcentre is effective in lowering the sex ratio among children in the SC-dominated communities. Mandal population significantly lowers the sex ratio, but it does the opposite in the villages with Subcentres. Paved roads and unpaved roads contribute equally to fewer female births and survival, while RMP does not seem to have any impact. Sex ratios are lower in larger mandals but higher in mandals with higher ST population.

Propensity score matching estimates on the level effect are smaller than DID estimates, implying that village fixed effects that increase the relative male birth survival are negatively correlated with the (probability of) Subcentre construction. This is evidence of regressive targeting, because the villages with lesser female survival are further away from the unconditional biological mean of sex ratio, and are generally considered to benefit more from Subcentre construction. The village fixed effects that increase relative male birth survival are negatively associated with female literacy and positively correlated with male literacy. These conform to the conventional wisdom in gender preference of parents and collective household models.

The results show that Subcentres might not just have been unsuccessful in lowering the sex ratios, but they may have been increasing the relative male birth-survival when the SC population is small. So, one can infer that selective births and/or selective parental care by child gender persist in villages after the construction of Subcentres. At the same time, although the Subcentres are built in SC- and ST-dominated, remote villages, and they are targeted toward villages with higher female births and survival than males. So, their choice of villages is inconsistent with one of their policy goals, protection of female children. Thus, we are led to conclude that the mere construction of facilities does not suffice and that the government must select targets to better suit its objectives. Positive DID estimates of ATE also suggest that we need to look into how the personnel perform in the periphery where there is no effective monitoring.

7.3 Discussion

The above analysis shows that even though the state has constructed many health centres, this has not led to an improvement in health outcomes. This indicates that mere construction of buildings is not enough. Whether a health centre contributes to the improvement of villagers' health depends on the quality of healthcare service that the centre provides.

There is a set of evidence implying the inefficiency or malfunction of public health centres in India. Chaudhury et al. (2005) report the results of a national representative survey of Indian health sectors and show that health workers were often absent. The absence rate among health workers was as high as 40 per cent and doctors are more likely to be absent than other health workers. This high frequency of absence is not due to a limited number of 'ghost' doctors who are posted there in name only, but is rather fairly widespread among the doctors. Another study by Banerjee, Deaton and Duflo (2004) in rural Rajasthan also found that 45 per cent of medical personnel were absent in Subcentres and aid posts, and 36 per cent were absent in PHCs and CHCs. Subcentres closed 56 per cent of the time during regular office hours and only in 12 per cent of cases was a nurse to be found in one of the villages served by her Subcentre. There seemed to be little regularity regarding which day of the week and which time of the day medical officers were present, suggesting that it was difficult for villagers to predict whether medical officers would be present when they went to the health facilities.[9]

Even if doctors are present, it does not ensure a good-quality healthcare service. Das and Hammer (2005) conducted a survey in urban Delhi, utilizing medical vignettes in which doctors were asked to diagnose and prescribe treatment to role-playing patients and it was found that doctors in poorer areas were less competent than those in richer areas. Studies in other countries such as Tanzania (Leonard and Masatu 2007) and Indonesia (Barber, Gertler and Harimurti 2007) also found a similar pattern. This low competence of health staff in rural health centres might partly explain why we do not observe a positive impact from health centres on health outcomes.

A more important point is made by Das and Hammer (2007). They used not only medical vignettes but also direct clinical observation to identify the effort level of the doctors. Whereas medical vignettes capture the doctors' knowledge (what they know), the information from direct clinical observation reveals the doctors' actions (what they actually did). By comparing what they know and what they do, it is possible to grasp whether and how much the doctors shirked their duties. The study found that doctors at public clinics exerted significantly lower efforts than their private counterparts. Although public-clinic doctors are far more competent than private, unqualified, non-degree doctors, their performance level is worse than the latter since the former utilized less than 30 per cent of what they knew while the latter utilized almost everything they knew.

Comments of health service users in Andhra Pradesh collected by Probe Qualitative Research Team (2002) support the findings of Das and Hammer (2007). Users report that private doctors 'speak well, inquire about our health' and 'treat us quickly', whereas public doctors 'do not tell us what the problem is, first check, give us medicines and ask us to go' and 'do not attend to us quickly'. Further, many of the 'public' doctors worked as 'private' doctors outside the operating hours of public health centres with a very different attitude. According to their report, '(t)he same government doctor who was not easily or conveniently accessible, whose medication was not satisfactory and whose manner was brusque and indifferent, transformed into a perfectly nice and capable doctor when he was seeing a patient in his private practice'. Quite a few users prefer to go to a government doctor in the evening when he works as a private doctor.

A study by Banerjee, Deaton and Duflo (2004) in Rajasthan provides quantitative evidence on users' preference for private health facilities over public ones. It found that only about a quarter of users' visits to health facilities were to public facilities and that poor households were more likely to visit traditional healers than were wealthier households, although health personnel in the private sector are often untrained and largely unregulated. They also found that visits to public facilities were generally not free. For the poor, each visit to a public health facility cost Rs. 71, compared to Rs. 84 for visiting a private doctor and Rs. 61 for going to a traditional healer. Although medicines and services at a public health facility are supposed to be free, the reality is different. When the medicines in the government supplies are depleted, additional medicines need to be purchased from the market. It is also often the case that patients are told to buy the medicine from the private stock of the health provider at the public facility. There are reports that some public health providers charge for their service. These practices also discourage villagers from utilizing public health centres.

Currently there is a large amount of evidence suggesting that public health centres do not function well. The fact that the same doctor performs very badly as a public doctor and very well as a private doctor indicates that the current public system does not provide good incentives for doctors to provide good healthcare service and suggests that by correcting the incentive system, we can improve the quality of healthcare services provided by public health centres.

7.3.1   Improving incentive systems

The quality of healthcare service provided by health workers depends on their competence, which is determined by their knowledge and skill, and their effort level, which is determined by their intrinsic motivation and the incentives they face. Considering the fact that the performance level of public doctors is lower than that of private, unqualified, non-degree doctors in spite of their advantage of higher competence (see Das and Hammer 2007 noted above), we need to consider ways to boost doctors' intrinsic motivation and incentives so that they will provide better service to the poor.

With regard to economic incentives, the high effort level in the private sector provides some suggestions. In private practice, more patients mean more income. In the private sector, people have some power over health workers because they directly influence health workers' earnings. This makes health workers more responsive and makes them pay attention to their patients. On the other hand, compensation for public health staff is fixed and not dependent on the number of the patients. Thus, in public practice, more patients lead only to more exhaustion (and no benefit). Though people might influence the earnings of the health staff through under-the-table payments, unless the amount of the bribe is large enough, doctors still have an incentive to reduce the number of their patients. As a result, in private practice they tend to provide good healthcare service in order to increase the number of their patients, whereas in public practice they tend to interact with their patients in an inaccessible way to reduce the number of their patients and to lessen their work burden, or even choose to be absent.

It is indeed the case that a number of doctors work very hard despite the lack of monetary incentives (see Leonard, Masatu and Vialou 2005) and it may be true that many doctors are socially motivated to work in healthcare facilities in poor rural areas. However, their own need to look after their families and ensure their own well-being runs counter to increasing services to people (World Bank 2003). In order to improve the healthcare service provided by public doctors and other health staff, we should improve the incentive system for them instead of merely relying on their social motivation and altruism.

An understanding of the incentive mechanisms in healthcare services is also important when considering the introduction of decentralization and public-private partnership (PPP), which are receiving attention in recent policy debate. Unless the incentive mechanisms are designed well to solve the incentive problems embedded in the current system, they will not improve the situation. Merely delegating authority to state governments or a lower tier of government will not ensure improvement of services unless this delegation brings about substantial changes in the incentive system in public sector. For example, one of the merits of decentralization is believed to be that local governments have more information concerning the local situation and are more responsive to local demands. However, if the quality of service is not an election issue or if local officials are colluding with public workers including PHC staff, then there is little scope for service improvement from decentralization. Likewise, merely contracting out the PHC service to the private sector or using contract doctors in PHCs (public-private partnership) may not improve the situation unless the incentive mechanisms are appropriately redesigned. For example, if the benefits and renewal of contract are not linked to performance, contracting out or using contract doctors will not change the situation. The success of decentralization and PPP depends on whether and how it can change the incentive system. Below, we discuss some potential strategies to make health workers more responsive to local needs and set out their limitations as well. We do not confine our discussion to decentralization and PPP, but rather try to convey some ideas that can be applied to any kind of reforms.

7.3.2　Community participation

One way to make health staff more responsive to the local poor is to utilize the community. Given that: 1) it is the users who can monitor the performance of health staff most inexpensively; 2) clinical service is discretionally and interaction-intensive, which makes it difficult for the state authority to monitor and assess whether or not the provided service is adequate; and 3) sometimes the state monitoring authority has few incentives to effectively monitor doctors' absence and performance, the strengthening of the beneficiary control seems to be a desirable option (World Bank 2003). However, there are some conditions that must be in place for beneficiary control to function well, and in many cases, these conditions are not met. Banerjee and Duflo (2006) point out that the following conditions should be satisfied in order for beneficiary control to affect absence, and these conditions are also applicable to more general cases, including the issue of healthcare quality: 1) beneficiaries must have a real demand for the service so that they have enough incentives to monitor providers; 2) the group of beneficiaries (for example, the community) must have some institutions or mechanisms to overcome a collective action problem, since whoever it is that monitors the providers all the beneficiaries can enjoy the same benefit, and thus everyone would like to have someone else do the monitoring; 3) beneficiaries must have a mechanism for affecting providers (through decision on hiring and firing, the amount of payment or promotion, or through social reward, for example).

Experiences with community participation have had mixed results. Banerjee and Duflo (2006) report disappointing results in two randomized experiments on absenteeism. The first, which was done in India, simply paid members of the community to check the presence of health workers. The results show that this intervention did not affect the absence rate. In this experiment, the community did not have any formal authority to affect providers and many communities did not seem to have any effective mechanisms for overcoming the collective action problem. The fact that conditions (2) and (3) above were unmet was the cause of the failure. Banerjee and Duflo (2006) also argue that condition 1) might not have been met as well: people seem to have had low expectations of the healthcare system and, as a result, had little desire to invest time and energy into making it better. A second experiment on teachers' absences in Kenya tried to satisfy conditions (2) and (3). In this experiment, school committees consisting of the students' parents were facilitated to have a meeting with school administration at the subdistrict level to ensure that the information the school committees had on the functioning of the school was transmitted to the hierarchy. In addition, the school committees were given funds to give a prize to the teachers whom they judged to have performed the best. However, the results were not encouraging: no statistically significant improvement in absence rates was found.

On the other hand, a successful case was reported by Bjorkman and Svensson (2007). They conducted a randomized field experiment in Uganda which entailed a more elaborate community-based monitoring project called 'Citizen Report Cards (CRCs)'. The first step was to conduct a survey of healthcare providers and a survey of healthcare users. The data from these two surveys were analysed and a small subset of the findings was assembled in CRCs on aspects such as utilization, quality of services, informal user charges and comparisons *vis-à-vis* other health facilities in the district and the country at large. This comparison was intended to affect the expectations of the community toward the health facilities and thus induce the community to demand improvement, thereby meeting condition 1. In addition to the report cards, posters were also designed so that even the non-literate could understand the information. After receiving this information, a community meeting was organized with the help of facilitators from various community-based organizations (CBOs) who utilized the participatory approach, and the community's suggestions for improvements were summarized in an action plan. This provided a community with a tool to overcome the collective action problem (condition 2) since the facilitators had the very mission and motivation to overcome it. Alongside this, a health facility meeting was also organized to review and analyse its performance and compare it with other health clinics in the district and across the country. After that, an interface meeting with community members and health facility staff was held to devise a strategy, or 'contract', for improvement based on the action plan developed in the community meeting and the discussions from the health facility meeting. After these initial meetings, a mid-term review, including a community meeting and an interface meeting, was conducted with the help of facilitators from the CBOs. This interface meeting can give the community the ability to affect providers (condition 3) even though the community, CBOs and the interface meeting do not have authority over the personnel or budget of the health facility. The results were encouraging. The implementation of the CRCs significantly reduced the absence rate by 19 per cent. The project also significantly increased equipment usage by healthcare providers, villagers' health facility utilization and immunization of children, reduced child mortality rates and increased infant weights. This suggests the possible effectiveness of this elaborate community-based monitoring, in which community meetings and interface meetings are organized systematically and regularly with the help of the facilitators.[10]

The result of the CRCs experiment is very encouraging, but there are some remarks to be noted, which also apply to other forms of community participation.

First, CRCs may have a potentially adverse effect on vacancy. In our field interview, a nurse in a PHC where the medical officers' posts had been vacant for several years responded that one reason for the long vacancy was the excessive 'political power' of the community, that is, the community was too demanding. Since doctors' salaries at the PHCs are only one-sixth of those at private hospitals[11], if the community becomes 'empowered' and begins to censure doctors for their absence more severely, it is possible that fewer doctors would accept work at PHCs, especially in rural areas.[12] Without increasing the benefit of work-ing at rural PHCs, empowering the community and making monitoring effective might increase vacancies at PHCs in the future, though it would induce the doctors currently working at PHCs to refrain from being absent. However, it is still possible that CRCs would induce the commu-nity to cooperate more with doctors and that doctors would highly value this cooperation and commendation from the community for improve-ment of community health conditions. Thus, whether the introduction of community-based monitoring has an adverse effect on vacancy is an empirical question that should be evaluated, and we leave this for future research. On the adverse effect on vacancy, monitoring mecha-nisms other than community-based monitoring would be worse given the same level of wages because commendation and cooperation from the community would not be available. Duflo and Hanna (2005) ran a 'camera experiment', in which they gave cameras with a tamper-proof date and time function to teachers in non-formal single-teacher primary education centres in rural Udaipur district, India, and required them to take a picture of themselves and their students every day at opening time and at closing time. Their salary depended on the number of 'valid' days, which was defined as days when the opening and closing pictures were separated by at least five hours and a minimum number of chil-dren were present in both pictures. The results displayed an immediate and persistent improvement in teacher attendance within the same level of average salary. However, the cautionary note is that teachers' salaries in the Indian public sector are high relative to their private counter-parts, and they would still agree to work there even if the monitoring system were introduced. On the other hand, the salaries of PHC doctors are remarkably lower relative to their private counterparts, and there is already a noticeable number of vacant posts in rural PHCs. We suspect that if such a monitoring system were introduced in PHCs with the same level of average salary, then the vacancy rate would worsen. Furthermore, if the community expects that strict monitoring will discourage poten-tial doctors from working in their community, as noted above, then the community will choose not to effectively monitor and discuss absen-teeism and performance. This implies that ensuring doctor availability

234 Making Health Services More Accessible in Developing Countries

in the future is critical. This point holds not only for CRCs but also for every kind of community monitoring and community empowerment programme. In addition, local authorities would have no incentive to implement a stricter monitoring scheme if there were a risk of increasing vacancy.

The last point is the sustainability of CRCs. The CRCs experiment in Uganda, which consisted of data analysis, summarization of the findings, community meeting, facility meeting and interface meeting with the help of facilitators, and regular follow-up meetings, was quite well-designed for overcoming the collective action problem. However, it is questionable whether that intensive community-based monitoring would be sustained after the external donor and research team had left the site, especially because everyone would have an incentive to shirk the monitoring and other duties. In order to increase the project's sustainability, therefore, the community (or government) needs to establish some institutional device to alleviate the collective action problem and, to save the monitoring burden, the minimum size of an effective monitoring mechanism should also be identified. Bestowing the community or the interface meeting with some authority over the personnel and budget of the health facilities might increase the benefits from the collective action and induce the community members to exert more effort to some extent.

CRCs are not the only means of community participation. One extreme is to let the community directly manage the health facilities, a task that requires a high level of community institutional capability as well as a pool of alternative health workers. The World Bank (2003) provides a rather comprehensive review of the experience of community participation around the world.

7.3.3 Increase the benefits of working for PHCs

As noted above, the threat of vacancy discourages communities and authorities from implementing any effective monitoring system. Thus, it is necessary to increase the benefits of working for rural PHCs in order to reduce the vacancy rate in rural areas. We should note that the increase in benefits would not directly reduce absenteeism or increase the effort expended by the health providers. Rather, it should be regarded as a prerequisite for implementing an effective monitoring system which could induce lower absence rates and a higher level of effort.

One straightforward way of increasing benefits is to increase salaries since the current salary level is too low, at just one-sixth that of private counterparts. However, a small increase in salary might not lead to a substantial improvement in the vacancy rate in rural PHCs, and a large salary increase would not be feasible due to government budgetary constraints. A more feasible option would be to attach a substantial weight to 'performance' at the PHC in promotion decisions. This would not only alleviate the problem of vacancy but would also attract more competent doctors to work at PHCs, since they are more likely to produce higher performance, which would greatly assist their prospects for promotion. The important factor in implementing this is how to measure the performance. We will discuss this issue later.

It might be also a good idea to provide scholarships, with the condition that the stipendiary should work for rural PHCs for several years after becoming a doctor. This will directly increase the number of doctors prospectively working for PHCs and also help to locate those students who are intrinsically motivated but who have financial difficulties themselves to serve rural poor people. Leonard, Masatu and Vialou (2005) found evidence that 'altruistic' health providers exerted greater effort irrespective of incentive schemes, and so increasing the ratio of such 'altruistic' doctors in rural PHCs would enhance the quality of healthcare service there.

Shorter office hours and allowing staff to work privately outside office hours, on the other hand, would also improve the working conditions at rural PHCs. However, this should be supplemented by a good monitoring mechanism of 'performance' in PHCs. Without monitoring, doctors might treat their patient badly in the public practice and treat them well in the private practice in order to induce them to come to the private practice, resulting in degradation of the quality of health services at PHCs. Holmstrom and Milgrom (1991) theoretically analyse a multitask moral-hazard model and show that if it is easy to measure the performance of the contracted activity, then more private outside activity should be allowed to save the amount of reward, but if it is difficult to measure the performance of the contracted activity, on the other hand, then the private outside activity should be limited. Thus, how to measure doctors' performance and reflect it in their salary, promotion or non-monetary valuation is a critical issue.

7.3.4 Measuring the 'performance' of health workers and introducing an incentive system in the public sector

Measuring performance in clinical service is difficult since the desired treatment is heterogeneous and dependent on patients' conditions, which are usually unobservable to the government, and the question of whether the patients are cured or not is largely influenced by factors other than the quality of the healthcare service provided (World Bank 2003).

One way to measure the performance of health workers is to utilize patient or community information such as CRCs. Even though individuals and communities would be one of the least costly sources for obtaining information on the quality of healthcare, there is a drawback. Since the patients' evaluation is mostly determined by whether they felt better or not after their visit to the facilities, doctors might have incentives to prescribe treatments that lead to short-run improvement in symptoms, such as steroid shots, but which are not medically effective or are contraindicated (Das and Hammer 2007). Actually, this is the very reason why more than a few villagers prefer visiting RMPs, who are unqualified and just give a shot without diagnosing the patient's condition. The problem with patient evaluation is that it is subjective and not backed by medical knowledge. However, this does not mean that individual and community information should not be used. Such information has its own merits. Utilization of patient-provided information is inexpensive and would make health providers more responsive to their patients.

The drawback of utilizing information provided by patients and the community can be tackled by using other objective information that examines whether the prescriptions and treatments are medically adequate. Such objective information includes standard health outcome measures such as mortality rate and morbidity rate, and more direct observation of individual interaction such as medical-chart checks with random sampling. Since there is the possibility that doctors do not write true information on charts, it might be better to create a medical card for each patient, to which would be attached a prescription sheet that doctors would be required to write something concerning the problem of the patient and the prescribed treatment. By collecting these prescription sheets along with CRCs, we might be able to collect reliable information on the performance of health workers, though the information would not be perfect.

Once the information on the performance of health workers is obtained, there are many ways to link their performance to their reward. However, given the evidence suggesting that monetary incentive might kill intrinsic social motivation (Gneezy and Rustichini 2000a, 2000b), it might be good to link the performance to promotion and dismissal instead of to monetary salary. As noted above, if the performance at rural PHCs is favourably weighted in promotion decisions, then more competent doctors will work in rural areas where vacancies are high and the competence of current health workers is miserable. If reliable information on performance is available, then it would also be possible to allow some private practice, to ensure that doctors could obtain additional income, which would make it easier for them to accept to work in rural PHCs.

One concern is the political feasibility of introducing these incentive schemes, which may include punishment or other sanctions. In particular, it would be very difficult to fire underperforming public doctors. When these political constraints become serious, contracting out or PPP would be required.

7.3.5   Utilizing a market-based reward system

In addition to utilizing the subjective and objective information, the government might be able to discipline health service providers through a market-based reward system. Klemick, Leonard and Masatu (2006) found that doctors in the private sector were less likely to be absent in Tanzania, and Das and Hammer (2007) found that doctors in private clinics exert more effort than doctors in the public sector. These results seem to imply that privatization would be a workable option for improvement.

However, the market and private healthcare service provision is not free from drawbacks. The first drawback is that markets are not pro-poor. Though the market is responsive to potential customers' demands, it is not responsive to the needs of those who have no purchasing power. Thus, unless there is an increase in the purchasing power of the poor, the market-based reward system will not benefit them. This is why poor rural villages face underdevelopment of the private health sector. Furthermore, if there are no competitors in the region, then the provider could set a monopoly price, which makes the service even more inaccessible to the poor. The second drawback is related to the problem of asymmetric information. Most patients lack medical knowledge and tend to highly evaluate those treatments that lead to short-run improvement in symptoms but which may not be medically effective. Since this second drawback can be tackled by collecting adequate information, as noted in the previous section, here we focus on how to increase the purchasing power of the poor so that a market-reward system can become pro-poor.

One way to increase the purchasing power of the poor is to provide the poor with health insurance with targeted subsidized prices. A challenge along this line is an additional asymmetric information problem: adverse selection and moral hazard. Currently in India, there are a number of NGOs that provide health insurance tailored for the poor, called health micro-insurance, but almost none of them employ any mechanism for curtailing adverse selection and moral hazard. One problem is that the insurance premiums are the same for healthy and unhealthy persons, with the result that only the unhealthy will purchase the insurance. This adverse selection issue has been drawing the attention of practitioners recently. On the other hand, little attention has been paid to moral hazard, which is also a major problem in the insurance market. It would be valuable to conduct research identifying how serious adverse selection and moral hazard are and how we can alleviate these problems.

Provision of medical vouchers to the poor also empowers them with purchasing power and makes health workers more responsive to their needs. Compared to insurance, vouchers would suffer less from asymmetric information. Vouchers provide the poor with the 'right' to use healthcare service a certain number of times, and the unused vouchers could be sold to those who need them if a market for vouchers were available. Individuals would have an incentive to take care of their health and reduce unnecessary visits to clinics because they could earn money by selling their unused vouchers in the market. There would be no adverse selection since everyone would be willing to receive the vouchers from the government, and there is no participation decision in effect. However, a downside of medical vouchers relative to health insurance is the restriction on the number of free consultations. Since some diseases require repeated consultation and also make individuals more vulnerable to other diseases, this restriction would have a serious impact on those poor patients who are vulnerable to illness due to nutritional deprivation.

Although there are some limitations, these market-based reward systems can be compatible with public health provision by relating the reward for health workers to the revenue of the facility. Furthermore, these interventions increase the voice of the poor and make the providers more responsive to the poor, which strengthens the effectiveness of community participation. Market, public organization and community are not substitutes but complements.

However, these market-based reward systems might not be effective in remote areas with low population densities. In such areas, there are no other competing health providers, and the marginal benefit of effort is not as high as in more competitive areas, since if there are competitors, their improved efforts will attract both the ex-customers of competitors and potential users who have chosen not to visit any facilities heretofore; if there are no competitors, their improved effort will only attract the latter. Thus in remote areas with low population density, the role of the incentive system in public organization and community participation is important.

7.3.6 Remarks

Above, we presented and analysed the possible solutions for improvement of the public health sector rather optimistically. Indeed, there are a great number of policies and reforms with a similar spirit to that of our argument, and they have been implemented with mixed results. There are many other factors affecting the results in addition to the points we have argued above, and they could affect the results substantially. Correcting incentive mechanisms is like repairing a bucket. Even if we repaired most parts, if there still remained a single hole, then water would leak from the bucket. Likewise, even if we corrected most of the incentive system, if there still remained a loophole, then people would find a way to pursue their own self-interest which would run counter to the social benefit.

Corruption is a good example. In spite of the great efforts expended on anti-corruption policies in many countries, experience shows that it remains impossible to plug up the hole in the bucket in many cases. Our policy suggestions are no exception. There is a possibility for collusion between doctors and politicians, health staff and community leaders, and evaluators and doctors. In this sense, our suggestions above are far from complete, and should be supplemented with a set of well-designed anti-collusion schemes that impose large costs on colluders. However, we believe that first plugging up the big holes and dealing with the smaller holes one by one is a practical way to repair the whole bucket.

One short route to improvement is to use a pre-existing, well-functioning bucket instead of repairing the broken bucket from scratch. It is reported that in some countries, NGO clinics function fairly well. Leonard and Masatu (2007) and Leonard, Masatu and Vialou (2007) report that, in Tanzania, many NGO clinics with a decentralized system (that is, the chief of each NGO clinic has significant authority in hiring and firing, setting of fees and deciding staff salaries) achieve significantly higher performance than public ones, although there is no significant difference in competence between public doctors and NGO doctors. An experiment in Cambodia shows that contracting out primary health services to NGOs achieved significant improvement of some health outcome measures (World Bank 2003). Although it is important to know what components of NGOs are really important in producing good outcomes in order to ensure accurate scaling up and replication, it might be a good idea to contract out some health services to credible NGOs when they are available.

7.4   Conclusion

In this chapter, we described the current situation of public primary health centres in India and pointed out that they do not seem to have had a significant impact on health outcomes. We argued that it is time to shift our focus from merely building facilities to improving incentive systems to motivate health providers. The analysis showed that Subcentre construction did not improve the male-female sex ratio, which suggests that merely building Subcentres did not contribute to improving health outcomes in rural areas. Furthermore, Subcentre construction was associated with an increase in the number of RMPs, who are medically unqualified and whose treatments are often inadequate, and the increase in the number of RMPs did not have any impact on the male-female ratio. The inability of Subcentres to drive away RMPs also suggested that Subcentre construction had not improved health outcomes.

Community participation could contribute to improvement of the quality of health service provided by public health facilities, but community participation also has its own limitations. In order to achieve a higher quality of healthcare service, we need to supplement it with an incentive reward system backed by reliable measurement of performance. Though the community and individuals suffer from a lack of the medical knowledge needed for assessing the quality of healthcare provided, it might be possible to combine their subjective information with a set of objective information which together could assess whether the treatment is medically adequate. By combining the interventions that empower the purchasing power of the poor together with these schemes, health service might be made more pro-poor.

Our point is that a given policy, such as decentralization, PPP or a performance-based reward system, can generate totally different results depending on the set of incentives affecting the providers. Currently, there are many experimental trials that attempt to evaluate the impact of specific policies, but the important means of making these experiments replicable is to understand the structure of incentives the providers face.

Table 7.A1: Probit estimates of health facility establishment

variables	PHC			Subcentre			CHC		
	(1)	(2)	(3)	(4)	(5)	(6)	(7)	(8)	(9)
intercept	-2.561***	-2.894***	-1.669***	-2.146***	-1.933***	-2.037***	-3.197***	-3.184***	-3.018***
	(0.066)	(0.153)	(0.330)	(0.047)	(0.082)	(0.151)	(0.139)	(0.192)	(0.340)
total population	19.087***	30.778***	28.258***	121.573***	120.161***	117.256***	-2.672	-5.582	-3.817
	(6.366)	(6.584)	(6.708)	(5.022)	(5.132)	(5.208)	(5.413)	(5.524)	(5.661)
population below age 6	-43.304	-60.302**	-40.566	-268.036***	-262.105***	-244.538***	42.954*	47.965**	38.950
	(28.421)	(28.779)	(29.701)	(22.130)	(22.305)	(22.913)	(23.881)	(23.973)	(25.008)
ST population	20.016***	1.542	5.850	41.094***	36.809***	33.159***	-3.420	-5.655	-2.182
	(4.621)	(5.305)	(5.406)	(4.030)	(4.530)	(4.583)	(4.949)	(5.424)	(5.393)
SC population	-13.218**	-2.488	-5.160	28.827***	26.982***	28.688***	-8.882	-4.490	-7.859
	(6.425)	(7.453)	(7.491)	(4.893)	(5.642)	(5.660)	(5.514)	(6.313)	(6.382)
literate population	5.342	-8.789	-9.963	-96.144***	-92.504***	-92.757***	14.071***	14.857***	14.670***
	(5.918)	(6.104)	(6.144)	(5.275)	(5.423)	(5.528)	(5.202)	(5.264)	(5.332)
water tap	0.074	0.110*	0.125**	0.124***	0.134***	0.138***	0.137***	0.152***	0.173***
	(0.057)	(0.060)	(0.061)	(0.032)	(0.032)	(0.033)	(0.053)	(0.053)	(0.054)
paved road	-0.022	0.359***	0.419***	0.700***	0.703***	0.701***	0.837***	0.862***	0.872***
	(0.065)	(0.074)	(0.076)	(0.047)	(0.050)	(0.050)	(0.136)	(0.141)	(0.146)
unpaved road	-0.143**	0.187***	0.249***	0.449***	0.439***	0.431***	0.480***	0.508***	0.530***
	(0.063)	(0.070)	(0.072)	(0.047)	(0.049)	(0.050)	(0.137)	(0.142)	(0.146)
distance	883.296***	195.790	205.137	153.832***	288.956***	298.516***	470.522***	593.904***	517.802***
	(64.478)	(125.723)	(130.613)	(46.430)	(94.848)	(95.381)	(89.877)	(198.609)	(194.334)
number of CHCs	0.276*	0.253*	0.264*	1.042***	1.020***	1.025***			
	(0.148)	(0.151)	(0.151)	(0.142)	(0.142)	(0.143)			
number of PHCs				0.689***	0.680***	0.692***	0.458***	0.494***	0.514***
				(0.055)	(0.055)	(0.056)	(0.057)	(0.057)	(0.058)
number of Subcentres	0.333***	0.538***	0.557***				0.010	0.059	0.101
	(0.060)	(0.075)	(0.076)				(0.064)	(0.076)	(0.076)
number of RMPs	0.022	0.032	0.030	0.107***	0.100***	0.102***	0.016	0.012	0.004
	(0.034)	(0.035)	(0.035)	(0.024)	(0.024)	(0.024)	(0.029)	(0.029)	(0.029)

(Continued)

Table 7.A1: Continued

variables	PHC			Subcentre			CHC		
	(1)	(2)	(3)	(4)	(5)	(6)	(7)	(8)	(9)
mandal Subcentre norm		-0.353***	-0.305***		-0.596***	-0.586***		-0.101	0.025
		(0.081)	(0.082)		(0.046)	(0.053)		(0.087)	(0.092)
mandal population		0.381**	-0.191		-0.268***	-0.079		0.010	-0.524**
		(0.194)	(0.221)		(0.098)	(0.109)		(0.188)	(0.214)
STD of village population		-15.622***	-12.957***		-1.474	-3.496***		5.987***	5.083**
		(2.925)	(3.043)		(1.270)	(1.345)		(2.009)	(2.163)
area of mandal		-0.001	-0.001		-0.000	-0.000		-0.001	-0.001
		(0.002)	(0.002)		(0.000)	(0.000)		(0.002)	(0.002)
average distance of villages in mandal		138.260	-19.224		-250.348**	-264.304**		-272.014	-228.652
		(176.984)	(185.197)		(122.148)	(123.055)		(254.024)	(251.903)
mandal ST population ratio		0.942***	0.560***		0.064	-0.032		0.140	-0.330*
		(0.142)	(0.169)		(0.078)	(0.089)		(0.155)	(0.185)
mandal SC population ratio		-0.403	0.450		0.087	-0.544**		-0.573	-0.633
		(0.434)	(0.499)		(0.196)	(0.230)		(0.409)	(0.477)
district Subcentre norm			-0.234			-0.150			-0.260
			(0.221)			(0.116)			(0.201)
STD of mandal Subcentre norm			1.106***			0.695***			-0.473
			(0.355)			(0.171)			(0.367)
district PHC norm			-1.007***			-0.025			-0.634**
			(0.269)			(0.114)			(0.255)
STD of district PHC norm			0.161			-0.175***			0.217*
			(0.125)			(0.053)			(0.119)
district population			-0.035***			0.003			-0.004
			(0.007)			(0.003)			(0.007)
STD mandal population			4.192***			-2.620***			6.812***
			(1.317)			(0.605)			(1.306)
district ST population ratio			0.002			0.977***			0.443
			(0.416)			(0.199)			(0.412)
district SC population ratio			-1.591**			1.852***			-0.053
			(0.804)			(0.384)			(0.856)

Note: Regressors are round 1 values. Population, literacy and distance are divided by 100,000

Table 7.A2: Probit and DID estimates of KMP presence

variables	(1)	(2)	(3)	(1)	(2)	(3)
intercept	-2.102***	-2.047***	-2.777***	-8.183**	-10.414***	-11.350***
	(0.051)	(0.085)	(0.161)	(3.956)	(3.996)	(4.027)
total population	52.903***	50.231***	63.691***			
	(4.370)	(4.432)	(4.612)			
population below age 6	-88.138***	-83.691***	-171.720***	-80.080***	-78.770***	-73.912***
	(19.265)	(19.343)	(20.318)	(14.239)	(14.247)	(14.369)
ST population	22.769***	34.315***	30.904***	42.055***	40.093***	39.187***
	(3.658)	(4.168)	(4.374)	(6.611)	(6.692)	(6.693)
SC population	35.176***	16.577***	19.317***	12.097***	24.026***	32.387***
	(4.418)	(5.013)	(5.179)	(6.015)	(6.383)	(6.384)
literate population	-52.752***	-47.194***	-44.116***	75.639***	76.462***	74.062***
	(4.668)	(4.744)	(4.948)	(3.464)	(3.494)	(3.548)
water tap	0.020	0.005	0.036	0.101***	0.089***	0.005
	(0.033)	(0.033)	(0.034)	(0.013)	(0.014)	(0.015)
paved road	0.969***	0.827***	0.820***	-0.052*	-0.071**	-0.081***
	(0.052)	(0.056)	(0.059)	(0.027)	(0.028)	(0.028)
unpaved road	0.778***	0.631***	0.576***	-0.009	-0.017	0.003
	(0.052)	(0.055)	(0.058)	(0.026)	(0.026)	(0.027)
distance	-185.349***	342.197***	325.599***			
	(49.475)	(107.583)	(108.792)			
number of Subcentres	-0.256***	0.055	0.074	0.258***	0.249***	0.254***
	(0.043)	(0.050)	(0.052)	(0.016)	(0.016)	(0.016)
number of PHCs	0.190***	0.229***	0.234***	0.103***	0.100***	0.120***
	(0.048)	(0.049)	(0.050)	(0.039)	(0.039)	(0.039)
mandal Subcentre norm		-0.565***	-0.100*		0.020**	-0.074***
		(0.046)	(0.052)		(0.010)	(0.016)
mandal population		-0.208**	-0.139		0.298*	-0.516**
		(0.099)	(0.113)		(0.172)	(0.212)

(Continued)

Table 7.A2: Continued

variables	(1)	(2)	(3)	(1)	(2)	(3)
STD of village population		6.721*** (1.246)	4.987*** (1.355)		−3.562** (1.439)	−0.486 (1.599)
area of mandal		0.001*** (0.000)	0.001*** (0.000)			
average distance of villages in mandal		−400.525*** (136.996)	−382.673*** (141.184)			
mandal ST population ratio		−0.415*** (0.084)	−1.174*** (0.108)		0.070 (0.444)	−0.506 (0.484)
mandal SC population ratio		1.097*** (0.193)	−0.488** (0.239)		−2.615*** (0.446)	−1.083** (0.531)
district Subcentre norm			−0.863*** (0.102)			−0.013 (0.031)
STD of district Subcentre norm			−2.406*** (0.181)			0.602*** (0.084)
district PHC norm			−0.259** (0.114)			−0.022 (0.025)
STD of mandal PHC norm			0.672*** (0.054)			−0.032 (0.039)
district population			0.034*** (0.003)			−0.009 (0.010)
STD of mandal population			1.073* (0.636)			7.189*** (0.692)
district ST population ratio			2.542*** (0.208)			−0.057 (2.020)
district SC population ratio			1.610*** (0.431)			−6.458*** (1.035)

Notes: 1. (1) to (3) are probit estimates RMP presence in round 2 on the sample with no RMPs in round 1. Size is 23,277.
2. (4) to (6) are difference-in-differences estimates on full sample. Size is 26,730.
3. Population, literacy, and distance are divided by 100,000.

Notes

1. NHP-2002, 2.2.3 also states: 'It is a principal objective of NHP-2002 to evolve a policy structure which reduces these inequities and allows the disadvantaged sections of society a fairer access to public health services.'
2. Figures are from the 2001 AP survey.
3. Strictly speaking, some RMPs have medical licences. They were given licences to practice medicine in the early days as an official compromise due to the lack of qualified doctors in rural areas. We use the term 'licensed' in the way that it is supposed to imply. See also Radwan (2005) for a description of RMPs.
4. AYUSH stands for Ayurveda, Yoga and Naturopathy, Unani, Siddha, and Homoeopathy.
5. The norms for both Subcentres and PHCs are lower for hilly areas where ST population resides, at 2000 and 20,000, respectively. As a nonnegligible portion of AP is covered by hilly terrain, use of plain norms undervalues the gravity of the lack of access.
6. Efficiency here thus refers to additional population coverage by a new establishment, and is not concerned with the difference in input costs depending on location.
7. Having a paved road approach to the village increases the chance of having a PHC, but so does having an unpaved road. This is due to the fact most of the villages have both, with a high correlation of .84.
8. Districts with high SC ratios get more, and the size of effect is twice as large as the ST ratio, suggesting that the SC population has stronger political influence than the ST population because political influence usually works at district level, but not at mandal level.
9. This is also observed by the people from several mandals we have talked with during our field visits.
10. A prototype of the CRCs started to be implemented in Bangalore, India in 1994, which has been spread to other states and other countries including Uganda (stated above), the Philippines, Vietnam, Bangladesh and Ukraine. The details of the projects and the outcomes have varied (Wagle, Singh and Shah 2004; World Bank 2003).
11. From our field interview with a PHC doctor.
12. Chaudhury et al. (2005) argue the possibility for implicit contract between the state authority and doctors, which permits the doctors to be absent from the PHCs to some degree in order to work privately in exchange for agreeing to work in undesirable rural areas where they can hardly find good educational conditions for their children, exciting entertainment and opportunities to interact with other educated people.

References

Banerjee, Abhijit and Esther Duflo (2006) 'Addressing Absence', *Journal of Economic Perspectives*, Vol. 20, No. 1: 117–32.

Banerjee, Abhijit, Angus Deaton and Esther Duflo (2004) 'Health Care Delivery in Rural Rajasthan', *Economic and Political Weekly*, 28 February 2004: 944–9.

Banerjee, Abhijit and Rohini Somanathan (2007) 'The Political Economy of Public Goods: Some Evidence from India', *Journal of Development Economics*, Vol. 82, No. 2 (March): 287–314.

Barber, Sarah L., Paul J. Gertler and Pandu Harimurti (2007) 'Differences in Access to High-quality Outpatient Care in Indonesia', *Health Affairs*, Vol. 26, No. 3: w352–w366.

Bjorkman, Martina and Jakob Svensson (2007) 'Power to the People: Evidence from a Randomized Field Experiment of a Community-based Monitoring Project in Uganda.' CEPR Discussion Paper No. 6344.

Chaudhury, Nazmul, Jeffrey Hammer, Michael Kremer and Karthik Muralidharan (2006) 'Missing in Action: Teacher and Health Worker Absence in Developing Countries', *Journal of Economic Perspectives*, Vol. 20, No. 1: 91–116.

Das, Jishnu and Jeffrey Hammer (2005) 'Which Doctor? Combining Vignettes and Item Response to Measure Clinical Competence', *Journal of Development Economics*, Vol. 78, No. 2: 348–83.

Das, Jishnu and Jeffrey Hammer (2007) 'Money for Nothing: The Dire Stratis of Medical Practice in Delhi, India', *Journal of Development Economics*, Vol. 83, No. 1: 1–36.

Duflo, Esther and Rema Hanna (2005) 'MonitoringWorks: Getting Teachers to Come to School.' CEPR Discussion Paper No. 5426.

Gneezy, Uri and Aldo Rustichini (2000a) 'A Fine is a Price', *Journal of Legal Studies*, Vol. 29, No. 1: 1–18.

Gneezy, Uri and Aldo Rustichini (2000b) 'Pay Enough or Don't Pay at All', *Quarterly Journal of Economics*, Vol. 115, No. 3: 791–810.

Holmstrom, Bengt and Paul Milgrom (1991) 'Multitask Principal-agent Analyses: Incentive Contracts, Asset Ownership and Job Design', *Journal of Law, Economics and Organization*, Vol. 7 (Special Issue): 24–52.

Klemick, Heather, Kenneth L. Leonard and Melkiory C. Masatu (2006) 'Understaffed or Underqualified? Health Care Staffing and Patient Access to Quality Care in Rural Tanzania.' Mimeograph.

Leonard, Kenneth L. and Melkiory C. Masatu (2007) 'Variation in the Quality of Care Accessible to Rural Communities in Tanzania.' *Health Affairs*, Vol. 26, No. 3: w380–w392.

Leonard, Kenneth L., Melkiory C. Masatu and Alex Vialou (2005) 'Getting Clinicians to Do Their Best: Ability, Altruism and Incentives.' Mimeograph.

Leonard, Kenneth L., Melkiory C. Masatu and Alex Vialou (2007) 'Getting Doctors to Do Their Best: The Roles of Ability and Motivation in Health Care Quality', *Journal of Human Resources*, Vol. 42, No. 3: 682–700.

Ministry of Health and Family Welfare (2005a), *National Rural Health Mission: Meeting People's Health Needs in Rural Areas*, at: http://mohfw.nic.in/NRHM/Documents/NRHM% 20-%20Framework%20for%20Implementation.pdf

Ministry of Health and Family Welfare (2006a), *Health Sector Reforms in India: Initiatives from Nine States*, Volume I, at: www.whoindia.org/LinkFiles/Health Sector Reform HSR in India Vol I.pdf

Ministry of Health and Family Welfare (2006b), *Health Sector Reforms in India: Initiatives from States*, Volume II, at: www.whoindia.org/LinkFiles/Health Sector Reform HSR in India Vol II. zip

Probe Qualitative Research Team (2002) 'Healthcare Seeking Behavior in Andhra Pradesh', Mumbai: Probe Qualitative Research.

Radwan, Ismail (2005) 'India – Private Health Services for the Poor: Policy Note', Health, Nutrition and Population (HNP) Discussion Paper, World Bank.

Registrar General, India (2006), *Maternal Mortality in India: 1997–2003, Trends, Causes and Risk Factors*, at: www.health.mp.gov.in/Maternal Mortality in India 1997–2003.pdf

Wagle, Swarnim, Janmejay Singh and Parmesh Shah (2004) 'Citizen Report Card Surveys – A Note on the Concept and Methodology', World Bank Social Development Note No. 91, Washington: World Bank.

World Bank (2003) *Making Service Work for the Poor People,* World Development Report 2004, New York: World Bank and Oxford University Press.

8
Health Services for Socially Excluded Tribes: Learning from the Asha Kiran Society's Intervention in Orissa, India

Cheryl D'Souza and Anugrah Abraham

Introduction

The articulation of global experiences in healthcare provision in the scattered poor regions of the world reflect the impressive effort being made towards expanding the knowledge-sharing base for those involved in actually making these initiatives realizable for the poor. This chapter finds expression within this larger knowledge base, attempting to trace a small yet significant case of the struggles of a primitive tribal group tucked away in inaccessible hill tracts of the Eastern Ghats of the Indian subcontinent.

While the preceding chapters deal in-depth with a cross-section of issues that affect the provision of health services to the poor, this chapter highlights one tribe's experiences in accessing modern healthcare. This is done by tracing an NGO's (the Asha Kiran Society) attempts at reaching out to a tribe considered by all to be unreachable. Outlined in the next few pages is a brief background of the intervention area and the people group, primary barriers that affect the utilization of healthcare, the specific Asha Kiran Society intervention and primary outcomes and lessons learned in working among this marginalized tribal group. The extreme nature of vulnerability/poverty that characterizes this context means the gains have been limited, but worth examining since these may provide some insights into bringing healthcare to the extreme poor.

The Asha Kiran Society is a faith-based non-profit organization in Koraput district of Orissa, India and was established in 1991 with a vision to work towards holistic development of the needy in the area. From the original team of eight, the team today consists of 70 full-time staff and about 170 community health volunteers. The operation of Asha Kiran's secondary-level hospital provides the resources for the organization to provide low-cost healthcare and to engage in community level work.[1] Occasionally, additional external financial support is accepted for specific projects.

The Asha Kiran Society (AKS) has been working with several tribal groups, one of which is the Bondo tribe. This paper limits itself to examine Asha Kiran's engagement with the Bondos and to draw lessons from its experiences. It is likely that not all the lessons from this experience can be generalized across contexts. Some may be of direct application to a tribal context; however the authors believe that this experience as a whole will find resonance with others engaged in bringing healthcare to the marginalized and extreme poor around the world. There exist numerous instances that illustrate the extent of social exclusion and its directly devastating link with the distressing health status of an entire tribe. Picking up on some of these, this chapter attempts to look beyond fragmented explanations to seek an integrated understanding of a complex reality.

This chapter briefly delineates the backwardness of rural Orissa, especially the regions where the Bondo tribe resides. Healthcare provision in the tribal districts of Orissa is grossly underdeveloped, and it is here that AKS started its intervention. In section 2, four prominent barriers to utilizing the government-provided healthcare services are discussed, namely, geographical, economic, organizational and cultural barriers. AKS had been successful, in relative terms *vis-à-vis* government, in all these aspects. But the most important efforts lie in lowering the cultural barriers facing the tribal – AKS healthcare workers speak their language and with health services at the village level, the tribal no longer feel intimidated or harassed as they regularly do outside of their hamlets. These all contributed to a significant change in healthcare-seeking behaviour and receptiveness to external interventions. Section 3 elaborates AKS's interventions in tribal healthcare, including construction of a secondary-level hospital and a peripheral clinic, provision of micro-insurance, employment and training of village health workers, and provision of promotional and preventive medicine jointly with the state government. Section 4 provides a glance through the visible achievements in terms of increased utilization of healthcare and improved maternal and child health, followed by conclusions and key generalizable lessons.

8.1 Background to the tribal context in Orissa, India

The state of Orissa accounts for 3.5 per cent of India's population (as of 2001) but a disproportionate 6.5 per cent of India's poor reside in this state (Mehta and Shah 2001). Indigenous people groups comprise 23 per cent of the population and are some of the most disadvantaged and excluded groups in the country. In undivided Koraput in southwestern Orissa, the proportion of tribal populations living in extreme poverty is as high as 60 per cent. According to the latest Orissa Human Development Report (Government of Orissa 2004) the high levels of poverty within which these tribes subsist translates into poorer levels of human development.

With a concentration of tribal population, the districts of Koraput and Malkangiri (where the NGO Asha Kiran Society works and whose intervention in the area this study traces), are among the districts with the lowest Human Development Index (HDI) values. This part of the state attracts particular attention in terms of policy intervention, being among the poorest regions in the country. Chronic drought conditions, food insecurity, income poverty, distress migration, lack of safe drinking water, starvation deaths, severe undernutrition and malnutrition, inadequate health infrastructure and poor rural infrastructure characterize this region (Government of Orissa 2004).

The healthcare dimension of development is wholly undermined in the state of Orissa. The public provision of health services in Orissa has been evidenced as inadequate, inequitable and disproportionate for the majority of the poor in urgent need of such services. The dual prerequisites to provide health services are insufficient – human resources (manpower) and physical infrastructure. Besides these, the low extent of immunization coverage points to the particular vulnerability of these populations to diseases that are routinely vaccine-preventable. The infant mortality rate (IMR) in Orissa is 69 per 1000 births, being significantly higher than the other Indian states (Government of Orissa 2006). The maternal mortality rate (MMR) is 358 per 100,000 live births, comparatively higher than the national average of 301 (Government of Orissa 2006). Health indicators such as low life expectancy at birth, infant mortality and maternal mortality can be attributed to inappropriate public expenditure and inefficient intervention.

The Bondos, inhabitants of this region for centuries, and of Austro-Asiatic origin, are scheduled by the government of India as a primitive tribal group (PTG) and a most vulnerable tribal group (MVTG). With a dwindling population of about 5500, they inhabit the upper hill tracts of the Malkangiri forests of southwestern Orissa. Despite their geophysical isolation and economic and social neglect, their very existence is a remarkable display of the inherent resilience of this people group. Dreaded and feared by the government and neighbouring tribes as a hostile people, they have a reputation for being prone to violence, with high homicide and suicide rates. Death due to curable and vaccine-preventable ailments and maternal and reproductive health complications are very high in the Bondo Hills, due to their geographical isolation, low levels of awareness about disease, traditional beliefs and poor or no access to a reliable health facility. Theirs is a barter economy with minimal use of cash. However, reliance on largely out-of-pocket cash expenditure is one of the main mechanisms of financing health needs and this bears cruelly on the already impoverished tribal people. Coupled with this is poor physical, social and economic access, which affects the utilization of public health facilities.

8.2 Barriers to healthcare

Accessibility of health services is not just about the physical availability and affordability of services but is a multidimensional concept (Frenk 1992). It also depends on factors such as the cultural and social acceptability of health intervention, traditional beliefs about health and illness, social support systems facilitating use of services and the primary interactions between the range of providers and patients. Although these determinants are interdependent, in this paper we shall classify them as geographical, economic (affordability), organizational and cultural (acceptability) factors.

Although there exists a debatable line distinguishing demand-side factors and supply-side factors that have a bearing on health outcomes, for the sake of discussion these are listed separately. Each demand-side barrier contains a significant supply-side element and vice versa. It has been established (Ensor and Cooper 2004) that the determinants of demand and supply may in turn generate barriers to utilization that arise when factors influence these determinants in a way that reduces utilization of services.

8.2.1 Cultural barriers

This aspect is most pertinent in a multicultural context such as India where health and development interventions need to acknowledge and appreciate differences in belief systems and world views to be truly people-centred. Tribal societies the world over have depended on evolving traditional systems of healing over many generations. Some of these beliefs have even withstood the scrutiny of modern science while most are still considered questionable.

However, these traditional systems have been the mainstay of tribal culture and are thus trusted by the tribal. Since modern medicine in the form of public health services are novel and unfamiliar, the tribal begins with distrust and gradually learns to fit this into his own understanding of healing. Thus the hesitancy of tribal societies to access healthcare, which may seem like a demand-side cultural barrier, may find its roots and solution in addressing the supply-side cultural barriers. These are the negative attitudes of providers in the form of officials, nurses and paramedics towards the tribal ng effect on access and utilization of healthcare services and further compound their inhibitions. Representatives of the government health system are usually non-tribal and this cultural and cognitive distance between provider and user stands as a major barrier. The non-tribal typically despises the tribal and his ways and often mocks his language, mannerisms and dress, and stereotypes him as ignorant and stupid. They therefore lack understanding and the insider perspective, and are crippled by a genuine fear of an unpredictable people (in the case of the Bondos). Thus, human interactions have the potential of disabling the health system due to a cultural abyss. Additionally, there has been a persistent lack of interest in crossing the linguistic barrier, which curbs communication and respect between provider and user.

Often health interventions fail to be culturally sensitive. Tribals often find the very buildings that house PHCs (primary health centres) and hospitals to be alien and intimidating and are overwhelmed by rigidly complicated procedures. At home, a patient is cared for by his family, but in a hospital the family is kept outside and care is provided by strangers.

All these manifestations of severe social exclusion, when put together, show why, justifiably, the tribal approaches the public health system with deep mistrust and apprehension. The cultural barriers are mentioned first since this has been the foundation for systemic exclusion of the tribal and works to strengthen all other barriers. Interventions that bridge this contribute to overcoming other barriers as well.

8.2.2 Geophysical barriers

Vulnerable populations that inhabit excluded regions suffer from poor access to healthcare by virtue of their isolated habitations, the difficult terrain that often characterizes these regions and the absolute unavailability of public transportation as a means of access to and from these areas. Private transportation is usually reserved as the last resort and when utilized has a crippling effect on the household due to its exorbitant costs. The tribals usually live in forests far from urban centres and often the only paths through these regions are made of mud and gravel and are exposed to the vagaries of the seasons. Inaccessibility to the more interior regions, especially during the rainy season, hampers adequate provision of health services. Roads and public infrastructure that would connect these socially excluded tribal regions are nonexistent. Sick patients – often on the brink of death – are often brought to widely scattered health facilities in makeshift stretchers as ambulances, carried for several kilometres by relatives. Long walks through forests to and from health facilities carry the additional risk of attack from wild animals.

Besides this, isolated hamlets also suffer the impact of geographical imbalances in the distribution of the health workforce (Dussault and Franceschini 2006). Due to the non-availability of infrastructure, electricity, housing, schools and so on, health workers choose not to live in tribal hamlets. Poor or no roads with no public transportation and the exorbitant cost of private transportation together form a strong disincentive for them to travel to the primary health centre to which they are posted. This translates into the non-availability of providers in or near the tribal hamlets. In addition, the very location of primary health centres further acts as a barrier since these are usually located near main roads and agglomerations of human settlements far from scattered tribal hamlets.

8.2.3   Organizational barriers

The poor performance of the public health sector in reaching tribal populations may be ascribed to several organizational barriers. Primary among these is a lack of accountability and responsiveness to the general public (Radwan 2005) characterized by absentee doctors, unresponsive ANMs (Auxiliary Nursing Midwives), informal payment due to corruption, and limited or no community participation in the functioning of the PHC. In some places private practice is permitted; hence, patients are referred to the doctor's private clinic. In this situation, the very poor patient does not receive even minimal care at the government facility and has to pay heavily at the doctor's private clinic. Besides this, the health system suffers from an erratic drug logistics and supply system. This results in non-availability of drugs and supplies, as a result of which the poor are required to purchase drugs that were meant to be supplied free of charge by the PHC from private pharmacies and unregistered drug dealers.

Another important aspect is the lack of public health management capacity (Radwan 2005). Although PHC doctors and district health officers may be good physicians, they generally possess little or no public health management skills. Neither are they permitted flexibility to reallocate financial capital and human resources to achieve better outcomes. This leads to poor management of the PHC (including staff, ANMs and so on) and a lack of monitoring and quality assurance. The poor condition of the PHC infrastructure and limited incentives for doctors in terms of low salaries and poor living conditions strike the final blow in an already battered situation.

The absence of mapping of satellite services creates an information vacuum as to the types of services available, their location and proximity. Hence, to access any auxiliary medical service, such as laboratories and x-rays, the poor patient may have to travel great distances with all the attendant difficulties and additional cost, even though these services may be available closer to home.

8.2.4   Economic barriers (affordability)

Non-cash economies such as that of tribal groups are disadvantaged right at the outset when faced with having to pay for healthcare. The non-availability of cash, especially during lean seasons, further compounds the vulnerability of a household seeking healthcare. High out-of-pocket expenditure is still the most common mechanism for financing the health needs of the very poor (Meessen et al. 2003). In this context, inadequate public health expenditure may be described as the primary barrier that keeps the state from hedging the health of the extreme poor. This is compounded by the absence of social security such as appropriate health financing mechanisms (health insurance) to protect against overall health hazards.

8.3   The Asha Kiran intervention

Working within this context of chronic poverty and disadvantage that characterizes the extremely poor regions in India, the NGO Asha Kiran Society (AKS) was set up in 1991 with the overall objective of facilitating holistic development among the largely tribal groups of Southern Orissa. The primary commitment at the inception of its work was in providing holistic healthcare to the populations of the Lamtaput block (Koraput district) and Bondo Hills (Khairput block, Malkangiri district). The focus was on people's access to a more reliable and equitable healthcare system that in turn would ensure a transformed and more just society. Since the team that started the Asha Kiran Society was mostly medically trained, their core competencies were health-related. Hence, from starting out as healthcare providers, they gradually diversified into what they perceived as other needs of the communities.

Besides a secondary-level hospital, some of their other initiatives are in primary healthcare, nutrition, agriculture and animal husbandry, training, education, language development and mother-tongue literacy.

8.3.1 Provision of curative health services (the Asha Kiran Hospital and Bondo Clinic)

Healthcare through first referral services (including family welfare and rural health services delivered through primary health centres) are underfunded in Orissa (Government of Orissa 2004). With this recognition of the inadequate public health system, AKS began the provision of healthcare through village-level health visits and the secondary-level Asha Kiran Hospital in 1991 and later through a peripheral clinic in the Bondo Hills in 1997. The Asha Kiran Society was set up in 1991 by a team comprising five doctors and a teacher as a small clinic in Lamtaput block of Koraput district in Orissa. This hilly terrain was chosen after a survey of the state of Orissa. Nearly 200km – a stretch of Southern Orissa from Jeypore to Motu – had at that time no credible medical or surgical facilities (Thomas 2002).

The AKS experience in setting up a clinic in the Bondo Hills traces a remarkable journey of perseverance and courage. Initial contact with the Bondos was made via mobile clinics set up at weekly base markets in the 1994–1996 period. Further inroads into this tribe were made when a medical doctor from Asha Kiran began frequenting the villages, learnt the local language and gradually began treating minor ailments. Until then this tribe had no access to medical care and had not been introduced to modern medicine. The only government-run primary health centre, located 21km away, was perceived to only treat victims of assault from bear mauls and fights. With the doctor from AKS treating fevers, malaria and diarrhoea there came a gradual recognition of the tangible benefits of modern medicine. In 1997 this doctor began staying in a Bondo village, providing constant services and building relationships with the people. These tribals were then asked to contribute towards the health services and initial payments varied from Rs. 1 or 2 in cash or a few tomatoes or a handful of rice. In 2000, the clinic shifted to a disused government building in the village, which had been handed over to AKS by the then Collector of Malkangiri district. With this, basic laboratory facilities to investigate diseases such as malaria and tuberculosis (TB) were also set up. In 2002, a donor (Action Aid) began to support Asha Kiran's efforts through a Community Health and Development programme.

Meanwhile, the Asha Kiran Hospital started out in a shack and, when funding was provided, took the shape of a 30-bed secondary hospital. Before designing the hospital, the architect studied tribal housing in the area, and designed the buildings along those lines using low-cost appropriate technology and hence providing a culturally acceptable front for the health facility. Cultural and linguistic barriers were broken down right at the outset of the NGOs interaction with the community, as a persistent effort was made to set up the clinic within a Bondo village, learn the tribal language (which was also scripted for the first time) and participate in their way of life. The healthcare providers at the hospital were more easily approachable since they spoke the language and were more responsive to the patients' needs while still being able to take full cognizance of local health traditions.

8.3.2   Provision of a financial tool

The Asha Kiran Hospital gradually grew into a secondary-level 30-bed hospital providing outpatient, inpatient and surgical facilities. However these interventions formed only part of a learning curve for the organization. In setting up the hospital, they encountered a dilemma similar to that suggested by Chambers (1983) in that the development of modern hospitals was a major source of difficulties for the rural poor, who have been made to choose between letting a sick patient die without care on the one hand and impoverishment because of high healthcare costs on the other.

In working closely with these groups, it soon emerged that one of the immediate challenges for the poor was the reliance on largely out-of-pocket payments during times of illness and disease. Distress sales of assets were the most common means of meeting hospitalization bills. This not only proved wholly deficient in financing their health needs but also further compounded their impoverishment. The catastrophic implication of such healthcare expenditure on already impoverished households is that it pushed the poor to spiral downward in the poverty trap.

The Asha Kiran Society community health insurance scheme was initiated in order to hedge the economic accessibility of healthcare services by these underserved populations.[2] It formed an integral part of the Society's Health and Development programme serving these marginalized tribal groups. The healthcare scheme was designed in such a manner that people benefited from health services (at the village, peripheral clinic and secondary-hospital level) and were able to overcome economic and physical access barriers. A distinguishing feature of the efforts of the Society in introducing community health insurance to the people was the consistent effort made towards building on the existing system of solidarity within the local community, such as their common beliefs and values and their collective activities, especially in agricultural work and celebration. Building on these aspects, people were encouraged to pool resources for health. This aimed at building capabilities through community-initiated voluntary participation, community management and risk pooling. With an individual enrolment and a nominal premium of Rs. 30 per person for a year, the scheme provided its members with three-tiered benefits, with the village-level health worker, the clinic based in the Bondo hills, and treatment at the hospital. The removal of any co-payment while accessing services was an essential component of the scheme for the Bondo tribe, given their situation of extreme poverty. Other tribes that the scheme covered were required to pay a co-payment since their financial situation was generally better. Treatment costs at the hospital are heavily subsidised by the meagre salaries drawn by the dedicated health professionals serving these poor, while treatment costs at the Bondo peripheral clinic are further subsidized by a donor partner. So although complete financial viability of this community health insurance scheme is as yet distant, it is certainly an important step in ensuring health coverage for this tribe.

8.3.3 Provision of basic and preventive services

Given the context of extreme poverty within which the work of AKS was inaugurated – the poor disproportionately affected by disease and the lack of health services – Radwan's (2005) assumption that the primary healthcare system plays the most important role in reducing the burden of disease has a significant bearing on planned intervention by AKS in the field of health service provision. The large network of local, trained community health workers (CHWs) forms a formidable workforce providing primary healthcare at the doorstep in the villages. Crucial to tribal life are strong solidarity systems involving collective activities. Therefore, based on the concept of mutual help and survival, the CHW also places her role as a community volunteer within this aspect of her tribal lifestyle. Appreciating this, Asha Kiran's outreach efforts among the primitive tribal groups have primarily been through this network of CHWs who have contributed to overcoming geographical, cultural and economic barriers to healthcare by making basic preventive, curative and promotive healthcare a permanent presence in the village. This workforce, comprising members of the local community, possesses an insider's perspective in understanding the specific health needs of its community.

Their responsiveness and availability as they provide doorstep primary healthcare has played a crucial role. These health workers are equipped to provide the bulk of primary healthcare at the village level and treat minor ailments such as diarrhoea and administer dosages for malaria and tuberculosis (TB), common conditions for which no cure was known till the AKS health intervention in the area. This team has made concerted efforts at awareness generation and community mobilization for the prevention and cure of such ailments (routinely preventable diseases which account for high mortality rates) as well as enhanced risk-coping strategies to increase enrolment in the community insurance scheme. Monthly review meetings are held for the CHWs where they are encouraged to review the health situation in their villages, report on patients they have treated and replenish their stock of medicines.

From the peripheral clinic in the Bondo hills, community nurses, along with trainee health assistants, make routine health visits to the villages to follow up on pregnant women, lactating mothers, patients under TB treatment, and chronically ill and aged persons. During these visits community meetings are also conducted, involving the community in the health insurance scheme and discussing the importance of under-five weight monitoring, antenatal checkups, and disease prevention.

The emphasis of the health intervention for these extremely vulnerable and at-risk groups is thus aimed at addressing a basic need for quality and efficient healthcare, improving equity and reducing the out-of-pocket expenses that aggravate poverty. Especially in the context of a primitive tribal group such as the Bondos, the intervention is focused on preventing diseases, reducing infant deaths and ensuring safe motherhood through improved access to treatment and essential drugs, thus raising the health security of the poor.

To summarize, low-cost quality care has been provided through a range of processes:

- The bulk of care at community and peripheral clinic level
- Rational drug use
- Low-cost prescriptions
- Rational diagnostics
- Protocol-driven care
- Low overheads (meagre salaries of staff, basic, clean amenities)
- Staff with a commitment to serve the poor
- Cognizance of local health traditions.

The AKS health intervention in the area has been designed within a rights-based approach, thus making healthcare services available as well as incorporating a strong element of community participation and stakeholdership in the health services provided to these groups. At the core of the successful reception of the health intervention was the effort made by the team to leverage the relationship built up with the village community for their greater empowerment. Hence besides curative services at the hospital and clinic, a major component weaved into the healthcare programme has been awareness-generation on preventive health issues, aimed at building capacities and a more informed and healthy community. A range of training programmes on health rights and awareness of the public health system for CHWs and health assistants have had government grassroots workers attending as well. As a consequence their work has also gained in efficiency.

8.4 What has been achieved?

8.4.1 Overcome the barriers

Working within a context largely distinguished by the social dimensions of inequality, the work of AKS through the years, with its vision of human development and emphasis on holistic healthcare, has achieved an exceptional transformation for these communities. Each milestone in this remarkable journey has seen a positive transgression of the rigid barriers that have stood in the way of reaching the poor. The constant physical presence of Asha Kiran in the Lamtaput block since 1991 and in the Bondo hills since 1997 and its integration with the communities has earned it an enduring relationship of trust with the local inhabitants of the area. Teams comprising medical and development workers living in the villages have journeyed far in appreciating local culture and traditions. Participation in festivals and the tribal way of life has brought a sense of oneness which has been realised as a prerequisite for even approaching the poor. The use of tribal languages has lowered communication barriers and fostered an understanding of the realities of the poor.

Efforts to preserve and document local culture have borne fruit with local languages and oral traditions being analysed and scripted. Medical anthropological studies have rendered health interventions more appropriate through recognition of traditional health systems.

The positive effects of the AKS intervention on the health-seeking behaviour and consequently on the overall healthcare of this tribal group have been most significant. The approach has been towards building local capabilities and has been largely a people-centred development initiative. The initiative stressed the community's participation in healthcare in order to ensure sustainability. Significant in this respect is the formidable workforce that has been drawn from among the locals of this secluded region. Neo-literates can go on to form an impressive human resource for healthcare; young semi-literate women from the villages have been trained as Health Assistants who assist trained nurses in all routine procedures at the peripheral clinic and on health visits. They further provide a familiar face to healthcare provision, especially for the otherwise hesitant tribal who, due to their efforts, can then approach the health facility with more confidence. This and associated efforts at the cultural appropriateness of health interventions have thus formed the basis of the positive reception of the healthcare programmes by the tribal populations.

8.4.2   Increased utilization

The impact of community health workers (CHWs) in lowering geographical barriers may be evidenced in the rise over the years in the number of patients treated by them (Figure 8.1). A major component of their work is generating awareness of health issues. This emphasis on community mobilization and awareness generation has been the most effective incentive for the tribal to access health services and even approach the secondary hospital for basic services. This has more specifically resulted in an increase in safe institutional deliveries and surgical

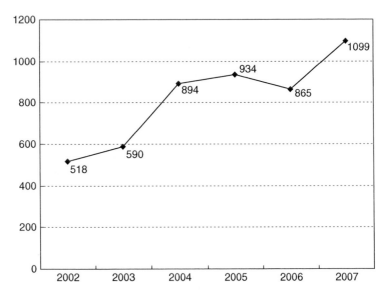

Figure 8.1:   Number of patients treated by CHWs
Source: The Asha Kiran Society.

procedures through which several lives have been saved. Using these net-works of local and accountable community volunteers providing basic diagnostic and treatment services at the village itself has contributed towards minimizing administrative costs to a considerable extent while avoiding unnecessary workload at the secondary hospital level.

Over the past few years the continuous presence of Asha Kiran's secondary-level hospital in Lamtaput and peripheral clinic in the Bondo Hills (especially in the absence of a public health facility in the inte-riors of the Bondo Hills), has resulted in a significant increase in utilization of health services by the target populations in the vicin-ity of these health facilities and particularly by those enrolled in the community health insurance initiative (Figure 8.2). Data shows that over the years health-seeking behaviour has seen a marked change. The Bondo Hills had been a region with no credible medical or surgical facil-ities (Thomas 2002). However, with the AKS-initiated health activities, institutional deliveries and surgical services were made available and uti-lized. Through this lives are being saved, especially those of children and pregnant women. This has been made possible, at least till the present, through a substantive subsidy from the Asha Kiran Hospital and from an external donor (Action Aid, for the Bondo tribe).

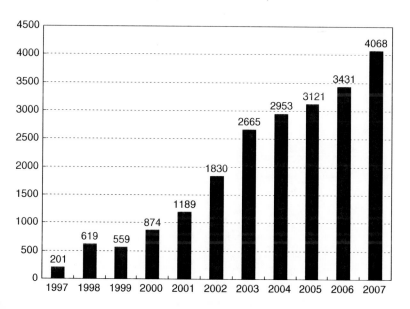

Figure 8.2: Number of patients treated at the Bondo Clinic
Source: The Asha Kiran Society.

8.4.3 Improved child and maternal health

This is a region where the number deaths due to common ailments and maternal and reproductive health complications is very high. This has been ascribed to low levels of awareness about disease and poor access to a reliable health facility. Thus the Asha Kiran initiative in the Bondo Hills was geared towards addressing the basic need for healthcare and averting such deaths.

The visits of the community nurses along with local health assistants in the nine focus Bondo villages has seen a reduction in splenomegaly from 62 per cent of the population in 2002 to 13 per cent in 2007. Similarly, third-grade malnutrition has also reduced, from 13 per cent to 5 per cent. After seven children died in March 2007 due to measles, the CHC (Community Health Centre) team conducted immunization in the largest village. Furthermore, one of the Integrated Child Development Scheme workers now monitors children's weight regularly and refers cases of malnutrition to the Khairput CHC. The health assistants additionally help the government workers with immunization and other tasks during their visits. Partnership with the government has seen the block CHC in Khairput providing medicines for tuberculosis and malaria to the AKS clinic and government staff (medical and others) visiting the villages.

As a consequence of awareness-generation campaigns, locals have become more aware of their entitlements and are now actively monitoring the visits of grassroots government workers to their villages.

The peripheral clinic has gradually become a lifeline in thousands of basic emergency cases. More than 4000 patients were treated here in 2007 while the number of inpatients was 100. Besides home deliveries, there were 10 deliveries in the clinic. During the enrolment period of January–March 2007, 204 households enrolled in the community health insurance scheme, which represented a high utilization of the scheme.

The pre-AKS intervention phase was set within a grim situation of pregnant women dying before being able to reach a health facility, lack of awareness of safe deliveries and many complicated cases not being given appropriate and timely service. With the AKS intervention in the area, with its strong focus on antenatal care and advocating the use of safe delivery kits, 10 per cent of the deliveries in 2007 were nurse-assisted and 4 per cent of complicated cases were successfully motivated to access referral support at the AKS hospital. Such small yet significant strides have characterized the perseverance of the team in carrying forward their goal of providing an enabling, safe and healthy environment for this tribal group. An important outcome of their advocacy with pregnant women was that 58 per cent of women used Safe Delivery Kits and 6 per cent even accessed the government hospital. Since the government recognized the Asha Kiran clinic all the delivery patients now receive Rs. 1450 (or US$36) per delivery from Janani Suraksha Yojana as an incentive from the government for institutional deliveries, and this has been a contributing factor in the tribal accessing of the clinic for deliveries.

Thus far, the Bondo Hills have witnessed either zero or inappropriate health intervention for preventable diseases such as malaria, which has contributed to the low level of awareness of prevention and cure. Ill-informed and unsuited governmental intervention in the form of an impersonal distribution of mosquito nets, for instance, contributed little towards malaria prevention, since these nets were used by the tribals as fishing nets. AKS nurses and health assistants have played a crucial role in generating awareness of malaria prevention through village visits and administering and monitoring medicine dosages.

8.5 Conclusions

From the outset, Asha Kiran's experience of extending healthcare to the Bondo tribe demonstrated the need for an insider's perspective while designing, implementing, monitoring and improving health interventions. This would further imply that there indeed exists no one-size-fits-all blueprint for extending healthcare to the extreme poor.

Asha Kiran's recognition of local resources within an extremely poor and vulnerable tribal group was a start. Their empowerment of local youth through literacy lessons and later through training some in basic nursing procedures has left the Bondos with a small but very capable human resource for healthcare. Their inputs to the network of community health workers have left a lasting resource in each village for tackling minor ailments. The initiation of community health insurance has given the tribe the confidence that they are able to collectively contribute finances to demand healthcare as their right. It took humility for the medical team to unlearn their own professional biases and learn instead from the wealth of traditional knowledge that they encountered, thus actively promoting healthy traditional practices and discouraging those that were evidently harmful. The role of the nurse practitioners in the peripheral Bondo Clinic has been pivotal and when combined with a robust network of CHWs has minimized the need for a doctor, thus saving on costs and proving more effective.

Health cannot be viewed as an isolated sector. Asha Kiran's simultaneous investments in literacy, education, agriculture and livelihoods have supported and hedged the gains made in health. The sectoral and departmental nature of typical government interventions requires a convergence at the household level, and civil society actors have a key role to play in this.

There are several lessons that were learned. First, community health insurance was effective in attaining financial security in relation to ill-health among the Bondos, compared to the government-provided free clinical services. We found this to be true because insurance gave the Bondos not just the purchasing power, but also the ability to choose a care provider other than the government services, and a sense of holding the right to quality care. As noted in this chapter and also in Chapter 7 by Ito and Kono, government-provided care frequently suffers from absenteeism and disrespectful treatment of patients, especially to the socially marginalized. By having the power to choose a care provider with their own purchasing power, the Bondos have achieved a firm sense of financial security and control, which are both important elements in healthy living.

Second, the Asha Kiran intervention has tried to understand local traditions/institutions and take advantage of them in collaborative efforts in healthcare. These are better understanding of the local livelihoods, education, local governance structure and traditions regarding healthcare-seeking behaviour, including traditional health practices. It was also vital to show visible commitment in understanding their traditions. All these efforts, we believe, built constructive and cooperative relationships which served to utilize local resources and to meet local preferences in healthcare provision. This allowed a reduction in the reliance on external, highly qualified health professionals and large-scale hospital-based interventions, which are costly and hard to sustain. This latter approach is often followed by the government, and it was found to be a little remote from reality on the ground because government-provided care often fails to adjust to local preferences, and ignores the existing (social, human, traditional medical) resources that can potentially work for care provision. In addition, building upon the relationship both with the Bondos and the government, AKS was able to connect existing government services to the Bondos, which in turn lowered the running costs of Asha Kiran hospitals.

Notes

1. A secondary hospital is a first referral unit that a primary-level clinic relies on in dealing with the symptoms that cannot be effectively dealt with in peripheral clinics.

2. Asha Kiran's community health insurance scheme was set up with the main objective of facilitating people's equitable access to reliable healthcare when needed without the barriers of requiring ready cash in hand, thus providing a level of health security to the poor of these tribal districts. The AKS scheme relies on the efforts of its village-level workers who are involved in executing the various stages of the insurance plan. Using these networks of local and accountable community volunteers minimizes the administrative costs to the scheme to a great extent. Over the past few years the continuous presence of the secondary-level Asha Kiran Hospital (AKH) and the Asha Kiran peripheral clinic in the Bondo Hills has resulted in a significant increase in utilization of health services by the members of the scheme. Data shows that since the initiation of the scheme, health-seeking behaviour has undergone a marked change. Institutional deliveries and surgical services are being utilized through which lives are being saved, especially those of children and pregnant women. This has been possible through a substantive subsidy from the AKH and an external donor (Action Aid).

References

Chambers, Robert (1983) *Rural Development: Putting the Last First*, Brighton: IDS.

Department of Health and Family Welfare (2006) *National Family Health Survey*, Delhi: DHFW.

Dussault, Gilles and Maria Cristina Franceschini (2006) 'Not Enough There, Too Many Here: Understanding Geographical Imbalances in the Distribution of the Health Workforce', *Human Resources for Health*, Vol. 4: 12

Ensor, Tim and Stephanie Cooper (2004) 'Overcoming Barriers to Health Service Access: Influencing the Demand Side', *Health Policy and Planning*, Vol. 19, No. 2: 69–79.

Frenk, Julio (1992) 'The Concept and Measurement of Accessibility', in K. White (ed.) *Health Service Research: An Anthology*, Washington: Pan American Health Organization, 824–855.

Government of Orissa (2004) *Orissa Human Development Report*, Bhubaneswar: Government of Orissa.

Government of Orissa (2006) *National Family Health Survey*, Department of Health and Family Welfare, Government of Orissa.

Meessen, Bruno, Gerald Bloom, Bart Criel, Wim Van Damme, Narayanan Devadasan and Zang Zhenzhong (2003) 'Iatrogenic Poverty', *Tropical Medicine & International Health*, Vol. 8, No. 7: 581–4.

Mehta, Aasha Kapur and Amita Shah (2001) 'Chronic Poverty in India: An Overview', Working Paper Series (Number 7), Chronic Poverty Research Centre, University of Manchester.

Radwan, Ismail (2005) *India – Private Health Services for the Poor*. Washington: World Bank.

Thomas, Joy (2002) 'Outreach from a Mission Hospital', *Christian Medical College Alumni Journal*, Vol. 36, No. 3: 11–13.

Index

Figures in **bold** refer to figures, figures in *italic* refer to tables